Bridging the Gaps

Bridging the Gaps

Faith-Based Organizations, Neoliberalism, and Development in Latin America and the Caribbean

EDITED BY TARA HEFFERAN, JULIE ADKINS,
AND LAURIE OCCHIPINTI

LEXINGTON BOOKS

A division of
ROWMAN & LITTLEFIELD PUBLISHERS, INC.
Lanham • Boulder • New York • Toronto • Plymouth, UK

LEXINGTON BOOKS

A division of Rowman & Littlefield Publishers, Inc.
A wholly owned subsidary of The Rowman & Littlefield Publishing Group, Inc.
4501 Forbes Boulevard, Suite 200
Lanham, MD 20706

Estover Road, Plymouth PL6 7PY, United Kingdom

British Library Cataloguing in Publication Information Available

Library of Congress Cataloging-in-Publication Data

Bridging the gaps: faith-based organizations, neoliberalism, and development in Latin
America and the Caribbean / edited by Tara Hefferan, Julie Adkins, and Laurie
Occhipinti.
    p. cm.
 Includes bibliographical references and index.
 ISBN 978-0-7391-3287-6 (cloth: alk. paper)
 ISBN 0-7391-3287-3 (cloth: alk. paper)
 ISBN 978-0-7391-3289-0 (e-book)
 ISBN 0-7391-3289-X (e-book)
 1. Neoliberalism—Latin America. 2. Religious institutions—Latin America. I.
Hefferan, Tara, 1972– II. Adkins, Julie, 1960– III. Occhipinti, Laurie A., 1968–
HN110.5.A8B75 2009
 361.7'5098—dc22

                                                                  2008046818

Printed in the United States of America

♾™ The paper used in this publication meets the minimum requirements of American
National Standard for Information Sciences—Permanence of Paper for Printed Library
Materials, ANSI/NISO Z39.48–1992.

For Quinn, Connelly, and Landry. *–T.H.*

For Thurman and Sue. *–J.A.*

For Joe and Paul. *–L.O.*

Table of Contents

Tables and figures

Chapter 1
Faith-Based Organizations, Neoliberalism, and Development: An Introduction
Tara Hefferan, Julie Adkins, Laurie Occhipinti

In an era of unprecedented global poverty, warfare, and suffering, faith-based organizations (FBOs) have proliferated, often filling the gaps born of state neglect and retraction by designing and delivering social services and development programming. They are essential conduits of information, resources, and "culture" between the global north and south. Yet, despite their rise in profile and practice, little is known about FBOs, what they are, what they do, or why they do it. From an anthropological perspective, this volume shines a much needed critical light on these organizations.

Drawing on in-depth case studies from across Latin America and the Caribbean, the chapters assembled here are concerned with relationships between international development, neoliberalism, and faith, particularly as they are (re)fashioned, rejected, and/or adopted in the day-to-day realities of people working in local organizational contexts. This, of course, is one of the hallmarks of ethnographic analysis: its ability to situate microlevel happenings within broader meso- and macrolevel frameworks, revealing both the complexity and patterns therein. It is also the strength of this volume, as the case studies provide an entry point for analyzing the contemporary restructuring of global economic and political realities in the Western Hemisphere.

In this volume, we look closely at how different organizational collectivities define and deploy development. Development in its "modern" form—which aims to combat poverty in the "global south" by raising per capita income levels (Martinussen 1997, 37)—has been a guiding set of global ideas and practices since the 1940s (cf. Maddox 1956). Often reflecting a messy entanglement of political over humanitarian concerns, U.S. foreign development aid, in particular, often has been preoccupied with moving those in the global south from a state of presumed "backwardness" toward a Western-defined notion of "progress" (Escobar 1995; Rist 1997). Since shifting national economies toward production was often seen as the mechanism through which to attain develop-

1

ment, states and their agencies were assumed to be the best, most logical designers and delivers of development programming.

In recent years, however, development's guiding ideas and practices have come under increasing scrutiny and challenge. Instead of adopting some vague notion of "modernization" as an appropriate goal of development, for everyone, everywhere, many practitioners and scholars—especially since the 1990s onward—have been embroiled furiously in debates over what constitutes development. What exactly does it mean to be developed? How should development proceed? With whom? Is it even desirable? As the chapters here reveal, FBOs often bring distinctive perspectives to such questions. Many adopt a deeply philosophical approach to the work of development, as they contextualize poverty within larger religious frameworks, sometimes employing a discourse of social justice. As grassroots organizations, their ideas may be shaped in dialogue with the population that the FBO serves, or, in other cases, they may represent an "outside" model that is enacted regardless of local culture and strongly echoes the more conventional notions heralded in government channels. In any case, the idea of "saving" people via development is often expanded in the work of FBOs—from simply "saving" bodies from poverty to saving souls and human dignity. Development, in such cases, is concerned with more than the material conditions of poverty, extending to the spiritual and emotional dimensions as well.

The volume also engages neoliberalism, a globally circulating ideology that stresses the "free market" should be the organizing principle of social life. Emphasizing individual responsibility and market-based solutions to social problems, neoliberal ideology suggests that governments take a "hands off" approach to development by letting the market discipline individuals, communities, and states according to their degree of market competitiveness. That is, neoliberalism encourages market-based rather than government-led development strategies, favoring the private over the public, the personal over the collective, and profit over all else. Accordingly, the neoliberal policies that arose in the 1980s and 1990s called for smaller governments less focused on social welfare provision and development programming.

In shrinking the size of the state and lowering its expenditures, neoliberal policies and practices have created space for "private" interests—including FBOs—to assume many of the duties and obligations typically associated with governments. As governments divest themselves of social spending as part of a neoliberal agenda, FBOs may pick up the pieces, operate in the margins, where government services leave off. As the chapters here reveal, some do so happily, enthusiastically embracing neoliberalism and its ideas on a number of different levels. Such FBOs oftentimes understand themselves to be "filling the gaps" born of state retraction, often positioning themselves as better, more efficient purveyors of services than the state. Yet, other FBOs see themselves very differently, as not so much working to fill the gaps as actively resisting the governmental policies and priorities that have created them. And yet other FBOs stand in the middle, working to impact policy while at the same time trying to mitigate the negative impacts of neoliberalism. Whatever their relationship with neoliberal ideology, many organizations find new funding sources, as international funding organizations encourage non-governmental organizations (NGOs) to move into social service provision. From providing education, credit, and technological inputs to serving as caregivers and healers, FBOs increasingly undertake a wide array of activities targeting the world's poorest, most vulnerable populations.

As the case studies presented here make clear, FBO perspectives on and responses to neoliberalism fall across a wide spectrum. At its base, conflict over neoliberalism, in the world of development and antipoverty programs, is often expressed as a conflict over the role of government itself. What ought a government provide for its citizens? What is the role of the state? FBOs, within different faith traditions, bring to bear long-term perspectives on the role of the state in the lives of its citizens, offering widely divergent and sometimes conflicting points of view.

Studying Faith-Based Non-Governmental Organizations

Theoretically, this volume builds on the work of anthropology of development scholars looking at development's discourses and practices, particularly those examining the "privatization" of development delivery via NGOs. Throughout the world, there are numerous non-governmental organizations working in the field of development and antipoverty programming. The label "NGO" includes an amazingly heterogeneous collection of organizations, encompassing a correspondingly wide range of theories, ideologies, practices, and strategies aimed at mitigating conditions of poverty. Some of these, such as the World Bank, United Nations Development Program, and the International Monetary Fund, are large and well-known multilateral institutions that draw resources from and strongly reflect the official agendas of the world's wealthiest, most powerful governments. Others—like World Vision and Catholic Relief Services—are likewise global in reach, but relatively "independent" in mission and goals, though perhaps still heavily reliant on official development aid flows originating in governments. There are also innumerable small agencies and organizations, many operating on shoestring budgets, in a single location, and perhaps relying solely on volunteers rather than paid staff. Thus, NGOs take many different forms: they may be sponsored by international or national charities, religious organizations, or corporations; they may be locally or externally initiated; they may work in agriculture, health care, education, or other fields; and they may be linked to a greater or lesser degree with other organizations or governments. In fact, "the heterogeneity of the universe of NGOs defies most analysts" (Carroll 1992, 23).

There are almost as many ways to classify NGOs as there are theorists examining them. Carroll (1992), for example, distinguishes between grassroots support organizations (GSOs) that are development organizations based outside of a community, and membership support organizations (MSOs), which include cooperatives and unions. The United Nations Development Program makes a general distinction between "people's organizations," or local grassroots organizations, and NGOs, which they classify as more formal (UNDP 1993, 84-85). David Leonard divides organizations into the categories of intermediate representative and local participatory (1982, 32-33). Robert Elias (1989) distinguishes private voluntary organizations (PVOs) from those staffed by paid professionals. There are INGOs (Intermediate NGOs) and GROs (grassroots organizations) (Storey 1998). The World Bank has recently moved towards using the term CSOs (civil society organizations) (World Bank 2007). Even as they leave us with a bewildering array of acronyms, such classifications become even more problematic when one considers religious organizations, which may have different operational levels within a single organization; as one example, a single church may support both international and local NGOs, or it may operate its own development programs through the congregation itself.

However they are classified, NGOs' presence in development has increased dramatically in recent years. At the beginning of the twentieth century, there were just over 1,000 international NGOs; by 2000 there were over 37,000 (UNDP 2002, 5). By some estimates there are more than 50,000 international NGOs in the global south (Streeten 1997, 193; Development Directory 2008), with millions more national and local organizations around the world (UNDP 2002, 5). Why so many organizations? Neoliberal reforms created conditions that favored NGOs during the 1980s and 90s, as development aid shifted from the public to the private sector. According to the 1993 *Human Development Report* of the United Nations, between 1970 and 1990 the global total that was transferred to international NGOs by government increased from under $200 million to $2.2 billion. During the same period, the total amount of money spent by international NGOs went from $1.0 billion to over $7.2 billion (UNDP 1993, 88), a level which seems to have remained relatively constant (UNDP 2002, 5).[1] Thomas Carroll attributes this enthusiasm for NGOs to a strong antigovernment ideology led by U.S. conservatives (1992, 23; see also Lehmann 1990, 201). NGOs have also enjoyed support from the left, as NGOs are framed as alternatives to corrupt or violent governments, as well as to governments overly focused on enhancing the capitalist marketplace at the expense of the poor (Sanyal 1997, 21). On both sides of the political debate, NGOs have been seen as a critical route to building and strengthening civil society (Feldman 1997). This wave of enthusiasm for NGOs has had material as well as ideological consequences, as NGOs have become the medium for many development projects and for much of the development money that is spent by both governments and private donors.

In practice, the relationships between different NGOs and the projects that they sponsor are also complex and interwoven. Most development programs are managed through a combination of central and local organizations with institutional linkages that include financial aid, technical assistance, regulation, representation, and informal influence (Leonard and Marshall 1982, x). In the last twenty years, many international organizations have become less involved in managing development programs directly, preferring to act as "partners" who transfer knowledge, technology, and money to smaller, locally managed organizations (UNDP 1993, 89; Lister 2000).

As NGOs have gained increasing importance in the development sector, they also have become of interest to scholars. A substantial body of literature has emerged on evaluating the institutional structure and effectiveness of NGOs and their programs, mostly written for and by the professional development community (see, for example, Esman and Uphoff 1984; Uphoff 1987; Leonard and Marshall 1982; Carroll 1992). This work, generally enthusiastic in tone, points out the advantages and challenges of small organizations working in local development, as well as the complexity of institutional networks that exist between different types of organizations. In a more critical vein, there have been a number of debates on issues such as the degree to which NGOs are, in fact, efficient and participatory agents of development (Lister 2000; Lorgen 1998); the relative strengths of NGOs compared to state-led development (Edwards and Hulme 1996; Riddell and Robinson 1995; Zaidi 1999); and the extent to which NGOs might operate outside of mainstream development discourses (Farrington and Bebbington 1993; Gardner and Lewis 1996; Grillo 1997). Anthropological studies of NGOs and their role in local communities have increased in the last decade, as well (Fisher 1997; Gardner 1997; Grillo 1997; Hefferan 2007; Lister 2000; Occhipinti 2005).

Despite the increase in number and profile of NGOs in recent years, the NGO literature has tended to ignore one particular type of NGO: the religiously driven or "faith-based" NGO (for exceptions, see below). From this, one might assume that FBOs are relatively insignificant "players" in the global development arena. This is far from the case. For example, The Boston Globe—as part of a year long investigation on the influence of the "religious right" in U.S. foreign policy—found that between 2001-2005, 179 faith-based organizations received more than $1.7 billion in USAID contracts, grants, and agreements (Boston Globe 2006). They also report that President George W. Bush during the same period nearly doubled the percentage of U.S. foreign aid funds flowing through FBOs, with over 98% of awardees Christian organizations (Boston Globe 2006). While these numbers reveal the magnitude of FBOs' U.S. government-backed reach into the developing world, USAID constitutes just one arm of the global development apparatus. Missing from this calculation are the thousands of privately funded FBOs originating in the U.S., as well as those both publicly and privately funded outside the U.S.

Given the growing importance of FBOs to international development, we agree with Holenstein (2005) and Ver Beek (2000) that the relative silence of the NGO literature on FBOs can be partially understood in relation to the ways faith and spirituality have been "stigmatized" and thus "taboo" and absent from development studies literature generally and from the anthropology of development literature, more specifically (Howell 2007). Some suggest this stems from the rooting of development in theories of modernization and secularization (Selinger 2004; Haynes 2008): the assumption—derived from Weberian thought—was that as societies "modernized," they also secularized, shedding religious or spiritual ways of knowing or experiencing the world in favor of scientifically grounded understandings. In such scenarios, religion and spirituality were cast as signifiers of the premodern, with their absence taken as a signal of modernity. Given development's preoccupation with moving societies from "traditional backwardness" (Gerschenkron 1940) to modernity, religion and spirituality have been understood as little more than obstacles to be overcome and, as such, perhaps "legitimately" ignored.

A shift in development studies is occurring, however, as an emerging literature examining faith, spirituality, religion, and their affiliated organizations begins to form (Clarke 2006; 2007; Clark and Jennings 2008; Haynes 2008; Mayotte 1998; Selinger 2004; Sweetman 1999; Ver Beek 2000). Focused, in large part, on teasing out the commonalities and linkages between religion and development, recent works often have had an applied focus explicitly intended to promote "dialogue" between the worlds of faith and development (e.g., Belshaw, Calderisi, and Sugden 2001; Tyndale 2000), with much of this writing more descriptive (Marshall 2001; Tyndale 2006) than analytical. Frequently underlying these recent works is an assumption about and endorsement of the power and promise of faith-based organizations to make international development more efficient, effective, and relevant than it is currently (Hoksbergen 2005; Hoksbergen and Ewert 2002; Marshall and Keough 2004; Marshall and Marsh 2003; Tripp 1999). That is, much of the emerging literature assumes that FBOs are somehow inherently "positive" additions to the development equation. Such framing links with the broader political context in which FBOs at the turn of the century are working. For example, in justifying his creation of the Office of Faith-based and Community Initiatives, President George W. Bush in 2001 argued that the best, most efficient purveyors of social services were faith-based organizations, since they often worked with low overhead and volunteer labor.

Yet, not all embrace FBOs as positive forces in the world of the international development. For many, FBOs have inherently negative connotations, associated with evangelizing the desperate in exchange for needed services and motivated by smug self-importance. Those concerned with the separation of church and state are troubled by what they see as the intermingling of the two, as they accuse the U.S. government, in particular, of state-sponsored Christian evangelization. In this volume, we nuance the polarizing debates between pro- and anti-FBO perspectives to consider the complex ways FBOs engage with the ideas and practices of international development in diverse and often contradictory ways, and how they themselves sometimes critically evaluate the role of evangelization in their work. Defying simple classification as either "good" or "bad," FBOs instead inhabit a space right at the intersection of globalization, neoliberalism, and international development, where multiple meanings and competing agendas play out.

Understanding and Comparing FBOs

Notably, like the label "NGO," the term "faith-based organization" is nebulous, for it endeavors to capture a wide range of organizations with differing philosophies, motivations, programming, size, scale, areas of interest and expertise, scope of activities, relationships—or lack of—with states, and means of support. In addition, those NGOs that describe themselves as faith-based mean a variety of things by that term. Some focus on evangelizing and converting the populations with whom they work; others engage faith only insofar as it motivates the individuals who provide services within the organization. Some prefer to focus on simple charity and meeting of immediate human needs (a "praxis of altruism"; see Fogarty this volume); others emphasize the creation of relationships of solidarity between the haves and have-nots who come in contact through the NGO's work. In the work of development, as they variously define it, most faith-based NGOs focus their attention on the communities or populations that are in need; a few, however, also draw attention to and demand responses from the state and market forces, which they perceive have behaved unjustly toward deprived communities and populations.

So, what makes an organization "faith-based"?[2] Gerard Clarke and Michael Jennings (2008, 6) suggest that a "faith-based organization" is one "that derives inspiration and guidance for its activities from the teaching and principles of the faith or from a particular interpretation or school of thought within a faith." Helen Rose Ebaugh et al. (2006, 2259) suggest the term traditionally has referred to "a religious congregation with primary missions of worship and religious education." But since the creation of the Office of Faith-based and Community Initiatives by George W. Bush in 2001, the term has been expanded to include a wide range of organizations, which may or may not be linked to congregations but do have an element of "religiosity." Drawing on Glock and Stark (1965), Ebaugh et al. (2006, 2259) conceptualize religiosity in relation to "religious commitment," identifiable in ritual activities, ideology or belief, experience, and knowledge of religious matters. In studying 612 faith-based social service organizations, Ebaugh et al. (2006, 2269-70) identified three dimensions on which FBOs differ in terms of religiosity: service religiosity, the ways in which the FBO relates to its clients; staff religiosity, meaning the ways in which staff are hired and relate to one another; and organizational religiosity, by which they mean the "public face" that the organization produces and presents.

A useful framework for understanding the role played by religion in faith-based organizations was laid out by the Working Group on Human Needs and Faith-Based and Community Initiatives in 2002. Appointed by United States Senator Rick Santorum, this working group was convened to find the "common ground" uniting faith-based organizations within the United States. Representing constituencies that ranged from Americans United for the Separation of Church and State and the ACLU, on the one side, to Evangelicals for Social Action on the other—as well as a broad spectrum of Christian, Jewish, and Muslim organizations in the middle—the Working Group, among its contributions and conclusions, put forth a descriptive matrix through which the level of faith engagement of a particular FBO might be analyzed. This typology has been further elaborated by Sider and Unruh (2004). We have reproduced the descriptive table developed by Sider and Unruh on the following pages (Table 1.1, pages 10-15) in order to begin our discussion of the chapters in this volume and our analysis of "how much" faith and/or religion infuses an FBO's missions, goals, funding, and practice.

As the table shows, the typology attempts to distinguish along a number of dimensions (e.g., the circumstances surrounding the organization's founding, where financial support comes from, connections between religious content and programming, etc.) how "faith-based" or religious a particular FBO might be, and in what ways. At one end of the typology are those organizations that might be classified as "faith-saturated," meaning that religious and faith elements provide an explicit organizational basis in all aspects of the FBO and are central to the programming and goals of the FBO. At the other end are those organizations considered "secular," where religious and faith elements are completely absent, forming no part of the organization's mission, goals, funding, or practice. Sandwiched between these two poles are a range of organizational types, where faith and religion come together in differing configurations that are more "moderate" than those at either pole.

In discussing the typology that Sider and Unruh proposed in 2004, Thomas H. Jeavons (2004) raises three critiques, which are important to consider here. First, he questions the Protestant Christian origins of the framework, asking whether such a typology is applicable to organizations outside the Judeo-Christian tradition. Second, Jeavons (2004, 142) asks whether the division Sider and Unruh make between "internal" and "expressive/external" manifestations of faith is not "too clean and facile." For, as he notes, the Christian notion of separation between "faith and work" is not necessarily shared across religious traditions. Finally, Jeavons poses the question of whether congregations should be considered FBOs, according to the typology. His concern is with congregations that directly sponsor programs or projects not separately incorporated as NGOs.

The case studies in this volume offer a valuable lens through which to consider both the usefulness of the Sider and Unruh typology and the critiques of it that have been introduced by Jeavons and others (e.g., Ebaugh et al. 2006). In fact, there is considerable overlap between the first and second concerns Jeavons raises about the origins of the typology and its usefulness to FBOs outside Judeo-Christian religions. And, we agree with both critiques he raises: the typology is unmistakably Protestant Christian in origin, and the distinctions between "internal" and "external" expressions of faith and religiosity certainly minimize the complexity evident in practice. From our perspective, however, *all* "typologies" endeavor to capture an "ideal type" and so necessarily collapse, telescope, and render invisible the true diversity inherent in reality. This is the central weakness of any typology, but it is a weakness that need not cripple or render typologies passé. Since typologies really are little more than attempts to reduce the complexity of the world, an effort to categorize and make sense of diversity, the questions we ask of the Sider and Unruh typology include: does it "work" in helping demystify the role of the faith in FBOs working in Latin America and the Caribbean? How might it be improved to better account for the diverse FBOs engaging in international development? Like Jeavons, our interest is in identifying the weaknesses and limitations of the typology, but then drawing on those insights to retool the typology to make it more useful, more often.

In applying the typology to the case studies within this volume, we find that more often than not, the typology does accurately capture the ways faith and religion are manifested in goals, mission, programming, and funding of the FBOs under consideration. While most of the FBOs discussed here are Protestant, several are Catholic, one Buddhist, and one Rastafari. In all cases, the typology's six axes of faith (ranging from faith-saturated to secular) accounted for the diverse ways these FBOs were organized and engaged. For example, the two chapters here dealing with Buddhist and Rastafari organizations are understandable vis-à-vis the typology. Suzana Ramos Coutinho Bornholdt describes the Buddhist Soka Gakkai International organization of Brazil as an evangelical organization strategically deploying development programming as a way to recruit converts to Buddhism. Buddhist Soka Gakkai International might be understood here as a "faith-centered" organization, whereby there is a division between the "internal" and "external" manifestations of religion. Bornholdt describes, for example, a self-conscious decision to position Soka Gakkai International as largely secular to the Brazilian public while to its internal membership Soka Gakkai International emphasizes religious doctrine and practice.

Bretton Alvaré's chapter considers the founding and transformation of the National Rastafari Organization of Trinidad and Tobago (NRO), from an organization with an explicit and militant antineoliberal mission to one focused on neoliberal "individual economic improvement." NRO might be classified as a "faith-background" organization, where the historical connection to Rastafarianism has become tenuous and those leading NRO have little concern with "faith commitments." From our perspective, then, the six "types" that Sider and Unruh have formulated make sense in the context of development FBOs in Latin America and the Caribbean analyzed here, though—as described below—the *criteria* (e.g., selection of senior management) for determining which of the six categories might be appropriate are not always applicable.

To return to the broader critiques introduced above, Jeavons's third concern stems directly from a practical consideration: should congregations and synagogues—85 percent of which directly sponsor social services delivery and educational programs—be eligible for government funding? The 1996 U.S. Charitable Choice initiative was, in part, intended to make it easier for these organizations to receive such funding (Bartkowski and Regis 2003). But Jeavons's feeling is that congregations and synagogues are not FBOs—by any typology—because the people comprising them do not think of them as FBOs.

Table 1.1 – FBO Typology – Sider and Unruh (2004)
Part 1 – Characteristics of Organizations

	Faith-Permeated (Faith-Saturated)	Faith-Centered
Mission statement and other self-descriptive text	Includes explicitly religious references	Includes explicitly religious references
Founding	By religious group or for religious purpose	By religious group or for religious purpose
If affiliated with an external entity, is that entity religious?	Yes	Yes
Selection of controlling board	Explicitly religious. May be (a) self-perpetuating board with explicit religious criteria, or (b) board elected by a religious body	Explicitly or implicitly religious; may be (a) self-perpetuating board with explicit or implicit religious criteria for all or most members, or (b) board elected by a religious body
Selection of senior management	Faith or ecclesiastical commitment an explicit prerequisite	Faith or ecclesiastical commitment an explicit or implicit prerequisite

Table 1.1 continued

Faith-Affiliated (Faith-Related)	Faith Background	Faith-Secular Partnership	Secular
Religious references may be either implicit or explicit	May have implicit references to religion (e.g., references to values)	No reference to religion in mission of the partnership or the secular partner, but religion may be explicit in mission of faith partners	No religious content
By religious group or for religious purpose	May have historic tie to a religious group, but connection is no longer strong	Faith partners founded by religious group or for religious purpose; no reference to religious identity of founders of the secular partner; founders of the partnership may or may not be religious	No reference to religious identity of founders of the secular partner (sic)
Often	Sometimes	May have dual religious/secular affiliation	No
Some, but not all, board members may be required or expected to have a particular faith or ecclesiastical commitment	Board might have been explicitly religious at one ·time, but is now inter-faith; very little concern for faith commitment of board	Board selection typically controlled by secular partner, with little or no consideration of faith commitment of board members; input from faith partners	Faith commitment of board members not a factor
Normally (perhaps by unwritten expectation) share organization's religious orientation; explicit religious criteria are considered irrelevant or improper	Religious criteria considered irrelevant or improper	Required to respect but not necessarily share faith of religious partners	Religious criteria considered improper

Table 1.1 continued
Characteristics of Organizations

	Faith-Permeated (Faith-Saturated)	*Faith-Centered*
Selection of other staff	Faith commitment is important at all staff levels; most or all staff share organization's religious orientation, with faith an explicit factor in hiring decisions	Faith commitment may be an explicit factor for jobs involving religion but may be less important in other positions
Financial support and nonfinancial resources	Intentional cultivation of support from religious community, policy of refusing funds that would undermine religious mission/identity	Intentional cultivation of support from religious community, often has policy of refusing funds that would undermine religious mission/identity
Organized religious practices of personnel (such as prayer or devotions)	Religious practices play a significant role in the functioning of the organization; personnel are expected or required to participate	Religious practices often play a significant role in the organization; personnel may be expected to participate
Characteristics of Programs/Projects		
Religious environment (building, name, religious symbols)	Usually	Usually

Table 1.1 continued

Faith-Affiliated (Faith-Related)	Faith Background	Faith-Secular Partnership	Secular
Staff expected to respect but not necessarily share the religious orientation of the organization; religious beliefs motivate self-selection of some staff/volunteers	Little to no consideration of faith commitment of any staff; religious beliefs may motivate self-selection of some staff/volunteers	Staff expected to respect faith of religious partners; program relies significantly on volunteers from religious partners	Religious criteria for any staff considered improper
May cultivate volunteer and in-kind support from religious community	May or may not cultivate support from religious community	Significant cultivation of volunteer and in-kind support from faith partners	Little cultivation of support from the religious community
Religious practices are optional and not extensive	Religious practices are rare and peripheral to the organization	Faith partners may sponsor voluntary religious practices; secular partners do not	No organized religious practices
Often	Sometimes	Sometimes (program administration usually located in a secular environment; program activities may be located in a religious environment)	No

Table 1.1 continued
Characteristics of Programs/Projects

	Faith-Permeated (Faith-Saturated)	*Faith-Centered*
Religious content of program	In addition to acts of compassion and care, also includes explicitly religious, mandatory content integrated into the program; beneficiaries are expected to participate in religious activities and discussions of faith	In addition to acts of compassion and care, also includes explicitly religious content that may be segregated from provision of care; beneficiaries have the option not to participate in religious program components; beneficiaries may also be invited to religious activities outside the program parameters
Main form of integration of religious content with other program components	Integrated-mandatory (engagement with explicitly religious content is required of all beneficiaries)	Integrated-optional or invitational (engagement of beneficiaries with explicitly religious content is optional or takes place in activities outside program parameters)
Expected connection between religious content and outcome	Expectation of explicitly religious experience or change, and belief that this is essential or significant to desired outcome	Strong hope for explicitly religious experience or change, and belief that this significantly contributes to desired outcome

Table 1.1 continued

Faith-Affiliated (Faith-Related)	Faith Background	Faith-Secular Partnership	Secular
The religious component is primarily in acts of compassion and care; program includes little (and entirely optional) or no explicitly religious content; staff may invite beneficiaries to religious activities outside program parameters or hold informal religious conversations with beneficiaries	No explicitly religious content in the program; religious materials or resources may be available to beneficiaries who seek them out; the religious component is seem primarily in the motivation of individual staff and volunteers	No explicitly religious content in program activities designed by secular partners; faith partners sometimes supplement with optional religious resources and activities	No religious content
Invitational, relational, or implicit (engagement of participants with explicitly religious content takes place in optional activities outside the program parameters or in informal relationships with the staff)	Implicit (beneficiaries only encounter religious content if they seek it out)	Implicit, invitational, or relational, depending on the staff/volunteers of the faith partners	None
Little expectation that explicitly religious experience or change is necessary for desired outcome; some believe that acts of compassion and care alone have an implicit spiritual impact that contributes to outcome	No expectation that religious experience or change is needed for desired outcome	No expectation that religious experience or change is needed for desired outcome, but the faith of volunteers from religious partners is expected to add value to the program	No expectation of religious experience or change

Moreover, labeling them FBOs has policy implications, potentially diluting the U.S. constitutional separation of church and state, and allowing U.S. politicians to create "patronage system[s]" by funneling money to religious leaders in exchange for their political support (2004, 143). These are interesting questions that reveal the importance of context in framing debates about FBOs, especially as they operate within international or transnational environments.

Both Tara Hefferan and Julie Adkins (this volume) describe congregations that organize outreach activities and development projects within the congregational context without incorporating such programs as separate entities. Yet, unlike Jeavons, both authors characterize such programming as FBO situated. Hefferan analyzes a relationship between two Catholic parishes, one in the U.S. and the other in Haiti, focused—in part—on promoting development in Haiti. The projects that result from this partnership (educational, microcredit, agricultural extension, among others) are funded solely from parishioner contributions and implemented through parish channels. The work of these congregations fits neatly—though not perfectly—within the "faith-centered" typology: there are certain assumptions made about shared faith between donors and recipients, and religious discourse is integrated into the provision of services, but there is no insistence that recipients subscribe to a specific set of religious beliefs and practices. One important assumption that the original typology makes is that those working within an organization are necessarily "staff." This is certainly not the case in Catholic Church partnering, where "lay" members of the parish organize and operate most dimensions of the project, at least at the U.S. end.

While some of those involved with Catholic Church partnering might be open to receiving U.S. government funds to supplement their Haiti budget, many—including those who are the focus of Hefferan's case study—explicitly adopt a neoliberal perspective that disallows for government funding of such programming. Perhaps this is one difference between U.S. domestic FBOs and certain FBOs engaged in international development: often the concern is less with government flows to such organizations than on bypassing government channels, which, especially in the global south, are seen to be corrupt, inefficient, and bureaucratic. Though, as Ethan Sharp's discussion in Chapter Two of prison reform and substance abuse treatment in Mexico makes clear, even "neoliberalizing" FBOs often see government coffers as important resources for "scaling up" their operations. A second key difference relates to the notion of church-state relationships. The U.S. distinction between church and state is not universal. Many countries in the global south make no such division, thereby rendering Jeavons's concerns about the constitutionality of such church-state funding streams irrelevant, while also problematizing Sider and Unruh's consideration of "financial and other support" as one indicator to discern FBO type. Indeed, Ethan Sharp describes "faith-saturated" outreach programs for drug-addicted prisoners and others in Mexico, which insist that conversion to evangelical Christianity is the only permanent cure for such addictions. And yet, in terms of financial support, Sharp's description also suggests that the most "successful" of these programs actually engage in "faith-secular partnerships," working with the government to formalize substance abuse treatment centers. Therefore, it might be more useful to think about funding streams in terms of potential donors—is an FBO positioned to draw support from religious communities or actors, even if that is not its exclusive means of financial support?

To summarize up to this point, the "types" that Sider and Unruh identify—despite their rooting in Judeo-Christian understandings—seem adequately to capture the range of diversity present in the FBOs described in this volume. Among the chapters in this volume, we find organizations that are situated in each of the faith-based columns of the table. At one end, Javier Pereira, Ronald Angel, and Jacqueline Angel outline the work of an NGO in Chile which, though inspired by its "faith background" to care for the indigent elderly (among others), does not include religion as part of its programming and demands no particular religious affiliation from its staff, volunteers, or clients. Laurie Occhipinti and Carmen Martinez Novo describe Roman Catholic-originated NGOs which are best understood as "faith-related." Based in liberation theology, they see value not only within their own religious tradition but also in the values expressed by the indigenous communities that predate the arrival of Christianity. Because liberation theology in general does not insist that a person must be Catholic—perhaps not even Christian—in order to be "saved," there is less concern about converting individuals and more emphasis placed on changing unjust social orders simply because the gospel demands it. Thus, faith enters into the conversation frequently but is not a prerequisite for participation and/or solidarity. Tara Hefferan and Suzana Bornholdt describe "faith-centered" organizations that draw explicit inspiration from their religious traditions, but they do not require that beneficiaries participate in the religious practice in order to access program resources. And, as described above, Ethan Sharp describes "faith-saturated" programs that insist that conversion to evangelical Christianity is the only cure for drug addiction and criminal behavior.

In suggesting the usefulness of such a typology, we recognize that such categorizations often can conceal as much as they reveal. We recognize that no one organization is a perfect fit for any column in the table, and that diversity is the norm rather than the exception. Nevertheless, we have found the framework useful in drawing comparisons and highlighting differences across the organizations discussed here. That said, in applying the typology to FBOs in Latin America and the Caribbean, we propose a number of changes to better capture the diversity that characterizes such organizations. First, we want to address the notion of a "mission statement" or other self-descriptive text that an organization uses to define itself and its purpose. Most obviously, many people who live in poverty are also often illiterate. As such, their organizations may not have any sort of written text describing who they are or what their "mission" is. The notion of "mission" is particular to a milieu where formalization and professionalization are the norm. Not all such organizations are so formalized. Moreover, even when they are, missions can change over time—sometimes very quickly, as Bretton Alvaré demonstrates in his analysis of NRO. In assessing what role faith and religion play within an organization, it is important to be attentive to such changes and to the reality that what the "rules" say should happen is often different from what actually occurs "in practice" (Bourdieu 1972; Ortner 1994). This is one strength of anthropological analysis—its ability to discern what organizations, and the people within them, actually do on a day-to-day basis, often in spite of what they *say* they do.

Second, because most FBOs in Latin America and the Caribbean are not organized according to the requirements of the U.S. tax code, their organizational structure may look very different than that outlined by Sider and Unruh. For example, there may be no "controlling board" or "senior management" whose religious beliefs a researcher might query. The typology, as it exists, assumes that all organizations have highly developed hierarchies, and that those at the top set the agenda for those down below. That may or may not be the case. In fact, there may be no "staff" or "personnel" at all, as in the case of Catholic parish partnering, where the programming is largely formulated and fund-raising undertaken solely on a volunteer basis. Or, it may be that the organization's structure might change over time, as documented by Bretton Alvaré. As such, the typology requires more flexibility to account for "participatory" and "collaborative" organizations without multiple administrative levels and that perhaps depend entirely on volunteers.

Finally, the importance of funding and other support must be assessed carefully. The typology as is presupposes a split between the church and state, a division that may or may not characterize the local context in which an FBO is working. Alternatively, even in contexts where there is supposed to be a division between church and state—like the U.S.—the actual line separating the two might be tenuous or shifting, as seen in George W. Bush's promotion of his Office of Faith-based and Community Initiatives. Thus, as described above, a "faith-saturated" organization—like those described by Ethan Sharp—may well see forming partnerships with the government as enhancing its ability to evangelize. FBOs, like all organizations, often act strategically in securing the resources that will allow them to continue their work, and deciding whether funding sources would "undermine their religious identity/mission" is subjective, meaning any one organization might have several conflicting perspectives on what constitutes "undermining." As within all collectivities, multiple and competing agendas exist within FBOs, as they—like their secular counterparts—attempt to design and deliver development programming.

Given these concerns, we propose a retooling of the Sider and Unruh typology, one that allows for a greater flexibility with regard to the issues outlined above. See Table 1.2 (pages 20-25).

As FBOs respond to neoliberalism, and the shift in the role of the state that it implies, we find that their responses and contributions depend very much on the context—their religious background, understandings of poverty and development, and the specific relationship of the FBO to the communities in which it works. This diversity is captured in the ethnographic studies in this volume, which offer richly contextualized analysis of FBOs, what they are, what they do, and why they do it. The case studies presented here offer fresh perspectives on the study of FBOs, which until now has been overwhelmingly U.S.-based (Bart-kowski and Regis 2003; Reese and Shields 2000; Smith and Sosin 2001; Wuth-now 2004), focused on evaluating the "effectiveness" of FBOs vis-à-vis secular organizations (e.g., Clerkin and Grønbjerg 2007; McGrew and Cnaan 2006), and concerned with measuring organizational religiosity and faith (Jeavons 1998; Monsma 2004; Sider and Unruh 2004). The aim of this volume, by contrast, is to examine the relationships between international development, faith, and neo-liberalism in the quotidian realities of people engaged with FBOs in Latin America and the Caribbean.

While much of the writing to come out recently on faith-based international development has focused on FBOs in Africa (Bornstein 2005; Hearn 2002; Hope and Timmel 2003; Nieman 2006; Ter Haar and Ellis 2006; Belshaw, Cal-derisi and Sugden 2001) and Asia (Bano and Nair 2007; Tomalin 2006), little has been written on FBOs in Latin America and the Caribbean (Hefferan 2007; Occhipinti 2005). Yet, this region is often heralded as the "original" site of globalization, as people, "culture," trade items, and ideas have circulated in and out of the area over the past five centuries (Trouillot 1992). Moreover, U.S. for-eign policy has often cast the region as part of "America's backyard," and as such targeted it for military intervention and foreign aid. In recent years, how-ever, as U.S. attention increasingly shifts to the Middle East in its "war against terror," official development aid flows to the region have dwindled sharply. Thus, the "gaps" we spoke of earlier might be understood to be intensifying in many parts of this region, as neoliberal pressures continue to compel states to "downsize" at the same time that official development aid flows through U.S. government channels decline. As the presence of FBOs grows in response to these changes, the multiple roles they play—both as new forms of imperialism and authentic agents of empowerment and change—are critical to discern.

Taken together, the chapters in this volume demonstrate the vital impor-tance of ethnography for understanding the faith-based "turn" in development, and what it means for those involved in the organizations and communities in which FBOs are operating. Through grounded analysis of the specific dis-courses, practices, and beliefs that imbue faith-based development with such power at the moment, the chapters reveal both the promise and the limitations of this "new"[3] mode of development.

Overview of the volume

Ethan Sharp's chapter on FBOs involved in the Mexican "war on drugs" offers a study of how evangelical Christian organizations are drawn into development work as an extension of proselytizing, as they seek out opportunities to offer their religious message to a new—and literally captive—audience. Sharp's analysis focuses on the common themes in the discourse of neoliberalism and the discourse of evangelical Christianity, including an emphasis on the role of

Table 1.2 – Revised FBO Typology

	Faith-Permeated	*Faith-Centered*
Self-description	Includes explicit references to faith	Includes explicit references to faith
Founded / Organized	By faith group and/or for faith purpose	By faith group and/or for faith purpose
Management / Leaders	Faith or ecclesiastical commitment an explicit prerequisite	Faith commitment understood to be a prerequisite (may be implicit or explicit)
Staff / Volunteers	Faith commitment is important; most or all share organization's faith orientation; faith an explicit factor in hiring/recruitment decisions	Faith commitment may be an explicit selection factor for tasks involving religion, but may be less important in other positions
Financial and other support	Garners support from faith community	Garners support from faith community

Table 1.2 continued

Faith-Affiliated	Faith Background	Faith-Secular Partnership	Secular
Faith references may be either explicit or implicit	May have implicit references to faith (e.g., references to values)	No reference to faith in mission of the partnership or of the secular partner	No faith content, but references to values are often present
By faith group and/or for faith purpose	May have historic tie to a faith group or purpose, but that connection is no longer strong	Faith partners founded by faith group or for faith purpose; no reference to faith identity of founders of the secular partner; founders of the partnership may or may not be religious	No reference to faith identity or spiritual views (if any) of founders(s)/ organizer(s)
Normally share the organization's faith orientation, but explicit faith criteria are considered irrelevant or improper	Faith criteria considered irrelevant or improper	Required to respect but not necessarily share faith of the faith partners	Faith criteria considered improper
Staff/volunteers are expected to respect but not necessarily share the faith orientation of the organization; faith beliefs motivate self-selection of some staff/volunteers	Little to no consideration of faith commitment; faith beliefs may motivate self-selection of some staff/volunteers	Staff/volunteers expected to respect faith of the faith partner(s); program relies significantly on volunteers from faith partners	Faith criteria for any staff/volunteer considered improper
Able to garner some support from faith community	Able to garner some support from faith community	Able to garner some support from faith community	Little to no ability to garner support from faith community

Table 1.2 continued

	Faith-Permeated	*Faith-Centered*
Organized faith practices of personnel/ volunteers (prayer, devotions, etc.)	Faith practices play a significant role in the functioning of the organization; personnel/volunteers expected or required to participate	Faith practices often play a significant role in the organization; personnel/volunteers may be expected to participate
Faith content of program	In addition to acts of compassion and care, also includes explicit and mandatory faith content integrated into the program; beneficiaries are expected to participate in faith activities and discussions of faith	In addition to acts of compassion and care, also includes explicit faith content that may be segregated from provision of care; beneficiaries have the option not to participate in faith program components; beneficiaries may also be invited to faith activities outside the program parameters
Main form of integrating faith content with other program variables	Integrated/ Mandatory (engagement with explicit faith content is required of all beneficiaries)	Integrated/Optional or Invitational (engagement of beneficiaries with explicit faith content is optional or takes place in activities outside program parameters)

Table 1.2 continued

Faith-Affiliated	Faith Background	Faith-Secular Partnership	Secular
Faith practices are optional and not extensive	Faith practices are rare and peripheral to the organization	Faith partners may sponsor voluntary faith practices; secular partners do not	No organized faith practices
The faith component is primarily in acts of compassion and care; program includes little (and entirely optional) or no explicit faith content; staff may invite beneficiaries to faith activities outside program parameters or hold informal faith conversations with beneficiaries	No explicit faith content in the program; faith materials or resources may be available to beneficiaries who seek them out; the faith component is seen primarily in the motivation of individual staff members and/or volunteers	No explicit faith content in program activities designed by secular partners; faith partners sometimes supplement with optional faith resources and activities	No faith content
Invitational, Relational, or Implicit (engagement of participants with explicit faith content takes place in optional activities outside the program parameters or in informal relationships with staff and/or volunteers)	Implicit (beneficiaries only encounter faith content if they seek it out)	Implicit, Invitational, or Relational, depending on staff/volunteers of the faith partner	None

Table 1.2 continued

	Faith-Permeated	*Faith-Centered*
Expected connection between faith content and outcome	Expectation of explicit faith experience or change, and belief that this is essential or significant to desired outcome	Strong hope for explicit faith experience or change, and belief that this contributes significantly to desired outcome
Faith symbols present	Usually	Usually

Source: Revised Table drawn from Working Group (2002) and Sider and Unruh (2004)

the individual, rather than the state or even the community, in creating and enacting change. Here, drug addiction and recovery are an extension of the moral strength of the individual, with external social or economic contexts ignored as extraneous. Even as structural changes created by neoliberal policies provide diminishing economic opportunities, the discourse emphasizes the "responsibilization" (Ferguson and Gupta 2002) of the neoliberal subject, as former state functions shift to private actors. This responsibilization created by neoliberalism may be precisely what some FBOs embrace, particularly those working from a more evangelical context, while it is what others resist as they attempt to shift this responsibility back to the state and even to the larger community.

Tim Fogarty's discussion of FBOs in Nicaragua suggests that the stance that an FBO takes in regard to neoliberalism hinges primarily on its attitudes and discourses towards charity. Like Hefferan, he suggests that while some FBOs

Table 1.2 continued

Faith-Affiliated	Faith Background	Faith-Secular Partnership	Secular
Little expectation that faith change or activity is necessary for desired outcome, though it may be valued for its own sake; some believe that acts of compassion and care alone have an implicit spiritual impact that contributes to outcome	No expectation that faith experience or change is necessary for desired outcome	No expectation that faith experience or change is necessary for desired outcome, but the faith of volunteers from faith partners is expected to add value to the program	No expectation of faith change or experience
Often	Sometimes	Sometimes (program's administration usually located in a secular environment; program activities may be located in a faith environment)	No

see themselves as espousing "alternative development," a more radical stance is an "alternative *to* development." The latter perspective does not simply seek out ways to help the poor, but rather challenges the institutional, structural, and economic frameworks that create poverty. Yet, Fogarty also points out that the practices and discourses of most FBOs in Nicaragua involve both stances, as organizations more or less reflexively elaborate their theological and economic strategies. Jill DeTemple, Erin Eidenshink, and Katrina Josephson's study of a Bolivian FBO provides an example of this, as they note that the attitudes and discourse of program and administrative staff may differ considerably.

The chapter by DeTemple, Eidenshink, and Josephson analyzes how a Bolivian FBO constructs gender roles according to what it sees as "Christian" norms, modeled largely on the (idealized) middle class North American family. Like Fogarty's, this study problematizes the role of the FBO as an organization that is simultaneously functioning as a development agency, concerned with material progress, and as a religious organization, whose function is to convey spiritual ideas and belief. In the work of this FBO, similar to those discussed by Sharp and Hogue, religious conversion is itself seen as a marker of development, a necessary condition for material progress. The emphasis is on the position of the individual, a theme common in both neoliberalism and in evangelical Protestantism.

Similarly, Emily Hogue's chapter on World Vision International in Peru demonstrates that, for some FBOs, the work of "development" may be inextricably intertwined with the work of spiritual transformation. As in the articles described above, World Vision International sees spiritual change as a step toward sustainable development, as material progress is understood to follow spiritual progress ("progress" in both cases as it is defined by the FBO). The FBO seeks to transform not only the material conditions of the communities in which it works, but the social and religious landscape. As described by Hogue, the FBO has something of a monopoly in highland Peru, as government resources, due to budget cuts resulting from neoliberal policies, are scarce or nonexistent. As Hogue remarks, and as the detailed ethnographic examples here illustrate, in highland Peru this has led to villagers espousing the values and beliefs promulgated by the FBO, including more commercialization of production.

Laurie Occhipinti describes how two Catholic NGOs in northwestern Argentina likewise seek to transform the material, social, and religious milieu in which they work. But, unlike World Vision International in Peru, these FBOs advocate less market involvement, instead employing a discourse based on a holistic notion of "development" that challenges conventional neoliberal ideologies and stands in opposition to unchecked global capitalism. Moreover, these organizations seek to preserve and promote a vision of local indigenous "traditional culture." Occhipinti's analysis skillfully demonstrates the ways that "liberation theologies" are adopted and deployed by these Catholic FBOs, and how this religious orientation fosters a notion of development stressing cultural autonomy and self-sufficiency.

Bretton Alvaré's chapter also considers the degree to which "external factors" come to influence visions of "culture" and "religion," though in this case the analysis focuses on how the visions of the FBO itself are transformed. Examining the founding and growth of the National Rastafari Organization of Trinidad and Tobago (NRO), Alvaré documents the shifts in organizational mission and practice that characterized NRO as it attempted to "scale up" its fundraising efforts and local-level community "uplift" projects in Trinidad and Tobago. Preoccupied with sponsoring projects that would draw donations while also "whitewashing" what U.S. donors might consider the more "radical" dimensions of Rasta belief, NRO ultimately lost the support of the local community it originally intended to "help." Alvaré argues that "the internalization of key elements of neoliberal ideology compelled NRO's leaders to revise their conception of social justice from one based on the promotion of Rastafari 'livity' (through collective rejection of destructive Babylonian culture—embodied in their original aims and objectives) to another based on individual economic improvement."

A similar set of shifts characterizes the church-to-church partnerships ("twinnings") described by Tara Hefferan. While initially predicated on creating authentic "partnerships" between Catholic parishes in the U.S. and Haiti, twinning in practice instead tends toward a managerial benefactor-beneficiary relationship between the two parishes. The radical critique of power structures that underlies liberation theology—which provided inspiration for twinning—is absent from the day-to-day functioning of twinning partnerships. Instead, neoliberal concerns about financial accountability, evaluations of program success, and individual transformation overtake the religiously-inspired visions of mutual respect, "familial love," and trust.

Employing some of the same discourse of "solidarity" as Fogarty, Julie Adkins describes the evolution of a partnership between one group of Presbyterian churches in the U.S. and a group of similar size in Guatemala. Bearing many similarities to the "twinning" relationships between Catholic parishes that Tara Hefferan analyzes, the U.S.-Guatemala partnership involves a long-term commitment on both sides and frequent renegotiation of roles and expectations. Several different levels of FBOs operate in this case study—from individual congregations to regional bodies of congregations to national-level denominations—as well as a singular FBO created for the purpose of mediating such transnational relationships. Rather than seeing solidarity as an alternative *to* development, Adkins suggests that these Presbyterian FBOs seem to understand solidarity as a *lens* through which to interrogate and re-envision "development." When solidarity and relationship-building are given first priority, they seem to argue, just and sustainable development is not only possible but necessary in order to build the world as it should be.

The chapter by Javier Pereira, Ronald J. Angel, and Jacqueline L. Angel examines neoliberal reforms in Chile, which encouraged NGOs to take on responsibilities such as elder care. The chapter explores how one NGO, Hogar de Cristo, balances its role as a service provider, dependent on the state for funding and legitimacy, and advocate, a role which implies the potential for conflict with the state. In such a relationship, NGOs may risk becoming "depoliticized," as the "anti-politics" of development (Ferguson 1994) transform them into proxy agents of the state itself rather than agents of social change. Pereira, Angel, and Angel suggest that FBOs, with the material, moral, and discursive support of religious organizations, may have greater potential to resist such depoliticization.

Paul Peters's chapter draws on the organizational studies literature to consider the ways that FBOs might have an advantage over secular NGOs in delivering social services. Looking at the work of Fe y Alegría, an FBO with a mission to educate poor and marginalized children in several South American countries, Peters suggests that FBOs—compared to NGOs more generally—do have perceived advantages and legitimacy in the eyes of local communities and funding agencies. This stems from their particular ability to construct myths and ceremonies that reflect and bolster their mission and goals. Particularly in the Latin American context, Peters argues, the Church as a social institution has a legitimacy that FBOs are able to adopt and take on as their own. This religious affiliation, he suggests, becomes an advantage when it informs organizational roles, ideological commitment, and program activities.

While Peters is concerned with the issues of legitimacy from the perspective of donors and constituent communities, Suzana Ramos Coutinho Bornholdt discusses from a different perspective the concern with legitimacy that characterizes the Buddhist Soka Gakkai International organization of Brazil. Bornholdt suggests that the Soka Gakkai International's prolific Brazilian projects—one focusing on education, the other ecology—are strategies for "carving space" for itself within the Brazilian context, essentially serving as vehicles for evangelization. In its bid for legitimacy, Bornholdt describes a self-conscious decision to position Soka Gakkai International differently among the Brazilian public than to its internal membership. The image produced for external consumption is largely devoid of religious features; rather, emphasis is on Soka Gakkai International as a militant NGO—operating in a context of material deprivation—seeking to educate Brazilian society and preserve its environmental resources; meanwhile, internally, Soka Gakkai International emphasizes religious doctrine and practice among its membership.

Carmen Martinez Novo approaches the role of FBOs by offering a historical examination of the role of Catholic Salesian missionaries in two regions of Ecuador. Her focus helps to illustrate the wide variety of initiatives and FBOs spawned by the church as an institution. In detailing shifting constructions of "tradition" and "modernity," as well as the Catholic Church's notions of a theology of inculturation, Martinez Novo shows how dynamic and dialectical such conceptualizations have been. Moreover, the analysis reveals how the changing sensibilities of the Catholic Church—from understanding indigenous culture as an impediment to be overcome to one that must be valued and preserved—have been manifested in multiple ways through the development programming and projects the Church designs and delivers to local populations. Through this dynamic engagement with poverty and development, the Church has had an enormous political role in building an anti-neoliberal political culture in the country.

Directions for future research

One of the strengths of the work collected in this volume is its representation of the incredible diversity of FBOs along a number of dimensions. This becomes particularly clear in the kind of detailed ethnographic case studies assembled here: organizations which may have similar qualities on paper may behave very differently in practice. Yet, the authors in this volume only just have begun to explore the complexities of FBOs in Latin America and the Caribbean. As this body of research develops, we hope to see more ethnographic studies of FBOs as they engage development, both in local contexts and beyond. As more case studies emerge, across the categories suggested by the typology above, we will gain a more nuanced picture of the roles of FBOs in development, one which will allow meaningful comparisons and generalizations to be made.

The study of FBOs offers a number of challenges for anthropologists. This research encourages, and perhaps demands, multi-sited, multi-vocal research strategies. Many FBOs span national boundaries, and nearly all are part of global religious movements. How do FBOs function as transnational agents? What kinds of relationships between localities do they create or encourage? How do they channel global discourses of religion, of development, of social justice?

There are also a number of dimensions to explore in terms of the relationships between FBOs and other agents of development. What kinds of relationships do FBOs have with funding agencies, both secular and religious? How do they create and maintain legitimacy in the largely secular sphere of development policy? Many of the authors here have examined the relationships of FBOs with governments, as we have focused specifically on neoliberal policies, but what is the role of FBOs in the "anti-politics machine" of development? Some of the authors here have argued that FBOs may offer up an alternative kind of development discourse; yet to be examined is whether this alternative discourse has any impact on the mainstream agents of development, and if so, what that impact might be. As Hefferan asks (this volume), if specific FBOs act as "alternatives *to* development," how have others responded to this alternative?

From a larger perspective, anthropologists have always approached cultures as holistic systems; it is one of the hallmarks of our discipline. We understand that religion and economics are inextricably linked, as are any dimensions of culture that one might choose to explore. But an examination of FBOs forefronts this holistic perspective, since the organizations themselves encourage us to think about the morality of economic choices, to see poverty as more than an economic condition. Questions of poverty and wealth are not only economic issues, just as they are not solely religious questions. Researchers studying FBOs are often highly aware of this convergence, and draw from studies on theology, economics, and development, among others, in their analyses. This body of research may open up nearly uncharted territory in terms of the intersection between anthropology and religion as it is practiced by dominant cultural groups. What does it mean, anthropologically, for evangelicals and Catholics and mainline Protestants to engage the larger society in ways designed to "help"? How does anthropology help us to take seriously both the emic and etic accounts of what is happening and why? These are important directions that require further systematic research in order to address.

Notes

1. This $7.2 billion represented about 13 percent of official aid to developing countries at that point in time (UNDP 1993, 93).

2. Gerard Clarke and Michael Jennings (2008) note that U.S. scholars have tended to distinguish "faith" from "religion." They suggest, "'Religion' normally refers to the values, rules and social practices stemming from belief in a spiritual and supreme being and codified in a sacred text such as the Bible, Qur'an or Bhagavad Gita. Key world religions include Christianity, Islam, Judaism, Hinduism, Sikhism, Buddhism, Daoism and Shinto. Three of these religions (Judaism, Christianity and Islam) share common roots in the Abrahamic tradition of monotheism and originated in the West or Occident, while the world's other major religions are largely polytheistic and originated in South or East Asia. 'Faith' is a more amorphous category, extending beyond the major or established religions. It includes political philosophies with religious elements such as Confucianism or Rastafarianism, modern sects or movements such as the Church of Scientology or the Falun Gong and traditional or indigenous belief systems such as shamanism, mysticism or folk religions which blend elements of mainstream religion with local and traditional beliefs and practices" (Clarke and Jennings 2008, 5).

3. We italicize "new" here, since there are many religious visions of what constitutes a "good life," what appropriate "good works" to express one's selflessness and virtue might be, and how to care for the most vulnerable members of a community that have been in existence for millennia. For example, Bano and Nair (2007, 3) note that the Rig Veda, the most ancient Hindu scripture dating from 1500 BC, "encourages charity and propagates the belief that the one who gifts '. . . shines most.'" However, it is only in the past decade or so that development donors and institutions have taken seriously the material and ideological participation of FBOs in development discourse and practice.

Works Cited

Bano, Masooda, and Padmaja Nair. 2007. Faith-based organisations in South Asia: Historical evolution, current status, and nature of interaction with the state. *Religions and Development Research Programme Working Paper* 12-2007.

Bartkowski, John P., and Helen A. Regis. 2003. *Charitable choices: Religion, race, and poverty in the post-welfare era.* New York: New York University Press.

Belshaw, Deryke, Robert Calderisi, and Chris Sugden, eds. 2001. *Faith in development: Partnership between the World Bank and the churches of Africa.* Oxford: Regnum Book International.

Bornstein, Erica. 2005. *The spirit of development: Protestant NGOs, morality, and economics in Zimbabwe.* Stanford: Stanford University Press.

Boston Globe. 2006. Bush brings faith to foreign aid: As funding rises, Christian groups deliver help with a message. Available online at http://boston.com/news/nation/articles/2006/10/08bush_brings_faith_to_foreign_aid (last accessed January 25, 2008).

Bourdieu, Pierre. 1972. *Outline of a theory of practice.* Cambridge: Cambridge University Press.

Carroll, Thomas F. 1992. *Intermediary NGOs: The supporting link in grassroots development.* West Hartford, CT: Kumarian Press.

Clarke, Gerard. 2006. Faith matters: Faith-based organisations, civil society and international development. *Journal of International Development* 18(6): 835-48.

———. 2007. Agents of transformation? Donors, faith-based organisations and international development. *Third World Quarterly* 28(1):77-96.

Clarke, Gerard, and Michael Jennings. 2008. *Development, civil society, and faith-based organizations: Bridging the sacred and the secular.* New York: Palgrave MacMillan.

Clerkin, Richard M., and Kirsten A. Grønbjerg. 2007. The capacities and challenges of faith-based human services organizations. *Public Administration Review* 67(1):115-26.

Development Directory. 2008. Directory of Development Organizations. Available online at www.devdir.org (last accessed February 26, 2008).

Ebaugh, Helen Rose, Janet S. Chafetz, and Paula F. Pipes. 2006. Where's the faith in faith-based organizations? Measures and correlates of religiosity in faith-based social service coalitions. *Social Forces* 84(4):2259-72.

Edwards, Michael, and David Hulme. 1996. *Beyond the magic bullet: NGO performance and accountability in the post-Cold War world.* West Hartford, CT: Kumarian Press.

Elias, Robert. 1989. Alternative development in Central America: A role for Oxfam? In *Dependence, development, and state repression*, ed. George A. Lopez and Michael Stohl, 1-32. New York: Greenwood Press.

Escobar, Arturo. 1995. *Encountering development: The making and unmaking of the Third World.* Princeton: Princeton University Press.

Esman, Milton, and Norman Uphoff. 1984. *Local organizations: Intermediaries in rural development.* Ithaca, NY: Cornell University Press.

Farrington, John, and Anthony J. Bebbington. 1993. Where from, where at, where next? In *Reluctant partners? Non-governmental organizations, the state and sustainable agricultural development*, 177-95. London: Routledge.

Feldman, Shelley. 1997. NGOs and civil society. *Annals of the American Academy of Political and Social Science* 554:46-66.

Ferguson, James. 1994. *The anti-politics machine: "Development," depoliticization, and bureaucratic power in Lesotho.* Minneapolis: University of Minnesota Press.

Ferguson, James, and Akhil Gupta. 2002. Spatializing states: Toward an ethnography of neoliberal governmentality. *American Ethnologist* 29(4):981-1002.

Fisher, William F. 1997. Doing good? The politics and anti-politics of NGO practices. *Annual Review of Anthropology* 26(1):439-64.

Gardner, Katy. 1997. Mixed messages: Contested "development" and the "Plantation Rehabilitation Project." In *Discourses and development: Anthropological perspectives,* ed. R. D. Grillo and R L. Stirrat, 133-56. Oxford: Berg.

Gardner, Katy, and David Lewis. 1996. *Anthropology, development and the post-modern challenge.* Chicago: Pluto Press.

Gerschenkron, Alexander. 1940. *Economic backwardness in historical perspective.* Cambridge, MA: Harvard University Press.

Glock, Charles Y., and Rodney Stark. 1965. *Religion and society in tension.* Chicago: Rand McNally.

Grillo, R. D. 1997. Discourses of development: The view from anthropology. In *Discourses and development: Anthropological perspectives,* ed. R. D. Grillo and R. L. Stirrat, 1-33. Oxford: Berg.

Haynes, Jeff. 2008. *Religion and development: Conflict or cooperation?* New York: Palgrave MacMillan.

Hearn, Julie. 2002. The "invisible" NGO: U.S. evangelical missions in Kenya. *Journal of Religion in Africa* 32(1):32-61.

Hefferan, Tara. 2007. *Twinning faith and development: Catholic parish partnering in the U.S. and Haiti.* Bloomfield, CT: Kumarian Press.

Hoksbergen, Roland. 2005. Building civil society through partnership: Lessons from a case study of the Christian Reformed World Relief Committee. *Development in Practice* 15(1):16-27.

Hoksbergen, Roland, and L. M. Ewert, eds. 2002. *Local ownership and global change: Will civil society save the world?* Monrovia, CA: World Vision.

Holenstein, Anne-Marie. 2005. Governmental donor agencies and faith-based organizations. *International Review of the Red Cross* 87(858):367-73.

Hope, Anne, and Sally Timmel. 2003. A Kenyan experience for faith-based transformative action. *Development* 46(4):93-99.

Howell, Brian M. 2007. The repugnant cultural other speaks back: Christian identity as ethnographic "standpoint." *Anthropological Theory* 7(4):371-91.

Jeavons, Thomas H. 1998. Identifying characteristics of "religious" organizations: An exploratory proposal. In *Sacred companies: Organizational aspects of religion and religious aspects of organizations,* ed. N. J. Demerath, Peter D. Hall, Terry Schmitt, and Rhys D. Williams, 79-96. Oxford: Oxford University Press.

———. 2004. Religious and faith-based organizations: Do we know one when we see one? *Nonprofit and Voluntary Sector Quarterly* 33(1):140-5.

Lehmann, David. 1990. *Development and democracy in Latin America: Economics, politics and religion in the post-war period.* Philadelphia: Temple University Press.

Leonard, David K. 1982. Analyzing the organizational requirements for serving the rural poor. In *Institutions of rural development for the poor: Decentralization and organizational linkages,* ed. David K. Leonard and Dale Rogers Marshall, 1-39. Berkeley: Institute of International Studies, University of California.

Leonard, David K., and Dale Rogers Marshall, eds. 1982. *Institutions of rural development for the poor: Decentralization and organizational linkages.* Berkeley: Institute of International Studies, University of California.

Lister, Sarah. 2000. Power in partnership? An analysis of an NGO's relationships with its partners. *Journal of International Development* 12(2):227-39.

Lorgen, Christy Cannon. 1998. Dancing with the state: The role of NGOs in health care and health policy. *Journal of International Development* 10(3):323-39.

Maddox, James G. 1956. *Technical assistance by religious agencies in Latin America*. Chicago: University of Chicago Press.

Marshall, Katherine. 2001. Development and religion: A different lens on development debates. *Peabody Journal of Education* 76(3 & 4):339-75.

Marshall, Katherine, and Lucy Keough, eds. 2004. *Mind, heart, and soul in the fight against poverty*. Washington, DC: The World Bank.

Marshall, Katherine, and Richard Marsh, eds. 2003. *Millennium challenges for development and faith institutions*. Washington, DC: The World Bank.

Martinussen, J. 1997. *Society, state and market: A guide to competing theories of development*. London: Zed Books.

Mayotte, Judith A. 1998. Religion and global affairs: The role of religion in development. *SAIS Review* 18(2):65-9.

McGrew, Charlene C., and Ram A. Cnaan. 2006. Finding congregations: Developing conceptual clarity in the study of faith-based social services. *Journal of Religion and Spirituality in Social Work* 25(3/4):19-37.

Monsma, Stephen V. 2004. *Putting faith in partnerships: Welfare to work in four cities*. Ann Arbor: University of Michigan Press.

Nieman, Anna. 2006. Churches and social development: A South African perspective. *International Social Work* 49(5):595-604.

Occhipinti, Laurie. 2005. *Acting on faith: Religious development organizations in northwestern Argentina*. Lanham, MD: Lexington Books.

Ortner, Sherry. 1994. Theory in anthropology since the sixties. In *Culture/power/history: A reader in contemporary social theory*, ed. Nicholas B. Dirks, Geoff Eley, and Sherry Ortner, 372-411. Princeton: Princeton University Press.

Reese, Laura A., and Gary Shields. 2000. Faith-based economic development. *Policy Studies Review* 17(2/3):84-103.

Riddell, Roger C., and Mark Robinson. 1995. *Non-governmental organizations and rural poverty alleviation*. Oxford: Oxford University Press.

Rist, Gilbert. 1997. *The history of development*. London: Zed Books.

Sanyal, Bishwapyira. 1997. NGOs' self-defeating quest for autonomy. *Annals of the American Academy of Political and Social Science* 554:21-33.

Selinger, Leah. 2004. The forgotten factor: The uneasy relationship between religion and development. *Social Compass* 51(4):523-43.

Sider, Ronald J., and Heidi Rolland Unruh. 2004. Typology of religious characteristics of social service and educational organizations and programs. *Nonprofit and Voluntary Sector Quarterly* 33(1):109-34.

Smith, Stephen Rathgeb, and Michael R. Sosin. 2001. The varieties of faith-related agencies. *Public Administration Review* 61(6):651-70.

Storey, Donavan. 1998. Towards an alternative society? The role of intermediary nongovernmental organizations (INGOs) in poor communities. *Urban Anthropology and Studies of Cultural Systems and World Economic Development* 27(3):345-92.

Streeten, Paul. 1997. Nongovernmental organizations and development. *Annals of the American Academy of Political and Social Science* 554:193-211.

Sweetman, Caroline, ed. 1999. *Gender, religion, and spirituality*. Oxford: Oxfam.

Ter Haar, Gerrie, and Stephen Ellis. 2006. The role of religion in development: Towards a new relationship between the European Union and Africa. *European Journal of Development Research* 18(3):351-67.

Tomalin, Emma. 2006. Religion and a rights-based approach to development. *Progress in Development Studies* 6(2):93-108.

Tripp, Linda. 1999. Gender and development from a Christian perspective: Experience from World Vision. *Gender and Development* 7(1):62-8.

Trouillot, Michel-Rolph. 1992. The Caribbean region: An open frontier in anthropological theory. *Annual Review of Anthropology* 21:19-42.

Tyndale, Wendy. 2000. Faith and economics in "development": A bridge across the chasm? *Development in Practice* 10(1):9-18.

———. 2006. *Visions of development: Faith-based initiatives.* Aldershot, England and Burlington, VT: Ashgate.

United Nations Development Programme (UNDP). 1993. *Human Development Report 1993.* New York: Oxford University Press.

———. 2002. *Human Development Report 2002.* New York: Oxford University Press.

Uphoff, Norman. 1987. *Local institutional development.* West Hartford, CT: Kumarian Press.

Ver Beek, Kurt Allen. 2000. Spirituality: A development taboo. *Development in Practice* 10(1):31-43.

Working Group on Human Needs and Faith-Based and Community Initiatives. 2002. Finding common ground: 29 recommendations of the Working Group on Human Needs and Faith-Based and Community Initiatives. Available online at http://www.sfcg.org/Programmes/us/report.pdf (last accessed January 10, 2008).

World Bank. 2007. Consultations with Civil Society. Available online at http://siteresources.worldbank.org/CSO/Resources/ConsultationsSourcebook_Feb2007.pdf (last accessed February 25, 2008).

Wuthnow, Robert. 2004. *Saving America? Faith-based service and the future of civil society.* Princeton: Princeton University Press.

Zaidi, S. Akbar. 1999. NGO failure and the need to bring back the state. *Journal of International Development* 11(2):259-71.

Chapter 2
Waging the War on Drugs:
Neoliberal Governance and the Formation of
Faith-Based Organizations in Urban Mexico
Ethan P. Sharp[1]

On August 15, 2005, the mayor of Ciudad Juárez, one of Mexico's largest cities, just across the border from El Paso, Texas, ordered a lockdown for a large prison under his jurisdiction in an attempt to end the trafficking and consumption of drugs by inmates. While he prevented the entry of most outsiders, including relatives of prisoners, he brought in evangelical Christian ministers to pray for the inmates and to help them through the processes of detoxification and rehabilitation, a move that generated humorous headlines in leading national newspapers.[2] By September, the mayor and the director of the prison, who are both evangelicals, declared operation *cereso limpio,* or clean prison, a success and lifted the lockdown. A few months later, a riot broke out and ended in the deaths of seven inmates. The director of the prison said the riot was an attempt to undermine the objectives of *cereso limpio*, and blamed gangs on the U.S. side of the border for the violence.

Despite the humor and mayhem surrounding the mayor's actions in Ciudad Juarez, I have found evidence of increasing and widespread cooperation between state agencies and evangelical organizations in the treatment of drug addictions both inside and outside of prisons.[3] In 2006, I conducted exploratory ethnographic investigations of evangelical programs for drug addicts in Mexico City, one of the world's largest urban agglomerations, and in Monterrey, Mexico's third largest metropolitan area, located in the northeastern state of Nuevo León. I made observations of three different prison ministries, as they were carried out within prisons, and four evangelical addiction treatment programs that operate independently from prisons. In addition to interviews with converted prisoners, recovered addicts and other individuals involved in these ministries, I interviewed prison administrators, public health officials, and representatives of governmental granting agencies who work closely with evangelical organizations. This comparative research on overlapping programs, conducted in multiple sites, yielded valuable perspectives on the processes that have transformed

35

the local evangelistic campaigns of conservative Protestant churches among prisoners and drug addicts into addiction treatment programs that have a regional or national reach and in some cases receive public funding.[4]

In this chapter, I contend that current patterns of neoliberal governance, many of which are carried out as part of the so-called war on drugs, have reinforced the growth and reorganization of evangelical churches, and birthed these new evangelical ministries which, while relatively free from the direct influence of organizations outside of Mexico, resemble in many respects evangelical faith-based organizations that have figured into major political campaigns in the U.S. The designation "faith-based" has no parallel in Mexico, and many of these new ministries have not yet found an appropriate discourse for representing their aims to a larger, secular public. Indeed, the term "faith-based" is a unique expression of the particular histories that have shaped the relationship of the U.S. state to religion. My argument, however, is that the war on drugs reveals a binational coordination of neoliberal politics and governance that is responsible for both the formation of evangelical organizations that have participated in the execution of public policies in Mexico and the rise to prominence of organizations like Prison Fellowship and Teen Challenge, a network of evangelical programs for drug addicts, in the U.S.[5] This process promises to realign the relationship between states and religion across the Americas along the lines of the current model in the U.S., for which the cornerstone is a strong ideological and political alliance between neoliberal regimes and evangelical missions.

In order to substantiate my argument, I begin with some clarifications about the war on drugs and suggest that the increasing public role of evangelicals amid the war on drugs has depended on the growth and political mobilization of megachurches. I then offer some specific examples of neoliberal technologies of governance that are employed in combating addictions to drugs, and consider the ways in which these technologies coincide with the practices of evangelical ministries. In conclusion, I describe some of the processes involved in building faith-based organizations that are able to seek and to obtain public assistance in Mexico. Throughout the chapter, I insert excerpts of discourses offered by representatives of the state, evangelical ministers, and their converts in order to convey the powerful affinities in these discourses. In the second half of the chapter, I consider more closely some of the testimonies that these ministries have produced, and the ways in which testimonies have been adapted to further the formation of faith-based programs for drug addicts in Mexico. Testimonies constitute the most important verbal genre for sustaining the work of evangelicals, and, if rendered in a language that affirms the transformative potential of faith without privileging evangelicalism, they can also confirm the public value of this work and assure it an enduring role in the war on drugs.

The War on Drugs

As the reports on the prison in Ciudad Juárez suggest, efforts to combat drug trafficking and consumption both originate with and are confounded by events in the U.S. Furthermore, as the drug trade has expanded, a drug addiction "crisis" has taken root in Mexico and opened new fronts in the war on drugs. Although there was once a relatively low rate of drug use in Mexico, incidents of drug use, especially cocaine and methamphetamine, have increased dramatically over the past few years in most parts of the country (Brouwer et al. 2006), and many of the men who have circulated through the country's prisons are addicts. One frustrated government employee who coordinates social programs in the poorest barrios of Monterrey claimed in exasperation that the drug problem "is not growing; it is invading us."

The standard explanation for this so-called invasion is that Mexican drug trade entrepreneurs have achieved a competitive advantage in the movement of cocaine from South America into the U.S., the principal market for cocaine. Because of their success, they have claimed the right to increasing percentages of cocaine shipments, some of which are retained for sale and consumption in Mexico (Boyer 2001, 72). Indeed, as the intercontinental drug trade has expanded, the market for cocaine has blossomed in Mexico, and now offers cocaine at very low prices, allowing poor urban youth to purchase drugs that were once beyond their reach. Unlike in the U.S., where federal and state governments have expanded their prison systems in order to absorb the massive number of drug consumers who have been prosecuted and sentenced as part of the war on drugs, the prisons of Mexico are notoriously overcrowded and largely ineffective for the purposes of the war on drugs. Except in a few cases, Mexican prisons remain important nodes in the drug trafficking network.

Regardless of the many strains that the war on drugs has placed on the state, the evolving drug abuse crisis has lent itself to media and political spectacles that can be used to mobilize the support of different segments of the population and to sustain exceptional actions by the state. The execution of the war on drugs in Mexico has created a state apparatus that both augments the power of the executive and infringes on the rights of individual citizens. As other scholars have shown, this process has been gradual, involving a series of changes over two decades, including the use of more aggressive police tactics, the criminalization of drug use, the implementation of longer sentences for drug offenses, increasing reliance on the military to enforce drug policy, and greater collaboration—both legal and extralegal—with U.S. agencies (See Freeman and Sierra 2005; Ramos Lira et al. 1999; Romero 1998). These changes, however threatening to democratic rule, must be understood in relation to the competitive state and national elections that have been taking place in Mexico, in which candidates are able to gain votes by making strong commitments to the war on drugs.

Since assuming the presidency, Felipe Calderón has received praise both in Mexico and abroad for leading a visible escalation in the war on drugs. The effects of this escalation have been profound in Monterrey. In a city that once had relatively low rates of violence associated with drug use and drug trafficking, drug cartels have begun carrying out a terrifying campaign of assassinations. In July of this year, Calderón visited the city in order to initiate his media campaign called *Limpiémos México*. The primary focus of this campaign, made clear in the many state-sponsored commercials that have been broadcast on radio and television about it, has been to address the drug abuse crisis, involving promises to prevent drugs from entering public school and to build more public facilities that can treat drug addictions. But it has also been tied to an even more aggressive stance against drug traffickers. In his speech in Monterrey, Calderón declared, "In this fight, we are absolutely committed, and we will persevere, and we will not take one step backward in the struggle against organized crime" (García 2007, 1A). This campaign by Calderón, as much as it is intended to strengthen his political position, also helps to sustain the state's continuing commitment to neoliberal policies and increasing economic interdependence with the U.S. Indeed, the war on drugs has helped to build up and to preserve political support in both countries for a binational neoliberal agenda, resulting in the increased movement of labor and capital across the continent.

The war on drugs, with its preoccupations with military campaigns, purposely obfuscates the causes of the drug trade and drug addiction. Part of the "long process of militarization and empire building" perpetrated by the U.S. (Lutz 2002, 723), this war is carried out principally by the Drug Enforcement Administration, which has helped to coordinate operations by the Mexican military and federal police forces, successfully extradited numerous suspected drug traffickers, and held out the promise of enormous aid packages intended to strengthen the Mexican state's effectiveness in the war on drugs. The influence of the U.S. in Mexico's execution of the war on drugs is so great that it was apparently responsible for the demise of a federal proposal in 2006 to decriminalize the possession of small quantities of marijuana. Several scholars have shown that Mexico's acquiescence in these matters is intended, paradoxically, to ensure that its sovereignty is not violated by the incursion of U.S. policing forces (Toro 1995). At the same time, the Mexican state does not want to jeopardize its interests in immigration and trade policy debates within the U.S. The broader set of transnational concerns, in other words, hinges on the pursuit of and adherence to a neoliberal model of economic integration and development in North America.

In the execution of this most recent stage of Mexico's war on drugs, the Mexican state also has sought to garner the support of evangelicals within its territories, although a relatively small proportion of the electorate, and to enjoin evangelical ministries in preventing and treating drug addiction. Indeed, the self-responsibilization that can be attained through evangelical communities can be a highly valued goal of neoliberal governance (Ferguson and Gupta 2002, 989; Cruikshank 1993, 330). Political scientist Alejandro Alvarez notes that the structural changes achieved by neoliberal policies since the 1980s have resulted in a dismantling of the social welfare infrastructure, yet have not generated additional opportunities for employment beyond the informal sector. In response, subsequent presidential administrations in Mexico have placed greater emphasis on "personal realization," a process that occurs "through intermediate structures between the state and the individual" (Alvarez 2004, 93). Evangelical organizations exist within this intermediate realm, providing paths to spiritual transformations that can help individuals to deal with the difficulties presented by the present economic situation.

The Expansion of Evangelical Ministries

The engagement of evangelicals with prisoners and addicts has become an important element in the growth of the evangelical movement. A number of faith-based addiction treatment programs that have gained prominence in the U.S. and Mexico are rooted in the early missionary work of Pentecostal churches, and have produced converts who have become leaders of their own missions and churches. In Mexico, Pentecostal churches like the Assemblies of God have maintained a presence since the first decade of the twentieth century, and have pursued missionary work among individuals who were perceived as "lost causes." In Monterrey, one Pentecostal church established a drug abuse treatment program called Barrios para Cristo in the city's red-light district in the 1970s. Barrios para Cristo later expanded into a network of treatment centers in northeastern Mexico, and no longer maintains close connections with a particular church or denomination. In Mexico City, a pastor affiliated with the Assemblies of God helped to establish Reto a la Juventud as a branch of Teen Challenge in 1979. Reto a la Juventud, even as it has lost most of its connections to the U.S.-based network and to the Assemblies of God, has evolved into a highly successful network of treatment centers, serving more than one hundred addicts per year.

These programs, which have grown in concert with the state's war on drugs, are focused on achieving a personalized, complete recovery through typical evangelical activities, such as Bible readings, sharing testimonies, and preaching—one that empowers the recovered individual to lead others through the same experience. Individuals who successfully complete the programs often model the kinds of conversions that evangelicals seek for all people and reflect their vision that only evangelism can provide solutions to the country's social problems. Because of this possibility, ministries to prisoners and to drug addicts are viewed as a very special work, often more important than missions concerned with meeting the basic needs of the poor.

Furthermore, the discourse that evangelicals often use to claim dramatic conversions and compel others to seek the same has parallels with the discourses employed in the war on drugs. They both invoke the language of military campaigns that can end only in total victory. This language was vividly on display in a sermon that I recorded in a large neo-Pentecostal church in Mexico City, in which the preacher declared, "Do you realize how in the nation of Mexico, how in Mexico City, we need men like these? Men and women, who are ready to shout, to pray, to plead, to fight the battle for this city?" He continued, "It is necessary that wherever you live, you raise your voice, you raise your voice, so that in this city, violence falls, crimes go down. And the gospel increases, and the Kingdom of God advances."[6]

Despite the discursive affinities between evangelicalism and the war on drugs, the building and expansion of the actual infrastructures for evangelical ministries among prisoners and drug addicts has depended on organizational changes in evangelical communities and the emergence of megachurches. As some urban evangelical congregations in Mexico have expanded into mega- churches over the last three decades, they have included more and more mem- bers of the middle class, boasting large modern buildings and teams of full-time ministers. Whether or not these megachurches have their roots in traditional Protestant churches, the growth of most megachurches has occurred through increasing interpenetration with Pentecostalism, a fact that begins to account for their highly skilled praise and worship bands, theatrical styles of prayer, and occasional glossolalia. These megachurches fit the consumerist, middle-class lifestyle, and provide a set of social connections that most suburban and urban dwellers would not find elsewhere. At the same time, they elevate or transform the place of evangelicals in the world. Having moved from dispersed, loosely affiliated small congregations, they now demonstrate remarkable organizational strength, and can pursue different avenues for gaining attention and recognition from outsiders. Megachurches can generate ministries that make use of more resources and achieve a greater impact than some longstanding private social services or state agencies. They also become highly desirable partners for politi- cal campaigns.

Both in Monterrey and Mexico City, there are a few well-known churches with congregations numbering in the thousands and offering a dazzling array of ministries. In Monterrey, for example, the Castillo del Rey is a network of churches throughout the metropolitan area, claiming over ten thousand mem- bers. Founded and led by a North American missionary less than twenty years ago, the Castillo del Rey network includes a comprehensive school and sponsors missionaries in different parts of the world. In 2003, its principal and largest congregation opened the Centro de Rehabilitación Ebenezer, a successful drug abuse treatment center that has treated an average of forty men each year. In Mexico City, Amistad Cristiana is one of the largest evangelical organizations, attracting thousands to its weekly services. Amistad Cristiana has maintained a strong alliance with Christ for the Nations, an organization based in Dallas, Texas; and with the help of missionaries from the U.S., spawned a network of prison and drug addiction ministries in the late 1990s, including Fundación Emmanuel. Although Fundación Emmanuel has staked out its independence from most evangelical churches and organizations, it draws volunteers for its ministries from the Castillo del Rey, Amistad Cristiana, and other mega- churches, as well as smaller traditional Pentecostal churches.

Fundación Emmanuel's principal mission is to minister to and to convert prisoners. This mission, however, has increasingly also involved helping prisoners to achieve freedom from drug addictions, and Fundación Emmanuel has instituted courses in prisons specifically targeted at addicts. Some inmates who have affiliated with Fundación Emmanuel have come to see their time in prison as a kind of rehabilitation program. A recovering addict to crack, whom I interviewed in one of Mexico City's vast prisons, claimed, "I can get out soon if I want. But the Holy Spirit has put it in my heart not to go and to let it be that the Lord really heals me." Fundación Emmanuel has also recently opened drug abuse treatment centers in Toluca and Guadalajara. It has received support from private donors, corporations, and state agencies in order to carry out its activities, and, like Reto a la Juventud, it has substantially increased its scope and impact in recent years.

At the same time that evangelicals have grown and become better organized, politicians like Felipe Calderón have begun to make appeals for support in evangelical megachurches. Calderón's campaign strategists, including some experts from the U.S., attempted to create a reliable block of voters among evangelicals. Calderón campaigned on the slogan "*Valor y pasión*," which sent subtle cues to evangelicals and other religious groups. Calderón and his wife met repeatedly with evangelical leaders in Mexico, and stated firmly their opposition to abortion and homosexual marriages in these meetings. In one interview with a newspaper produced by the Amistad Cristiana organization in Puebla, Margarita Zavala de Calderón explained her husband's slogan, "We realized . . . that many men and women want people with values, an approach to policymaking that protects the family and that lives with those values" (Amistad Comunicaciones 2006). These efforts clearly paid off. Although I found that evangelical Christians in Mexico proved to be significantly less interested in politics than their counterparts in the U.S., I did find more support for Calderón among them than for any other candidate.

The engagement of evangelicals in political campaigns provides a basis for their direct participation in neoliberal governance. Furthermore, as I have suggested, the war on drugs is well suited for evangelicals. Its discourse, emphasizing crises and combat, resonates with the apocalypticism of many evangelicals. To the degree that evangelicals become engaged with the state's war on drugs, the state can consolidate political support among evangelicals, and evangelicals can gain an increased measure of legitimacy and visibility. Furthermore, evangelicals can receive special access to state agencies and public resources that benefit their work.

Miraculous Modes of Governance

José Luis Velasco (2005) and other scholars have argued persuasively that changes in economic policies in accordance with neoliberal orthodoxy, accompanied by "democratization," have further marginalized already vulnerable segments of the Mexican population and rendered them even more disposed to involvement in the drug trade and violence.[7] This chapter has begun to describe some governmental strategies that the Mexican state has pursued under these circumstances—strategies that are consistent with neoliberal ideologies yet intended to counteract the disastrous effects of neoliberalization. For example, the state has created new social actors, assigned them responsibilities that once were believed to be the domain of the state, and facilitated international and transnational cooperation to fulfill these responsibilities.

As several scholars have argued, neoliberal governance does not involve a lessening of the state's reach, but is rather a process of the state achieving desirable goals, such as a more flexible and enterprising workforce, through reliance on new nonstate actors. Anthropologists James Ferguson and Akhil Gupta, for example, provide the following clarification:

> This is not a matter of less government, as the usual ideological formulations would have it. Rather, it indicates a new modality of government, which works by creating mechanisms that work "all by themselves" to bring about the governmental results through the devolution of risk onto "enterprise" or the individual, and the "responsibilization" of subjects who are increasingly empowered to discipline themselves (Ferguson and Gupta 2002: 989).

I propose, however, that neoliberal governance is not only a set of new and more efficient governing technologies, but also encompasses the political and cultural work that creates the conditions in which these technologies achieve viability.

I encountered examples of this kind of governance in the implementation of government programs, both in Monterrey and Mexico City. One is the program designated "*Todos en Tu Barrio*," through which federal, state, and municipal agencies collaborate with non-governmental organizations—including private universities and multinational corporations—in order to improve and to beautify neighborhoods that were originally squatter settlements. Through the program, residents received donations of concrete and paint, and were instructed to construct sidewalks and paint their homes. In Monterrey, many shared in the benefits of this beautification project because the unfinished and unpainted homes of these neighborhoods were often constructed on mountains and foothills, visible from different vantage points throughout the city, and therefore distractions from the desired image of a prosperous and sophisticated metropolis, the host city for the United Nation's 2007 Forum of Cultures. The Consejo de Desarrollo Social, which coordinates "Todos en Tu Barrio" in Monterrey, also has dispatched an employee of the state of Nuevo León in order to get to know the residents of these neighborhoods and to respond to their needs. In the neighborhood where he was concentrating his efforts in 2006—overrun with crack cocaine—he identified a number of addicts and managed to enroll a few of them in a private drug abuse treatment program at the expense of the state, although none completed the program.

Another example of this kind of governance, one which has directly involved evangelicals, is the grant competition. The Consejo de Desarrollo Social in Monterrey began in 2005 to solicit grant applications from non-governmental agencies, and at least two evangelical organizations in Monterrey received government grants for the first time. Both organizations provide services to drug addicts and their families. The parallel to the Consejo de Desarrollo Social in Mexico City, the Instituto de Asistencia e Integración Social (IASIS), began an annual competition for grants in 2003. Fundación Emmanuel applied for and received a grant to support its work with children of prisoners in the same year, and Reto a la Juventud has received a substantial grant from IASIS every year since 2003.

Aside from these grants, both Fundación Emmanuel and Reto a la Juventud have begun to work closely with prison administrators. For example, the office of the director for all prisons in Mexico City, known as Dirección General, included Fundación Emmanuel in a formal collaborative project for the first time in 2006. As part of this project, Fundación Emmanuel has begun to develop a re-entry program for thirty inmates. Dirección General also invited Reto a la Juventud to design and to implement programs for a new kind of prison that prepares inmates whose sentences are about to end for re-entry. Two prisons of this kind were opened in Mexico City in 2005, with the goal of reducing recidivism and beginning to solve the problem of prison overpopulation. The director of one of these new prisons told me that the work of Reto a la Juventud, Fundación Emmanuel, and another ministry affiliated with Amistad Cristiana has been essential to her success because it provides the inmates with "hope." Furthermore, she claimed that these organizations often do what most psychiatrists and state programs cannot do: they rehabilitate prisoners. I encountered several impressive testimonies generated by the ministries of Fundación Emmanuel that could bear out this affirmation.

Fundación Emmanuel, which coordinates ministries in most prisons throughout Mexico, has maintained a firm commitment to evangelism and the support of churches within prisons, despite its involvement in other projects. In Mexico City I entered several prisons with Fundación Emmanuel, and attended courses in "human relationships," Bible studies, and church services that Fundación Emmanuel sponsored within the prisons. On occasion, ministers of Fundación Emmanuel may distribute snacks, like day-old donuts donated by Dunkin Donuts, at church services in order to attract more inmates to the events. On other occasions, volunteers may distribute soap and deodorant, among other gifts. Because inmates are largely dependent on outsiders to provide them with clothes, hygiene products, and money, inmates whose families are unavailable or unwilling to give them these necessities often turn to Fundación Emmanuel or other prison ministries for help. José, an inmate released in 2006 and now living at a halfway house affiliated with the organization, recalled that he ultimately was drawn to Fundación Emmanuel because his family no longer visited him, and after several years he came to acquire an evangelical faith and eventually to overcome his addiction to drugs. In an interview in Toluca, he recalled his thoughts as the end of his sentence approached:

> And I said yes, but I never had intentions of continuing. Why? Because I had the idea to continue robbing. I said, "No, well after so many years robbing, how am I going to make such a radical change? . . . But thanks to God, I began to pray and to ask God. And I begin to make requests. . . . And so little by little I started believing.[8]

Just as the nicely painted homes achieved by "Todos en Tu Barrio" in the poor neighborhoods around Monterrey are intended to convey a successful campaign to alleviate poverty in Nuevo León, the testimonies of miraculous change offered by people like José may be used as evidence that evangelical initiatives can yield solutions to the epidemic of drug addiction and are worthy of widespread support. In this way, testimonies play important roles in the formation of faith-based programs, and provide these programs with increasing opportunities for collaboration with the state.

These testimonies also form the basis for other kinds of evangelical discourse that are more obviously engaged with neoliberal governance. For example, I witnessed numerous instances in which evangelical ministers insisted before groups of prisoners that disciplined labor and respect for authorities— after conversion and salvation, of course—could yield solutions to their problems. In the dozens of sermons, lectures, and discussions that I listened to, ministers emphasized repeatedly that inmates, by virtue of being in prison, have opportunities to change through not only prayer and other spiritual exercises but also by participating in educational programs and preparing themselves for work. In one Bible study session in a large prison on the southeast side of Mexico City, one man representing Fundación Emmanuel spent more than thirty minutes trying to convince the inmates that they were privileged, insisting that they were "spoiled by Papá," they had received a "fellowship from God," that they should not "throw away the opportunity to prepare themselves," and that God had a "respectable job" for them once they got out.

The possibilities for many inmates to get a respectable job, however, are quite limited. If there is any job for them to have, it is most often in the informal sector and does not pay well.[9] The dearth of good opportunities was made starkly clear to me when one of the ministers working with juvenile delinquents in Monterrey enthusiastically proposed that the young men in her charge should take classes to learn how to process and package soy products, like tofu, so that they could in turn sell it to their neighbors—an unlikely enterprise given that tofu is not very well known in Mexico.[10] She was certain that these classes could keep them from returning to the life that led them to prison.

The Formation of Faith-Based Initiatives

Faith-based organizations can work closely with the state to evaluate and adjust treatment programs, thereby fostering an ever more fortuitous convergence of the discourse of the church with the discourse of the state. I have heard several evangelicals who work closely with state agencies claim to speak two languages, the Spirit-inspired language of faith and the bureaucratic language of government. The degree to which both of these languages can mix within faith-based organizations—so that they can attract strong support from both evangelical networks and the state—will determine the long-term viability of these organizations. I have found that Fundación Emmanuel has not been fully committed to these processes, and its treatment efforts have failed to command the kind of support that evangelical organizations dedicated to residential addiction treatment have received.

The operation of prison ministries, however, when compared with the operations of residential addiction treatment centers, is relatively simple and inexpensive. Unlike prison ministries, addiction treatment centers must be involved in the following activities in order to carry out their mission effectively: building and acquiring of facilities that can house addicts, receiving support beyond evangelical networks, achieving accreditation from and acceptance within state agencies, including health departments, and pursuing different kinds of direct and formal collaboration with state agencies. The receipt of a government grant can represent the culmination of these activities. Of the organizations that I got to know, only Reto a la Juventud was successfully engaged in all of these activities; however, I encountered other evangelical ministries that aimed for the kind of institutionalization that Reto a la Juventud had achieved. This transition inevitably requires a more precise calibration of evangelical discourse so that it appeals to wider audiences, from which it can cull clients and request funds for its operations. Also, if an addiction treatment organization seeks support from the state, it must also employ a discourse that, in accordance with public consensus, supports and defends religious diversity.

By way of conclusion, I consider more closely the work and discourse of Reto a la Juventud. Over a period of almost twenty years, Reto a la Juventud has built a large campus in Mexico City and has opened facilities in other parts of Mexico. Its facilities have received accreditation from local health departments and related agencies. Unlike traditional evangelical ministries that rely on small donations, Reto a la Juventud requires that the families of interns make some kind of financial contribution, and also has a team of volunteers that are dedicated to obtaining additional financial support. Much of this additional support has come from sources outside of evangelical networks such as individual donors, private foundations, and government sources. The organization is recognized as an Instituto de Asistencia Privada, or IAP, under the laws of the federal district of Mexico City, and this legal standing allows it to receive donations from a wide range of sources. The transition of Reto a la Juventud from a small church-based program into a large and respected substance abuse treatment center that maintains its evangelical character is rare, but provides incentive for other evangelical organizations to pursue the same kind of expansion.

As part of this transition, Reto a la Juventud has also allowed for different kinds of evaluations of the program, and made changes as necessary, such as lengthening the amount of time required to complete the program. Today participants in the treatment program at Reto a la Juventud endure periods of separation from their friends and family that last nine months. Roberto, who passed through the program four years ago when it only lasted six months, and now serves as a volunteer at the headquarters of Reto a la Juventud in Mexico City, claims that the length of the program ensures a kind of success that is almost universally desirable. He explained to me, using a language that meets the interests of the state, "Because we don't want to just get away from the substances, but we also want to gain knowledge and skills . . . so that they can become incorporated into society." During the course of the program, residents are expected to pass through three stages. Roberto described the first stage as detoxification and the decision to make a "radical change," although he did not initially specify what this change entailed. The second stage is a process of self-discipline and restoration of the family, and the third stage is social reinsertion, which can include different kinds of job training.

The kind of change that interns experience at Reto a la Juventud is, of course, a religious conversion. Later, I asked Roberto for his testimony. He said he came to Reto a la Juventud after several years of addiction to alcohol, marijuana and other drugs. He decided to enter the program after his father gave him an ultimatum, telling him to get help or get out of the house. He recounted the process:

> So I stayed in the rehabilitation center. And from the beginning they started to talk to me about Christ, about Christ, and I didn't want anything to do with it. I started to read the Bible, and I didn't understand anything and I didn't like it. Until, after having been two months in the rehabilitation program, I stayed, I was convinced, and I continued to stay with it . . . So two months after having been in rehabilitation, I gave my life to Christ. I became convinced that only through his power I am going to be able to come out of all this. And more than that, you know, I became convinced that he is the best option for a style of life.[11]

Jorge, who also passed through the program and now works as a volunteer alongside Roberto, also helped to illuminate the experience of rehabilitation at Reto a la Juventud. He came to Reto a la Juventud at the age of twenty-three, after five years of addiction to cocaine. He called his addiction a "bitter" experience, which involved fruitless searches for liberation. He explained: "Before arriving at Reto a la Juventud, I went through clinics, through psychologists, with doctors, with witchcraft, and nothing of that could change me." After spending some time at the facility in Toluca, Jorge claimed:

> I understood that it was the goodness of God that allowed me to be there. . . . He helped me to change my character, to change my laziness, to change that thing that I could not stop, addiction. Those three months in Toluca were for me a honeymoon with God.[12]

The conversions of both Roberto and Jorge seemed to have saved them from a future of continued suffering, but as critics of faith-based organizations in the U.S. have pointed out, direct government support for these kinds of programs that push interns toward an encounter with God constitutes a violation of governing principles that guarantee religious freedoms. Furthermore, several critics insist that it is a diversion from more substantial, comprehensive solutions that the state could make. Emphasis on conversions, for example, can prevent addicts from acknowledging social and other kinds of sources for addictions.

By viewing this kind of government support through the lens of the war on the drugs, I find that these criticisms ultimately fail to respond to the increasing numbers of people that have come to expect religion to play a transformative role in the governance of the North American continent, a change that has depended on continuing innovations in neoliberal political strategies and the growth of evangelicalism. This chapter has sought to illuminate the powerful convergences between these two processes and to imagine some of the ways in which these processes are mutually constitutive. The carefully crafted testimonies of Roberto and Jorge, victors in the war on drugs, begin to convey the intricacies of these convergences. By presenting their recoveries as part of the natural course of strengthening one's personal faith, and evincing little of an aggressive commitment to evangelism, they present a model of faith-based action that many of us might readily endorse and, by so doing, begin to redress the crises that the implementation of neoliberal policies has occasioned—completing yet another circle that serves to reinforce the political consolidations that keep these policies in place.

Notes

1. I conducted research for this chapter through the support of a Transnationalism Fellowship from the Mexico-North Research Network. I am grateful to the Mexico-North Research Network for this support. Ultimately, this research was made possible by the generous collaboration of individuals affiliated with evangelical ministries discussed here, especially Fundación Emmanuel and Reto a la Juventud.

2. For a full account of the events in Ciudad Juárez, see De la Fuente 2005 and Nájera 2005.

3. Evangelicals resist simple definitions. I use the term in ways that are consistent with the uses of other scholars (See Bowen 1996 and Cahn 2003). The common characteristics of the organizations that I am referring to here are the use of rituals and discourse that are Bible-centered, an emphasis on evangelism and leading nonbelievers through a dramatic conversion experience, strong social networks among believers, and theological and institutional traditions that are rooted in conservative Protestantism.

4. Although none of the people whom I interviewed described their work, which was largely focused on the troubles of specific individuals, as part of the war on drugs, it is important to recognize that the war on drugs defines the broader contexts in which their work takes place.

5. Prison Fellowship and Teen Challenge programs have received substantial grants from state and federal governments in recent years. They are perhaps the best known evangelical faith-based organizations in the U.S., and are regarded as favorites of the current Bush administration. Studies have suggested that Prison Fellowship programs are successful in reducing recidivism, and that Teen Challenge programs are more successful than nonsectarian programs in treating addiction (See Dilulio 2004; Johnson 2002).

6. "¿Se da cuenta cómo en la nación de México, cómo en la ciudad de México, se necesitan hombres como éstos? Hombres y mujeres que estén dispuestos a clamar, a orar, a rogar, a pelear la batalla por la ciudad. . . . Se necesita, dondequiera que usted viva, se levante clamor, se levante clamor, para que en esta ciudad, la violencia caiga, los crímenes bajen. Y el evangelio aumente, y el reino de Dios avance."

7. See Portes and Roberts 2005. Philippe Bourgois also illuminates the "structures of segregation and marginalization" that lead to involvement in the sale and consumption of crack cocaine in the U.S. (Bourgois 1996, 18).

8. "Yo le dije que sí, pero nunca tenía la meta de seguir. ¿Por qué? Porque yo tenía la idea de seguir robando. Dije, 'No, pues si tantos años llevo robando, ¿cómo voy a hacer un cambio tan radical?' [. . .] Pero gracias a Dios, yo empiezo a orar y a pedirle a Dios. Y empiezo a hacer mis peticiones. [. . .] Entonces yo poco a poco fui creyendo."

9. Researchers have documented a general process of destabilization and segmentation of formal employment opportunities, together with a growth in informal economic activities and temporary work with low wages, in Monterrey and Mexico City. These developments are due in part to neoliberal policies that were formulated and enacted in response the economic crises of the 1980s and 1990s (Aguilar and Escamilla 2000).

10. As Donna Goldstein has shown, the emphasis on microenterprise programs reinforces the neoliberal view that poverty is a "personal problem" (Goldstein 2001, 238). These programs, which are intended to empower individuals to overcome this problem, are often poorly conceptualized and "undercapitalized."

11. "Entonces me quedo en el centro de rehabilitación. Y desde el principio me empiezan a hablar de Cristo, de Cristo, y yo no quería nada. Empecé a leer la Biblia, y no entendía nada y no me gustaba. Hasta que, como a los dos meses de que estaba adentro de la rehabilitación, me quedaba, me convencía y me seguía quedando. . . . Entonces dos meses después de estar rehabilitando, me entrego mi vida a Cristo. Me convenzo solamente a través de su poder voy a poder salir de todo esto. Y más que eso, ¿no? me convenzo de que el es la mejor opción para un estilo de vida."

12 "Comprendí que era la bondad de Dios que estuve allí. . . . Me ayudó a cambiar mi carácter, a cambiar mi pereza, a cambiar eso que no me podía dejar, adicciones. Esos tres meses en Toluca fueron para mí una luna de miel con Dios."

Works Cited

Aguilar, Adrián Guillermo, and Irma Escamilla. 2000. Reestructuración económica y mercado laboral metropolitano: Los casos de ciudad de México, Guadalajara, Monterrey y Puebla. In *Globalización y regiones en México*, ed. Rocío Rosales Ortega, 179-218. Mexico City: Facultad de Ciencias Políticas y Sociales, Universidad Nacional Autónoma de México.

Alvarez, Alejandro. 2004. Mexico: Relocating the state within a new global regime. In *Governing under stress*, ed. Marjorie Griffin Cohen and Steven Clarkson, 90-109. New York: Zed Books.

Amistad Comunicaciones. 2006. Una visita inesperada. *América Nueva* 8.

Bourgois, Philippe. 1996. *In search of respect: Selling crack in El Barrio*. New York: Cambridge University Press.

Bowen, Kurt. 1996. *Evangelism and apostasy: The evolution and impact of evangelicals in modern Mexico*. Montreal: McGill-Queen's University Press.

Boyer, Jean François. 2001. *La guerra perdida contra las drogas: Narcodependencia del mundo actual*. Mexico City: Editorial Grijalbo.

Brouwer, Kimberly, Patricia Case, Rebeca Ramos, Carlos Magis-Rodríguez, Jesus Bucardo, Thomas L. Patterson, and Steffanie L. Strathdee. 2006. Trends in production, trafficking and consumption of methamphetamine and cocaine in Mexico. *Substance Use and Misuse* 41:707-27.

Cahn, Peter. 2003. *All religions are good in Tzintzuntzan: Evangelicals in Catholic Mexico*. Austin: University of Texas Press.

Cruikshank, Barbara. 1993. Revolutions within: Self-government and self-esteem. *Economy and Society* 22(3):327-44.

De la Fuente, Daniel. 2005. El cereso de Dios y la "malilla." *El Norte*. September 9.

Dilulio, John. 2004. Getting faith-based programs right. *Public Interest* 155:75-88.

Ferguson, James, and Akhil Gupta. 2002. Spatializing states: Toward an ethnography of neoliberal governmentality. *American Ethnologist* 29(4):981-1002.

Freeman, Laurie, and Jorge Luis Sierra. 2005. Mexico: The militarization trap. In *Drugs and democracy in Latin America*, ed. Coletta Youngers and Eileen Rosen, 263-302. Boulder, CO: Lynne Rienner Publishers.

García, José. 2007. Dice Felipe: Dejemos de echarnos la bolita. *El Norte*. July 3.

Goldstein, Donna. 2001. Microenterprise training programs, neoliberal common sense, and the discourses of self-esteem. In *The new poverty studies: The ethnography of power, politics and impoverished people in the United States*, ed. Judith Goode and Jeff Maskovsky, 236-72. New York: New York University Press.

Johnson, Byron. 2002. *Objective hope: Assessing the effectiveness of faith-based organizations: A review of the literature*. Philadelphia: Center for Research on Religion and Urban Civil Society, University of Pennsylvania.

Lutz, Catherine. 2002. Making war at home in the U.S.: Militarization and the current crisis. *American Anthropologist* 104(3):723-35.

Nájera, Horacio. 2005. Matan a 6 en motín en penal de Juárez. *El Norte*. December 18.

Portes, Alejandro, and Bryan Roberts. 2005. The free market city: Latin American urbanization in the years of the neoliberal experiment. *Studies in Comparative International Development* 40(1):43-82.

Ramos Lira, Luciana, Enrique Pérez Campuzano, and Martha Romero Mendoza. 1999. La criminalización de la violencia juvenil: El caso del consumo de drogas. *Jóvenes: Revista de estudios sobre juventud* 3(8):108-21.

Romero, Bernardo. 1998. Las estrategias de seguridad pública en los regímenes de excepción: el caso de la política de tolerancia cero. *Cotidiano* 90:13-26.

Toro, María Celia. 1995. *Mexico's war on drugs: Causes and consequences.* Boulder, CO: Lynne Rienner Publishers.

Velasco, José Luis. 2005. *Insurgency, authoritarianism, and drug trafficking in Mexico's "Democratization."* New York: Routledge.

Chapter 3
Fighting for "Livity": Rastafari Politics in a Neoliberal State
Bretton Alvaré

Introduction

Despite their claims to autonomy, NGOs are connected with state governments, private funders, and local constituencies in complex and contradictory relationships that shape both their goals and their strategies for pursuing them (Fisher 1997). The missions, structures, and practices of NGOs can become compromised when, in addition to performing their intended functions, they are forced to focus on fundraising and compliance with government regulations (Goode 2006). Such compromises are especially significant for faith-based NGOs, which draw their inspiration from and strive to operate according to specific religious ideologies (Bornstein 2005). In the present era of NGO activism, a faith-based organization's ability to "keep the faith" depends less on the depth of its members' devotion to a set of religious ideals than on its relationships with and obligations to private donors and state governments that allow it to function.

The relationships NGOs maintain with state governments and private donors can be described as "dialectical" in that NGO missions, practices, and structures both shape and are (re)shaped by these relationships and their associated discourses. As organizations become transformed by the nature of support (or lack thereof) these linkages produce, so too are their relationships with local constituents—the people meant to benefit from their works. In this chapter, I will first describe how the nation of Trinidad in the British West Indies has adapted to the demands of neoliberalism over the past twenty years. Then, through ethnographic analysis, I will document the ways the mission, practices, and organizational structure of the National Rastafari Organization (NRO)—a small faith-based NGO in Trinidad that is at once locally (in its administration and ideology) and transnationally (in its staffing, fund-raising, and marketing activities) oriented—are being shaped by critical interactions with both the

Trinidadian and U.S. governments, and with private donors. For the leaders of the NRO, these critical interactions have transformed both their conception of social justice and their strategies for achieving it.

Motherless Children: Neoliberal Social and Economic Policy in Trinidad

Former Prime Minister A. N. R. Robinson summed up the hegemonic neoliberal discourse that has endured into the present era of Trinidadian politics when he stated without regret in 1990 that Trinidad could no longer be "a tireless mother, forever providing, a guarantor of welfare, and a haven of security" (in Rogozinski 1994). This disassociation of the state from the welfare and security of the people represented a departure from the policies and discourses of the post-independence era, when the People's National Movement (PNM), led by Dr. Eric Williams, took drastic interventionist measures to change the unequal distributional structure of the postcolonial economy. These included the expansion of public education opportunities, improvements in health and housing, and the direct employment in the expansion of infrastructural development (Henry 1990, 66). Williams himself, in his *History of the People of Trinidad and Tobago,* had proudly invoked the metaphor of the Trinidadian state as a tireless mother, striving to provide for all of her "children" (1962, 281). In the post-independence era the government enthusiastically took on the role of "guarantor of welfare," but by 1990 the Prime Minister was publicly declaring the end of the welfare state.

The Trinidadian government's initial embrace and subsequent abandonment of Keynesian welfare policies were directly influenced by global economic forces largely beyond its control. Throughout Trinidad's independent history (1962-present), the nation's economic and political fortunes have depended on revenues generated by oil extraction and export, activities that are highly susceptible to the whims of foreign-owned corporations and the fluctuations of foreign-dominated financial markets. In the post-independence period, bountiful oil revenues enabled the ruling People's National Movement (PNM) regime to develop a system of patronage that it used to cement and legitimize its rule (Hintzen 1989; Henry 1990; Premdas 1990). The regime distributed to the black and East Indian lower classes "direct allocations of jobs, services, facilities, loans, and housing . . . on a massive scale" (Hintzen 1989, 73). Following the Keynesian model, the government took a direct role in reducing unemployment by setting up a number of government programs, including the Special Works Program, Development and Environmental Works Division, and Carnival Development Committee to provide jobs for the unemployed in community works, housing, and infrastructure development (Hintzen 1989, 73-74). By 1982, twenty years after independence, direct state employment accounted for 22 percent of the total employment figures (*Trinidad and Tobago Review,* vol. 6(6):3; in Hintzen 1989, 74). The government also took a direct role in addressing lower class social problems by instituting free public transportation for the elderly, free school busing and meals programs, and school book grants for primary and secondary children; and by increasing its expenditures on direct welfare assistance for pensioners (Henry 1990, 70).

The dramatic expansion of the Trinidadian welfare state was made possible by the oil boom that lasted from 1973-1982. During this period, the GDP at constant prices increased by 58 percent and, thanks in large part to the high wages being paid to government and union workers, Trinidad approached the top of the World Bank's list of middle income countries (Henry 1990, 70). But in 1983, when the price of oil began to plummet, the PNM could not sustain its Keynesian economic and social policies. State subsidies were cut significantly in order to maintain a balance between spending and revenue, severely eroding the PNM's popular support. In the 1986 general election the people responded by sweeping the PNM out of office. However, the new ruling National Alliance for Reconstruction (NAR) party, faced with a TT$ 2.8 billion deficit and an annual foreign debt service obligation in excess of TT$ 1.7 billion, had little choice but to continue dismantling the welfare state that the PNM had created during the two previous decades (Premdas 1990, 147). State subsidies were reduced or eliminated, including the annual Cost of Living Allowance (COLA) and foreign food and drug import subsidies worth over TT$ 700 million (Premdas 1990, 147). Existing taxes were increased, new taxes were added, public servants had their salaries reduced significantly, and a national recovery levy was placed on all persons whose incomes exceeded TT$ 70,000 (Henry 1990, 71).

It was in this context of economic crisis that, having submitted the nation to a series of IMF-sponsored and supervised Structural Adjustment Programs, Prime Minister A. N. R. Robinson publicly proclaimed the death of the welfare state. Trinidad was forced to adapt to the demands of neoliberalism, which meant dismantling nonagricultural trade barriers, removing currency controls and establishing a floating currency system, and enacting aggressive policies to attract foreign investors (Griffin 1997, 188). Since the PNM returned to power in 1991, the government has continued to sell off state enterprises, reduce salaries of state employees, and outsource social services to private companies and NGOs. As oil revenues (and, consequently, Trinidad's national budget) have soared in the wake of 9/11 and the ensuing Iraq conflict, the PNM remains committed to governing according to the tenets of the neoliberal paradigm. Shunning the welfare state policies of the 1970s and 80s, the PNM proudly employs a network of NGOs to administer key social services to the population. This policy is based on the prevailing neoliberal assumption that "Government . . . cannot single-handedly address the myriad of social problems in the society" and that relying on NGOs "ensures there is wider coverage of the delivery aspect to the national community" (Trinidad and Tobago National Budget 2006-2007, 29). Unlike other nations in the region, Trinidad's current commitment to neoliberal economic and social policymaking is not necessitated by debt obligations, and therefore serves as a testament to the hegemonic power of "free market" ideology.

The government's present stance was articulated by trade minister Ken Valley, who recently reflected on the Keynesian principles that guided economic and social policy during the 1970s and 80s: "That is a paradigm of the past, because in today's business environment, government's fundamental role is that of a facilitator. . . . Government's focus is on creating the best environment for business to flourish, to be a facilitator for the private sector to derive economic growth" (Homer 2006). This position raises serious questions about the changing nature of government accountability in Trinidad. While the state seems eager to spend handsomely to meet the demands of foreign investors, neglected citizens' requests for basic services fall on deaf ears. During 2006-2007 no fewer than a dozen villages were forced to take to the streets to demand road repairs, bridge maintenance, and access to electricity and running water. In contrast, when the Alcoa corporation indicated that in order to begin construction on a new aluminum smelter it needed the government to build hundreds of miles of new roads and expand the capacity of the national electrical grid by 950 megawatts (an 87 percent increase), the prime minister was eager to comply (Browne 2006). This follows neoliberal logic regarding infrastructure expansion: when it can be used to accommodate the development of private industry, it is a sound investment, but when the collective needs of the population are the only things at stake, it is a sunk cost.

The government's adherence to a neoliberal paradigm has led it to increase its support of "civil society agencies" that are meant to produce "empowered young people who are able to make informed choices so they can lead meaningful, enjoyable lives" (National Youth Policy Document cited in Trinidad and Tobago National Budget 2006-2007, 36-37). Unlike the groups of residents that shut down streets and sparred with police to get their roads repaved (Charan 2006), such organizations work to cultivate relationships with the government and private donors to secure the funds and proper authority necessary to provide social services themselves. The government's belief in the efficacy of NGOs in addressing social problems is evidenced in expanding budget allocations to the sector, which increased by 99.7 percent (to TT$ 175,507,136.11) between 2004 and 2007 (Trinidad and Tobago National Budget 2007-2008, 53). In response to the proliferation of national and global discourses that blame poverty and unemployment on individuals' behavior, many NGOs are enacting strategies for social change that focus on reforming and training individuals as separate labor units (Goode 2006, 210). By "teaching them to fish," they seek to give local constituents "marketable skills" (literacy, basic computer skills) that will, presumably, enable them to escape poverty "on their own" (without direct state intervention) by joining the labor force. In faith-based NGOs, where religious belief is intended to provide the ideological foundation upon which organizational missions and practices are based, the penetration of these neoliberal discourses and practices (a product of their relationships with the state and private donors) represents an unforeseen consequence of social and political activism.

A Dream Come True: The Establishment of a Rastafari NGO

The following case study explores the process by which a specific group of Rastafari *bredren* (devoted brethren) created a faith-based NGO intended to promote a broad-based program of community uplift and empowerment, referred to as a *livity*. The *bredren* surely could not have known that the mission, practices, and structure of their organization would change significantly over time as a result of critical interactions with the government agencies and private donors. These relationships seriously altered their original conceptions of social justice, as well as their strategies for achieving it. Far from the *livity* they envisioned and struggled to create, the NRO's program has come to be based on the promotion of neoliberal themes of multiculturalism, individual accountability, and capitalist entrepreneurship. The events recounted below show a process through which external pressures contributed to a mission shift, followed by a change in the organization's administrative structure. These, in turn, produced internal divisions, as well as further departures from the organization's original ideology and practices. I do not in any way wish to devalue or criticize the efforts of these passionate, well-intentioned activists whose personal commitment to their community is unparalleled and whose devotion to the Rastafari *trod* (spiritual way of life) is beyond question. I merely want to illustrate the ways neoliberalism works to subtly transform people's understandings of social problems and, consequently, their strategies for addressing them.

The fieldwork which supports this analysis consisted of two and a half years of interviews and participant observation with the organization's administration, staff, members, and local constituents. This multi-sited research was conducted at the NRO headquarters in Trinidad, the NRO U.S. office in western Massachusetts, and at fundraisers the organization held up and down the East Coast of the United States. As the organization matured, I was able to directly observe, by monitoring its publications, internal communications, and administrative meetings, the evolution of the strategic processes by which it has recruited new members and staff, reached out to other Rastafari organizations, interacted with government agencies and private funding institutions, and implemented programs in the local community.

The NRO is a faith-based NGO embedded in the radical religion and culture of Rastafari, whose leaders are endeavoring to remedy a host of social maladies afflicting their home community of "South Village," including: high dropout rates, inadequate health-care services, and chronic un- and underemployment. These social problems have intensified in recent years in response to the state's adoption of neoliberal economic and social policies, including government divestment from the agricultural sector (which in 2007 brought an end to the 150-year-old sugar cane industry that once formed the backbone of Trinidad's plantation economy) and the relocation of oil and petrochemical production operations away from South Village to the Point Lisas industrial park as part of Trinidad's national industrialization and development program. Because government patronage and services in Trinidad have always been distributed on a clientelistic basis in exchange for electoral support (Hintzen 1989, Henry 1990, Premdas 1990), the negative consequences of neoliberal social and economic policies have hit hardest in the regions that consistently vote against the PNM, such as the Nariva/Mayaro and County Victoria regions of the South where unemployment rates have spiraled to 20.4 percent and 10.1 percent respectively despite a national unemployment rate that remains below 6 percent (Paul 2007). Faced with a crumbling infrastructure, massive government divestment, and little hope for gainful employment, the residents of South Village and the other neglected districts of the South have become the principal victims of Trinidad's deleterious neoliberal policies.

The relocation of oil production operations, combined with the disappearance of the lucrative employment opportunities once offered by direct state employment programs and state run enterprises, have transformed it into one of Trinidad's most depressed communities. Unemployment, poverty, and the associated problems of crime and alcoholism are rampant. The pavilion that once housed the local market stands rusting and empty, inhabited only by vagrants and stray dogs. Crumbling sidewalks and sewage-filled drainage ditches line the town's main road, along which a bank, bakery, grocery, and small appliance store are interspersed with the seedy rum shops that occupy the vast majority of South Village's storefronts. Like the rest of the island, which absorbed 145,000 East Indian indentured workers between 1836 and 1917 (Mars 1998, 24; Khan 1999, 252), South Village's population is made up of roughly equal numbers of people with African and East Indian ancestry. Local residents cite the town's relative poverty as the reason that South Villagers seem less prone to the fierce African-Indian racism that pervades Trinidadian culture and politics. They describe their shared economic and political marginalization at the hands of white and light-skinned elites as the source of a sort of class consciousness that functions to overpower racial divisions.

NRO conducts its fund-raising activities in the northeastern United States and then transfers funds to South Village, where local staff members implement its projects. NRO's administration and staff, which is made up of about a dozen Rastas both black and white, are unpaid and split into two groups, one based in Trinidad and the other based in the United States. NRO was created in 2004 by three Rastas from South Village who recruited members and staff from their community of origin as well as from the Rastafari community in the U.S. Over the past two and a half years, these *bredren* have had to navigate the discourses and demands of a diverse array of interest groups, negotiating with potential financial resource brokers such as the Trinidadian government and Rastafari populations in the northeastern U.S., while at the same time appealing to potential grassroots supporters, including other locally oriented Rastafari organizations in Trinidad and the greater Caribbean region. The discourses regarding efficiency, professionalism, and multiculturalism, meant to entice potential funders from the U.S. and draw support from the Trinidadian state, are very different from the traditional Rastafari discourses of racial solidarity and community uplift that they initially used to guide their mission and develop relationships with local constituents. The organization's struggle to reconcile these inherent contradictions has led it to dramatically shift its organizational mission and practices.

When the organization was conceived in November of 2004, NRO sought to accomplish many goals within a broad framework of community uplift. Their first program established a *true-brary* (as opposed to the English "lie-brary") on a small piece of land on the outskirts of South Village. The organization collected and purchased used books to start the *true-brary*, which was open one day a week to make Afrocentric, anticolonial literature available to all. Members of the local community were given an opportunity to come out, read, and reason with Rastafari elders in an informal learning atmosphere that provided an alternative to the "colonial miseducation" of the public school system. The *true-brary* created a lot of buzz around South Village, encouraging NRO to sponsor a "Rastafari Family Day and Sports Meet" where local community members interacted in an environment of friendly competition, strengthening collective relationships and promoting a sense of community solidarity.

In addition to these rather modest community programs, NRO also began publishing a Rastafari newsletter, *The Liberator*, which was distributed online to Rastafari web communities and message boards and in hard copy at the NRO headquarters in South Village. In the inaugural issue, NRO's leaders outlined the organization's aims and objectives (listed below). Despite their repeated insistence that they were "not a churchical order," NRO's number one objective (educating people about the living God: Haile Selassie I, born Ras Tafari Makonnen) indicated that the original organizational mission was firmly grounded in the Rastafari faith. The stated aims and objectives are:

1) To educate the community about H.I.M. Qedamawi Haile Selassie 1st Abbajonhoi and propagate the teachings of H.I.M. Haile Selassie 1st to foster good relations between the Rastafarian community and the general population.

2) Introduce and promote appropriate agricultural techniques, including organic regeneration of the land site so as to increase food production and coordinate other integrated rural and urban development through community-based programs.

3) To participate, promote, and conduct cultural exchanges between Rastafari in different parts of the Caribbean and the world.

4) Carry out literacy programs, health education, sanitation as well as other environmental conversations.

5) To provide the opportunity where adults and young people can get basic education and skill training.

6) Promote and develop athletic and other cultural and recreational programs for the youth of the area.

These aims and objectives illustrate NRO's original intention to offer a comprehensive program of community uplift. Taken together, these goals promoted the propagation of a *livity* built on traditional Rastafari cultural and religious principles: faith in the divinity of Haile Selassie I, organic vegetarianism, environmental preservation, and self-empowerment through educational, cultural, and spiritual development. Basic education and skills training was just one of the many services they intended to offer.

Over the course of the next two years, the rigors and realities of NGO activism reoriented NRO's efforts away from these original objectives. The dual burdens of fund-raising and compliance became the organization's primary concerns, and they eventually pared down their original aims and objectives until basic education and skills training were all that remained. This shift in mission and practice was accompanied by a penetration of neoliberal discourses regarding efficiency, multiculturalism, and the efficacy of the corporate model, which converged with reconfigured Rastafari discourses regarding entrepreneurship and the evils of racism. NRO, in order to comply with U.S. government requirements for nonprofit status, also adopted a hierarchical administrative structure and pay-based membership system that created divisions within the staff and administration and produced a gap between the organization and the local constituents it was originally meant to serve.

The Liberator was well received by online Rastas around the world, drawing accolades from readers in France, Ethiopia, and South Africa. The newsletter became a tool that NRO used to attract supporters and recruit staff from the Rastafari community in the U.S. Within four months of the first publication (November 2004), NRO had recruited a secretary (a white Rasta woman from Ohio), educational director (a brown-skinned Trinidadian Rasta originally from Point Fortin working as a professor in New York), and technical director (a white Rasta youth from rural North Carolina). My own involvement with NRO began in March 2005, when I contacted Ras Chaka, an NRO founder and director who resides in Massachusetts, after reading about the organization in *The Liberator*. An article at the end of the issue invited any and all who were willing to join the organization on its upcoming field trip to South Village, so I answered the call. At first I was unsure how I would be received, but Ras Chaka welcomed me, proclaiming, "What *Jah* (God) bring together cannot be torn asunder!" It took less than six months for NRO to build a support base among the local constituency and develop a ramshackle volunteer staff. As we began preparations for our field trip, everything seemed to be on stream and the prevalent attitude was one of unbridled optimism at the prospect of doing meaningful Rastafari works.

I traveled with the NRO U.S. team to Trinidad during July and August of 2005, where we met with Ras Sundyata and Ras Nelson, lifetime friends of Ras Chaka and cofounders of NRO. The majority of the trip was spent entertaining enthusiastic visitors from the local community who ventured out to the NRO's eleven-acre piece of land to *reason* about Rastafari and pledge their support to the organization. Local constituents brought gifts of locally-grown food and *ganja* (a Hindu-derived term for locally cultivated marijuana) to show their appreciation for NRO's works. Rastafari houses from the surrounding villages sent delegations to investigate or present letters of support. Around South Village everyone was wearing NRO buttons that featured images of Selassie I or the

NRO crest. There was a feeling of hope and excitement in the air, a sense that something had been set in motion which, with a little momentum, would have the power to transform the entire community. It didn't matter that the proposed NRO community center only existed in our imaginations or that we had no operating budget; based on the success of the *true-brary* and the Family Day and Sports Meet, everyone had faith that this was Jah's work, that people were responding to a call from the Almighty Haile Selassie himself, and that "what Jah bring together cannot be torn asunder."

The trip culminated with an enormously successful health workshop, where Cuban doctors on loan from the National Council for Cuban Solidarity donated their time to giving basic checkups (eye exams and blood pressure checks) to the hundred or so South Villagers who turned out. I was impressed by the magnetude and diversity of the crowd. Rastas and non-Rastas, young and old, came out to have their health checked and enjoy themselves. Local Rastafari *sistren* (devoted sisters) prepared and served *Ital* food (salt- and sugar-free vegetarian dishes prepared according to the strict dietary restrictions of Rastafari) while local elders delivered Rastafari-themed speeches to the crowd as they waited to see one of the doctors on hand. Senator Jennifer Jones of the United National Congress opposition party delivered a speech complimenting the efforts of NRO and other NGOs for their efforts to deliver social welfare services once provided by the state. The positive impact of the program was captured by a workshop attendee who submitted the following letter to the *Trinidad Express* daily newspaper:

> The show of unity was overwhelming. As I sat and listened to the speakers, I observed one woman in tears (she is not a Rasta); the conversations were exceptionally eloquent and to the point. The Rastas spoke of the declining social situation in Trinidad and what they could contribute to the restoration of some sort of civility to the population. . . . There were Rastas from all over the country at the opening, as well as members of the local community. There were also foreign visitors present. This is the kind of community involvement that we need. We all have to work together to ensure that the social environment changes for the better. I look forward to the NRO-sponsored community programme (Concerned Citizen 2005).

The workshop was only scheduled to last a few hours, but it ended up taking all day, stretching into the evening hours when dozens of Rastas from the surrounding area arrived to reason and give *ises* (praises) to the Almighty Jah Rastafari with Nyabinghi drums and chanting. Positive vibrations from the depths of our souls drew together as one and rose like the smoke curling from the fire up beyond the giant stands of bamboo and into the black sky.

A Dream Deferred: The Transformation of the NRO

Ras Chaka and the rest of the staff returned from the trip invigorated and ready to take the next step toward building the community center on the NRO land in South Village. Arrangements were made to have an electrical line run out to the ramshackle bamboo and plywood shed we had built on the NRO land, which had hosted the workshop (during the three-week trip an extension cord run from a neighbor's house a few hundred yards away was the only power source). Faced with the reality that construction costs would be substantial, NRO got down to the business of developing a fund-raising plan. They chose to utilize Ras Chaka's connections with the existing Rastafari cultural community in western Massachusetts to draw supporters to a series of fund-raisers which would be held at area colleges and community centers. In exchange for a small donation, they would treat attendees to a night of Rastafari cultural performances, including reggae music and Afrocentric speakers. They would sell concessions (*Ital* food and Rastafari merchandise like flags, buttons, pins, books, and photos of His Majesty) inside the venue to raise additional funds.

I flew in to Providence, Rhode Island, to help out with the NRO's first fund-raiser in the fall of 2005. When the event got underway, I was pretty surprised by what I saw. The Rastas in attendance bore little resemblance to the bredren we grounded with in Trinidad. White or light-skinned, affluent, and well-heeled, these donors occupied social and class positions that enabled them to become *consumers* of Rastafari culture. They wore dreadlocks and dressed like Rastas, but they had come to Rastafari from a totally different direction than the bredren in Trinidad, and their comfortable positions within the global capitalist system (symbolized by the Rastafari concept of *Babylon*) made me question whether their calls to "*bun* (burn) Babylon" were truly heartfelt. Austin-Broos once suggested (1992, 307) that "Rastafarianism . . . would have very little significance for [its] practitioners if its members did not also see themselves as materially dispossessed." These attendees were certainly not materially dispossessed, but NRO fund-raisers gave these consumers of Rastafari culture a chance to legitimize their claims to Rastafari identity by "contributing to the cause" (through small monetary donations) and associating with "authentic" Rastas from the Caribbean like Ras Chaka and NRO's educational director, Brother Fari, whose speeches were a staple at the fund-raisers.

I worked at NRO's fund-raisers by collecting money at the door and helping with mundane tasks like setup and cleanup. Working the door put me in the position of having to explain NRO's proposed projects to uninformed attendees who were curious about how their "suggested donations" were being spent. Ras Chaka specifically instructed me that, when people inquired, I should refer to the proposed community center as a "school" because people would be more inclined to make donations if they thought they were "helping children." However, the community center NRO envisioned was to be so much more than a school; it was to be the foundation for a genuine Rastafari *livity* for children and adults alike, a testament to Haile Selassie's suggestion that academic education is worthless without spiritual development. But Ras Chaka felt that the more NRO resembled a traditional development organization, the more people would be willing to donate. Representing the community center as a "school building project" (this was the phrase Ras Chaka emblazoned on the posters advertising the fund-raisers) was a clear attempt by the NRO to appeal to patrons' ideas about what a traditional development project should be.

Brother Fari's speeches provided another interesting window into the process by which NRO represented itself to private donors. Traditional Rastafari discourses regarding black empowerment and the need for the total destruction of the "world order of white supremacy," which had figured prominently in the pages of *The Liberator* and in the *reasonings* (spiritual philosophical discussions) I observed back in Trinidad, were conspicuously absent at the fund-raisers. In his speeches, Brother Fari made no mention of Rastafari's ultimate goals of reparations (for African slavery) and repatriation (to Ethiopia). He avoided discussing confrontational racial politics altogether, instead invoking statements by Haile Selassie ("the color of a man's skin is of no more significance than the color of his eyes") that promoted a kind of utopian multiculturalism, a vision of progress through international, interracial cooperation. His words contrasted sharply with the message of *The Liberator,* which the very same month had reprinted Malcolm X's statement that " . . . if the present generation of whites would study their own race they would be anti-white themselves" and published articles that railed against the "white world order" whose "'first world' status is derived from having slave labor in the formative stages of their economic development and from centuries of draining the natural resources of the world's non-white peoples." Race and racism were fundamental issues in the pages of *The Liberator* newsletter and in the *reasonings* in Trinidad, but the fund-raisers were a different story altogether. Clearly, in an effort to draw donations from the affluent white and light-skinned Rastas who attended NRO's fund-raisers in the U.S., NRO made the decision to alter its self-representations and political messages. Just as the community center was to be described as merely a "school," NRO's racial politics were severely watered down until they resembled the multiculturalism typical of neoliberal discourse.

According to Charles Hale, multiculturalism is an integral feature of neoliberalism's cultural project, which endeavors "to harness and redirect the abundant political energy of cultural rights activism" (2002, 495); in this case, away from the centrality of structural racism. Multiculturalism, which celebrates ethnic diversity and defines racism as an individual psychological problem rather than a structural one, stands at odds with traditional Rastafari cultural beliefs and discourses centered around a strong belief in African superiority and the necessity of black empowerment, as described by Marcus Garvey and Ras Tafari himself, His Imperial Majesty Haile Selassie I. In his 2005 master's thesis, "Unlearning White Superiority: Consciousness-raising on an online Rastafari Reasoning Forum," Christian Stokke describes, on the AfricaSpeaks website (run by black Trinidadians), how white Rastas who try to downplay their racial privilege by invoking multiculturalist discourses of universal equality and color-blindness become subject to "re-education" by their black counterparts, who are quick to identify multiculturalism as yet another form of white domination. NRO's fund-raising activities not only aligned it with donors who themselves could be construed as "agents of Babylon" but did so on a discursive pretense that removed the racial politics at the heart of the traditional Rastafari discourses I witnessed on the ground in Trinidad and in NRO's own publications and internal communications.

In addition to raising funds by hosting Rastafari cultural events in the Northeastern U.S., NRO also approached the Trinidadian state to request funding to support its organizational activities. Nationalist discourses promoted by the Trinidadian government focus on Trinidad's multicultural demography and history in attempting to construct a national identity that promotes diversity, tolerance, and equality (Green 1999). In this positive nationalist vision, Trinidad is portrayed as a cosmopolitan society in which people with vastly different cultures, religions, and beliefs live in relative peace and harmony (Green 1999). Such is the context in which NGOs in Trinidad compete with one another for state funding. Organizations that can represent themselves as working to further this positive nationalist vision through a program that promotes cultural understanding stand the best chance of being rewarded with government monies.

Fearing that Rastafari's traditional emphasis on black empowerment and racial solidarity would prevent their organization from being funded, NRO leaders presented a "whitewashed" version of their program agenda to the Ministry of Community Development. There was no mention of educating individuals about Haile Selassie or promoting Rastafari cultural exchange, even though these figured prominently in NRO's original "Aims and Objectives" (see above). As at the fund-raisers in the U.S., the project was cloaked in the multiculturalist discourse employed by the state. Wary that the organic farming and youth recreation aspects of the project might seem too ambitious to government agents, NRO's leadership emphasized that above all, the community center's goal would be to provide basic education and skills training that would remedy social problems by preparing individuals for participation in the labor force. The Ministry responded positively, offering a small grant to assist in the construction of the community center, a decision that ultimately validated NRO's discursive strategy.

Over the next eight months, NRO became increasingly preoccupied with its fund-raising activities. The penetration of neoliberal discourse represented an unintended consequence of this shift and had a significant impact on NRO's practices, which in turn drastically altered its relationship with the local community of South Village. At administrative meetings and in NRO internal communications, Ras Chaka and Ras Sundyata began stressing the need to run NRO on a "for-profit basis." The *true-brary*, Family Day, and Health Workshop events that had been so successful in getting the local community of South Village interested in NRO the previous summer were deprioritized because they did not carry the potential to generate funds. "Success" began to be measured in terms of dollars and cents. Ras Chaka's following open letter to an online Rastafari reasoning forum illustrates the gravity of the discursive and ideological transformation produced by NRO's engagement with state and private funders:

> Before we begin a barrage of Bible verses and admonitions from the annals of H.I.M., let's admit that economics is a major problem for most Rasta worldwide. . . . Some crucial restructuring of how we conduct gatherings is needed to improve productivity. . . . We don't have to argue about theology, philosophy, etc. We need to operate in the realm of practicality. Garvey says that we can't prove the race's worth by lagging behind in the van of civilization. H.I.M. does not condone lazy policy, uneducated guesses, wishful thinking. Don't get mad at me—talk to H.I.M. . . . There's no way that we as Rastafari can justify not setting up corporations. . . . After you get mad about what I said, let's ALL get money. Up! you mighty race! You can accomplish what you will (author's original emphasis).

In this statement, Ras Chaka explicitly endorses the capitalist corporate model, while simultaneously attacking the efficacy of traditional Rastafari practices; specifically, the structure and substance of the informal *reasoning* gatherings that in large part define and constitute Rastafari religious practice (Chevannes 1994; Edmonds 2002; Williams 2000). Furthermore, the Bible verses and "annals of H.I.M." (His Imperial Majesty Haile Selassie) that form the foundation of Rastafari theology are dismissed as irrelevant since economic improvement, presumably, can only occur through "improve(d) productivity" and "get[ting] money" by "setting up corporations." Ras Chaka's anticipation that his message would not be well received by the online Rasta community indicates his acknowledgement that his words represent a violation of many of Rastafari's core tenets, most notably rejection of the Babylon system and the promise of real life (practical) salvation through adherence to H.I.M.'s (spiritual) teachings. By stating that "H.I.M. does not condone lazy policy, uneducated guesses, wishful thinking" and "Garvey says that we can't prove the race's worth by lagging behind in the van of civilization," he attempts to situate his critique in Rastafari discourse while simultaneously elevating neoliberal understandings of social problems (which cite individual laziness and lack of initiative as root causes) to the level of Jah's holy word.

As part of NRO's growing obsession with fund-raising, compliance with U.S. regulations governing the operations of nonprofit organizations became a top priority. Obtaining official 501(c)(3) status would allow it to collect donations from online readers of *The Liberator,* whose table of contents Ras Chaka began prefacing with a cover letter requesting donations for NRO's "school building" project. Before the external pressure of compliance came to bear on NRO, it lacked anything resembling a hierarchical organizational structure. The line separating "staff" from "administrators" was ill-defined (if not nonexistent). Everyone collaborated to make decisions in an informal atmosphere and volunteered their efforts under the unspoken assumption that everyone was in this together and would do whatever they could. Similarly, members were not officially registered; they just showed up to participate in events and brought individual or family contributions without being asked. Attendance, participation, and membership were virtually synonymous. All of this changed when NRO began the process of registering as a nonprofit with the U.S. government. The application dictated the necessity of creating a board of directors with terms and elections, an annual dues system, and a membership registration system. They decided that, in order to comply, all members would be required to pay US$ 250 per annum in dues, the payment of which would distinguish the "free-loaders" from those who were really "dedicated." Thus "dedication," like "success," also came to be measured in dollars and cents.

These formal changes to the organization's structure created internal divisions and a sense of distance between the U.S.-based staff, who assumed the role of "givers," and the local constituents in South Village, who, unable to pay any annual dues, were relegated to the position of "receivers." They were no longer considered "members" with a stake in the organization. Instead, they came to be regarded as something else altogether: charity cases. Brother Fari, who had worked tirelessly for the organization, donating books and delivering speeches at fund-raisers, was alienated by a number of derogatory internal e-mails deriding his opposition to the dues system. He eventually left the organization.

When Ras Suji, a Trinidad bredren who had volunteered to watch over NRO's property for a modest remittance of $20 per month, was dismissed from the program for what was considered "unproductive behavior," a new discourse of personal responsibility was invoked, and the issue was discussed as a decision based on "business logic" and contractual obligations. Similarly, slow action on the part of other Rastas in Trinidad to join or support NRO began to be conceived as consequences of "laziness" and "hard-headedness." When they failed to complete an assigned task of photocopying and distributing copies of *The Liberator* within an expected period of time, Ras Chaka remarked that he was "sick and tired of dealing wit dem illiterate Rasses."

NRO's discursive, practical, and structural transformation had serious negative consequences on their relationship with the community of South Village, which became evident when I returned there with them in August of 2006. Over the course of the year, the organization had lost the interest and support of its local constituents. Gone were the NRO buttons that so many had proudly displayed on their clothing the year before. Only a handful of individuals, most of whom were close friends of Ras Chaka and Ras Sundyata, made the trip up to the land to *reason* and give *ises*. No Rasta delegations came to express their support. A sense of idleness pervaded the camp, which had become severely overgrown as a result of Ras Suji's dismissal. Without being taken out of their container for six months, the *true-brary* books had begun to rot. The pain on Ras Chaka's face was visible as he looked over the spoiled books, shaking his head. Only a year before, the path forward had seemed so clear, the local support so strong. Now it was difficult to figure out what had gone wrong, or why our return was so poorly received. A literacy and computer training workshop, which was meant to be the centerpiece of the service trip and was expected to bring as many attendees as the last year's health clinic, had to be cancelled due to lack of attendance. But no one seemed to understand the lack of interest.

NRO's commitment to the neoliberal paradigm prevented the administrators from recognizing that, for the local people, literacy and computer training and the employment it was meant to promise could not bring the sense of empowerment and community uplift they had gained from their visits to the *true-brary* or their participation in the Health Clinic or Rastafari Sports Meet and Family Day. The weak show of support during the 2006 service trip only pushed NRO further away from its original mission and practices. The organization slowed down considerably during 2007, thanks in large part to the loss of Brother Fari. There were fewer e-mails and only a handful of fund-raisers. For the first time in the organization's short history, there was no service trip to Trinidad. In adjusting its mission, practices, and structure to appeal to state and individual funders, NRO systematically removed the parts of the program that held the most appeal for the people it initially set out to serve.

Conclusion

As NRO devoted itself to the process of registering for official NGO status in Trinidad and the United States and worked to develop successful fund-raising strategies, it shifted its program emphasis away from community empowerment and uplift to the transference of technical skills to isolated individuals. A growing preoccupation with fund-raising and compliance narrowed the organization's vision of the possibilities for its political activism. The resultant penetration of neoliberal capitalist discourses regarding efficiency, profitability, and the efficacy of the corporate model led the organization to abandon the programs responsible for its initial success in connecting with local constituents in South Village. This disconnect was magnified by their decision to adopt a hierarchical structure, which alienated core staff and administrative members while dividing the organization along class and racial lines into North American "givers" and South Village "receivers."

Critical interactions with the state and private funders led NRO's leaders to abandon many of the core tenets of the traditional Rastafari ideology on which the organization was founded. Rastafari discourses were reconfigured to justify NRO's new practical alignments with the state and affluent consumers of Rasta culture in the U.S.; black liberation and solidarity were deemphasized in favor of multiculturalism, a core feature of the neoliberal paradigm (Hale 2002). Faith in the power of Jah to effect real change was eroded by a growing faith in the transformative power of free market principles like efficiency, productivity, and corporatization. The internalization of key elements of neoliberal ideology compelled NRO's leaders to revise their conception of social justice from one based on the promotion of Rastafari *livity* (through collective rejection of destructive Babylonian culture—embodied in their original aims and objectives) to another based on individual economic improvement (through successful participation in the labor market—embodied in their abandonment of all but the skills training aspect of their program). New strategies were enacted, dedicated to enhancing organizational efficiency and productivity in order to raise additional funds, and the organization subsequently lost connection with and support from its local constituents.

NRO's experiences demonstrate that NGOs often are not as autonomous as they are made out to be in political and popular discourse. Rather, their mission, practices, and structures are in large part determined by their relationships with state regulators and private funders (Fisher 1997). For small NGOs without a steady fund base, survival depends on the ability to navigate the demands of these relationships without losing sight of their original intentions. For faith-based NGOs founded on specific religious beliefs, this ability is far more critical, for, as this analysis has shown, even the most radical ideologies can become compromised by the process of NGO activism that characterizes the neoliberal era.

Works Cited

Austin-Broos, Diane J. 1992. Religion and the politics of moral order in Jamaica. *Anthropological Forum* 6(3):293-319.

Bornstein, Erica. 2005. *The spirit of development: Protestant NGOs, morality, and economics in Zimbabwe.* Stanford, CA: Stanford University Press.

Browne, Juhel. 2006. Additional electricity coming for smelters, says Manning. *Trinidad Express,* November 6.

Charan, Richard. 2006. Cops, soldiers take over: 10 arrested in midst of Fyzabad protest. *Trinidad Express,* October 5.

Chevannes, Barry. 1994. *Rastafari: Roots and ideology.* Syracuse, NY: Syracuse University Press.

"Concerned Citizen." 2005. Rastas of T&T stepping up. *Trinidad Express,* September 3.

Edmonds, Ennis B. 2002. *Rastafari: Outcasts to culture bearers.* Oxford and New York: Oxford University Press.

Fisher, William. 1997. Doing good? The politics and antipolitics of NGO practices. *Annual Review of Anthropology* 26(1):439-64.

Goode, Judith. 2006. Faith-based organizations in Philadelphia: Neoliberal ideology and the decline of political activism. *Urban Anthropology,* 35(2-3):203-236.

Green, Garth L. 1999. Blasphemy, sacrilege, and moral degradation in the Trinidad Carnival: The Hallelujah controversy of 1995. In *Religion, diaspora, and cultural identity: A reader in the Anglophone Caribbean,* ed. John W. Pulis, 189-214. New York: Routledge.

Griffin, Clifford. 1997. *Democracy and neoliberalism in the developing world: Lessons from the Anglophone Caribbean.* Aldershot, UK: Ashgate.

Hale, Charles R. 2002. Does multiculturalism menace? Governance, cultural rights, and the politics of identity in Guatemala. *Journal of Latin American Studies* 34:485-524.

Henry, Ralph M. 1990. Notes on the evolution of inequality in Trinidad and Tobago. In *Trinidad ethnicity,* ed. Kevin A. Yelvington, 56-80. Knoxville, TN: University of Tennessee Press.

Hintzen, Percy C. 1989. *The costs of regime survival: Racial mobilization, elite domination, and control of the state in Guyana and Trinidad.* Cambridge: Cambridge University Press.

Homer, Louis B. 2006. Local firms urged to invest globally. *Trinidad Express.* August 16.

Khan, Aisha. 1999. On the "right path": Interpolating religion in Trinidad. In *Religion, diaspora, and cultural identity: A reader in the Anglophone Caribbean,* ed. John W. Pulis, 247-76. New York: Routledge.

Mars, Perry. 1998. *Ideology and change: The transformation of the Caribbean left.* Detroit, MI: Wayne State University Press.

Paul, Anna-Lisa. 2007. Unemployment still high in certain areas. *Trinidad Express,* March 1.

Premdas, Ralph. 1990. Ethnic conflict in Trinidad and Tobago: Domination and reconciliation. In *Trinidad ethnicity,* ed. Kevin A. Yelvington, 134-53. Knoxville, TN: University of Tennessee Press.

Rogozinski, Jan. 1994. *A brief history of the Caribbean: From the Arawak and Carib to the present.* New York: Plume.

Stokke, Christian. 2005. Unlearning White superiority: Consciousness-raising on an online Rastafari reasoning forum. Master's thesis, University of Oslo.

Trinidad and Tobago National Budget 2006-2007. http://www.finance.gov.tt/ (last accessed October 23, 2007).

Trinidad and Tobago National Budget 2007-2008. http://www.finance.gov.tt/ (last accessed October 23, 2007).

Williams, Eric. 1962. *A history of the people of Trinidad and Tobago.* New York: Frederic A. Praeger.

Williams, Winston. 2000. The seven principles of Rastafari. *Caribbean Quarterly Rastafari Monograph* pp. 16-23.

Chapter 4
Encouraging Development "Alternatives": Grassroots Church Partnering in the U.S. and Haiti
Tara Hefferan

International development is both an ideology and a set of practices aimed at promoting social change in the "global south." While there is no agreement on what exactly constitutes development or how best to define it, conventional initiatives often have assumed that development is "a process whereby the real per capita income of a country increases over a long period of time while simultaneously poverty is reduced and the inequality in society is generally diminished" (Martinussen 1999, 37). As such, in the nearly sixty years since the rise of "the development machine" (Ferguson 1994), countless attempts to "grow" income levels in the global south have arisen. Unfortunately, more often than not, such efforts have been profound failures, serving not only to exacerbate global inequality but also to depoliticize poverty (Ferguson 1994) and further concentrate northern powers' disproportionate control over the global economy. Because of this, the past decade has been abuzz with "post-development" calls for the "death" of development (Sachs 1992; Escobar 1995a; 1995b; 2000; Rahnema and Bawtree 1997), or at least its significant reworking (Gardner and Lewis 1996). Can development be imagined in terms other than the global, neoliberal, capitalist models currently fueling conventional development initiatives?

The search for alternatives, many postdevelopment theorists suggest, must begin with grassroots mobilizations and social movements (Escobar 1995a) that offer visions counter to conventional development's hegemonic discourses and practices. In particular, by looking for alternatives among those who are not trained as development "experts" and who do not earn their livelihoods as development practitioners, there is the possibility of standing apart from the development apparatus and locating or exposing alternative visions. This chapter—by focusing on development initiatives that are designed, delivered, and evaluated by "ordinary" citizens untrained in conventional development theory and practice—attempts to delineate what "alternative" development means in the context of Catholic church-to-church partnering, also known as "twinning." As described below, twinning links individual parishes in Haiti and the U.S. together

69

in direct grassroots relationships focused, in part, on promoting development in Haiti. Finding that twinning is an "alternative" form of development—rather than an alternative *to* development—and that this orientation generates significant discord in these relationships, the chapter considers the possibilities for reducing local-level tensions and expanding twinning's alternative dimensions.

Whither alternatives to development?

Postdevelopment scholars understand international development to be problematic "not merely on account of its results but because of its intentions, its worldview and mindset" (Nederveen Pieterse 2000, 175). The "development" referenced here is that which arose in the post-World War II context, stemming from Harry Truman's 1949 "Four Point" address (Rist 1997; Matthews 2004). In it, Truman portrayed a world divided: one area was characterized by "modern" progress, with industrialization and democracy, urbanization, markets, education, consumption, and science; the other was "backwards," lacking each of these "modern" characteristics while also plagued by disease and poverty. In conjunction with such ideas, "development" was imagined as a "progressing" of people from traditional "backwardness" to a cosmopolitan modernity. A "can do" spirit bolstered the notion that poverty was manageable, maybe even reversible, with the proper external inputs: infrastructure, education, health care, and the like. And in due course, a wide array of state and international institutions arose to provide such inputs to the "developing" world. Yet, over the long decades since its emergence, development has been exposed as a cruel "deception," postdevelopment theorists argue. Rather than making good on its promises of mitigating poverty, development instead has worsened the disparity between the rich and the poor, while at the same time sowing environmental destruction, upsetting local social structures, creating networks of violence and corruption, and undermining local cultures. In short, far from bringing justice, dignity, or equality, development disproportionately has wounded the marginalized, plagued the powerless. Development has failed not only because it was badly implemented but because it was fundamentally misconceived (Matthews 2004), rooted as it was in Western values of science, rationality, "progress," and social engineering.

As a result, some scholars call for the creation of a "post-development" era, where "the centrality of development as an organizing principle of social life would no longer hold" (Escobar 2000, 11). Because development—both as an idea and as a practical enterprise—is fundamentally flawed, it must be rejected outright, they argue. One way to do this is to "call attention to diversity, highlight alternatives, show interconnectedness, and uncover the complexity of social and economic life" so as to challenge development's key assumptions and representations and provide alternative ways of seeing (Gardner and Lewis

1996, 50). One should look especially closely, they suggest, at alternative or "counter" visions to development as they are (re)created at "local" level "interfaces," where individuals with differing interests, resources, and power come together (Arce and Long 1992). This chapter exploring Catholic parish twinning is one attempt to do just that.

"We lend hope, solidarity, and love": Catholic Parish Twinning

The Parish Twinning Program of the Americas (PTPA) promotes Catholic parish partnering. As described on their website, PTPA focuses "on creating lasting sister parish relationships between parishes in the U.S. or Canada and parishes in the country of Haiti and elsewhere" (PTPA 2008). With over 340 pairings, twinning intends to promote "a mutual and enriching relationship of sharing, solidarity and understanding" among parish partners. In practical terms, this often means U.S. parishes send money to Haiti to support education, health care, and feeding programs. Indeed, "since 1978, our parishes have sent over $22 million in aid," PTPA (n.d.) reports. Moreover, three-quarters of Catholic parishes in Haiti are currently twinned with at least one parish or program in the U.S., making linkages like twinning crucial sources of transnational flows between Haiti and the U.S. (McGlone 1997).

My research has focused on one such pairing as a case study. Over a period of twenty-three months between 2000 and 2006, I collected qualitative data via in-depth interviews, participant observation, and content analysis of program documents regarding the twinning linking St. Robert of Newminster parish in Ada, Michigan with Our Lady of the Nativity in Verrettes, Haiti. The findings presented here are part of a larger project concerned with how these two parishes conceive of their relationship with one another, the ways the pairing intends to promote development in Haiti, and how these attempts relate to more "conventional" development discourses and practices (see Hefferan 2007). Here, I discuss more precisely the tensions, fissures, and possible "solutions" that characterize the St. Robert-Our Lady partnership, particularly as these arise around issues of twinning as an alternative to development.

Let me begin by briefly introducing these two parishes. St. Robert is a relatively affluent, predominantly white parish in an upscale suburban community in Michigan; Our Lady is a sprawling parish in Haiti's Artibonite region. It is described as including 55,000 people, twenty-one chapels in addition to the main church, as well as six parish schools. The main church is located in a town of about 8,000, with the chapels in the mountains surrounding the town. Most people in the parish are farmers, have an average income of $60 a year, and live without running water or electricity.

St. Robert and Our Lady have been twinned since 1995, with representatives from both parishes having approached PTPA requesting partners. As is standard in twinning, at the beginning of their partnership St. Robert sent a delegation to Verrettes to meet the priests and to gain an understanding of the milieu. During that trip, St. Robert's Haiti committee members asked the Haitian priests to come up with a "wish list" of needs that St. Robert potentially could meet. The priests devised such a list, which over the years has included a school student sponsorship program, a lunch program, a vocational school, and a microcredit program, among others. For the most part, St. Robert has responded positively to its Haitian twin's requests by raising money for desired programs and funneling those funds directly to the Haitian priests, who then redistribute the money through their parish-level networks. In many ways, this is just the type of "grassroots" needs identification and implementation currently in vogue in much of the participatory development literature (Chambers 1993; 1997; 2005). St. Robert is not imposing its vision for developing Verrettes through these programs; rather, it is letting Our Lady take the lead in identifying its most pressing needs and handing over the money so that Our Lady can attempt to address them.

There are many reasons why twinning might be considered part of an "alternative" development paradigm. What is alternative development? John Martinussen (1999, 291) suggests there are two varieties: 1) A redefinition of development's goals (rejecting the hegemonic discourse of economic growth as an end in itself and instead advocating welfare and human development); 2) A shifting of development toward civil society (emphasizing local communities as a means for promoting human well-being). Twinning incorporates both of these elements.

First, the goals of the twinning between St. Robert and Our Lady are framed in terms of "helping" Haitians to lead better, more secure lives by providing them educational opportunities and other possibilities for self-sufficiency (e.g., via the microcredit program). For St. Robert's participants, development primarily means meeting basic needs in Haiti, being sensitive to "local" conditions, and offering people the opportunity to better themselves—and their chances for "success"—via education. With this focus on promoting well-being in Haiti (food programs, education), twinning is intensely focused on the local level and almost entirely ignores the macroeconomic context. This "fits" with the first of Martinussen's criteria.

The second variety of "alternative" development, Martinussen suggests, is seated within civil society.[1] Historically, development has been the domain of states and their affiliated agencies. Especially in the past two decades, however, a "crisis" has befallen international development as its guiding principles, funding channels, and daily practices have come under increasing political, scholarly, and popular scrutiny (see this volume's introduction for a fuller discussion). From reduced flows of official aid for development activities in the world's poorest regions to a lack of "faith" (Rist 1997) that poverty ever will be eliminated in such areas, the crisis in development has been intensified by neoliberal economic models. Such models—which doubt the state's capacity as a social change agent (Salomon 1993)—suggest that states take a "hands off" approach to development by letting "markets" reward and punish economies according to their degree of openness, emphasis on trade, "comparative advantage," and the like. One result of this "crisis" is a transition in conventional development initiatives away from states and increasingly toward "private" initiatives, including those like Catholic parish twinning. Twinning, which rests wholly with "grassroots" participants acting within and across their local communities, exemplifies the shift in development toward "civil society," thereby reflecting Martinussen's point two.

Yet, an "alternative" development paradigm is not the same thing as an "alternative *to* development," as called for by postdevelopment scholars. While alternative development skirts conventional development's emphasis on growth and its state-centric underpinnings, it often continues to invest in development's guiding principles of a world divided by centers of "modernity" and "backwardness," where the modern have an interest—perhaps a duty—to help advance those who have been "left behind." This is certainly the case in twinning, where on the one hand St. Robert's participants conceptualize Haitians in very positive moral terms—that Haitians are superbly spiritual, family focused, and in touch with what is "real"—while on the other hand they view Haitians as overwhelmingly deficient: lacking knowledge, rationality, motivation, and health.

The "help" that St. Robert's extends to Haitians is not so much concerned with the structural conditions (e.g., structural debt, political economy, predatory states; see DeWind and Kinley 1998; Dupuy 1989; 1997; Farmer 1992; 1994; 2004) giving rise to Haitian poverty and vulnerability; instead, the "help" is very much targeted toward "empowering" Haitians to "act on their own behalf" (Cruikshank 1999, 39). That is, St. Robert's Haiti program tends to frame Haiti's problems in terms of individual or community-level shortcomings that can be overcome through education, by giving people the resources needed to "better" themselves (Cruikshank 1999).

Post-structural scholars like James Ferguson (1994) have critiqued conventional development for similar conceptualizations. Ferguson suggests that such framing is not harmless or incidental to development's functioning. Rather, it is central to it—an "instrument effect"—that shifts attention away from the structural features undergirding global poverty and instead focuses it on "technical" features that can be quantified, measured, and evaluated (Ferguson 1994; Escobar 1995a). Poverty then becomes cast as the result of something lacking—or abnormal—about the nation, society, or group labeled "poor." Power and domination, the global division of wealth, structural inequality, and the like remain unacknowledged while poverty is cast as a technical problem best resolved through apolitical "interventions," such as increasing industrialization, promoting trade, enhancing agricultural efficiency, reducing disease, and building roads. Or, in the case of twinning, by providing education, food, and access to credit.

Twinning fails as an alternative *to* development, at least as imagined by Escobar (1995b) and Nederveen Pieterse (2000), because it does not attempt to "undo" development in Haiti. Rather, it intends to extend its reach there, to "bring in" those who are perceived as having been neglected by more formal development initiatives. Twinning fails as an alternative *to* development, because in its "intentions, world-view, and mindset," it is very much characterized by "belief" in development and invested in fomenting its spread throughout Haiti.

Tensions, Fissures, Convalescence?

To some, evaluating whether twinning is best understood as alternative development or an alternative *to* development might seem purely academic. To the contrary, I suggest that understanding how and where twinning intersects with and diverges from international development is essential for making sense of the many problems St. Robert and Our Lady routinely encounter in their relationship with one another. From gaps in communication to concerns with accountability, the troubles these parish twins encounter in trying to make twinning "work" tend to rest squarely in those areas where twinning "overlaps" with conventional and alternative forms of development. To reduce tensions and mend fissures in these relationships, I want to propose that twinning more fully embrace the "alternative" visions *to* development it offers in its national-level rhetoric.

Let me first introduce the idealized vision of twinning, then talk about some of the problems afflicting the St. Robert-Our Lady pairing. In its promotional materials, PTPA frames twinning as building "bridge[s] whereby the love of God flows in both directions as parishes learn to care, share and pray for one another" (PTPA n.d.). Twinnings are supposed to be mutually rewarding partnerships among coequals bonded together in close relationships of respect and love. The term "twinning" itself, for example, deliberately was chosen to emphasize these features of equality and familial affection. These are intended to be relationships of solidarity, as described by Fogarty (this volume).

At an organizational level, liberation theology informs both the mission and goals of twinning. Liberation theology is a Catholic-inspired, radical critique of power structures that attempts to address and reform the political and economic conditions underpinning human suffering (Zweig 1991). Importantly, liberation theology conceptualizes these as conditions from which people need to be set free (liberated) rather than addressing them as problems of development or individual deficiencies (McGovern 1989).

None of the people I interviewed or observed at St. Robert framed their participation in twinning in terms of liberation theology; indeed, no one spoke of liberation theology at all. Instead, most everyone spoke about twinning in terms of development, of "producing" through education Haitians who would be able to care for themselves, to meet their own needs, to become independent. Repeatedly, I heard the clichéd adage, "give a man a fish, he'll eat for the day; teach a man to fish, he'll eat for life," the sense being here that people do not yet have the knowledge necessary to be successful. This focuses attention on what the "fisherman" lacks in "know-how" rather than looking to see whether the lake even has any fish, if those fish are edible, or if obstacles—like improvised explosive devices—might line the path to the lake.[2]

In assuming that Haitians are people who "do not know," the "mutuality" that is supposed to characterize twinning is undermined. Instead, one group—not coincidentally, the one who also controls the purse strings—imagines itself as having a "larger" worldview that permits it to take full account of the world and its operations while simultaneously framing the second group as somehow less fully aware, more partial in its knowledge and experiences. This potentially transforms Haitians into perceived "objects" of compassion rather than the more liberation theology-based understanding of the poor as dynamic agents of social change (McGovern 1989).

Twinning is supposed to inspire respect and appreciation for the "mutual gifts" that each parish has to offer the other. For St. Robert, those gifts include its ability to provide material resources for Our Lady. But, because the flow of money to Our Lady is so deeply intertwined with the idea of promoting development in the parish, St. Robert feels compelled to "protect the intentions" of their donors. That is, fund-raising efforts at St. Robert are often tied to specific projects (e.g., student sponsorship), so that when the money is transferred to the Haitian accounts, it is with the assumption that the money will be used for the specified purposes. So, while in principle the Haitian priests have control over the money, in reality they often have little maneuverability with regard to how those funds actually get used. For example, the priest in Haiti—Father Yvens—made a request to St. Robert for money to build pews for the church. St. Robert agreed, and sent the money. During their next visit to Our Lady, St. Robert parishioners found a new backyard improvement project had been completed. Inquiring about where the funds to pay for the project had come from, the parishioners were told that money left over from the pew project paid for the renovation. Not long after, Father Yvens approached St. Robert, asking for additional money to buy more pews. As one woman related to me, "We said no, they should've built more church pews with the money we gave them. Father probably felt he had a lot more discretion with that money than we felt. . . ."

This story is told by those active in the St. Robert twinning program to illustrate what they see as a real disconnect between their understanding of twinning and that of the Haitian priest. Whereas twinning is supposed to be based on trust and respect, St. Robert parishioners feel that the Haitian priest is, in many ways, not trustworthy._He does not provide them with the required accounting of funds, and when he does, they are "suspiciously" precise, "down to the penny." The question becomes, of course, who has the right to control that money: St. Robert or Our Lady? And, if it is Our Lady, how many "strings" come attached? In any event, rather than promoting a mutuality, these transfers of funds and calls for accountability setup a "benefactor-beneficiary" relationship that exacerbates rather than undermines the differences in power and position separating these "partners."

In conventional and alternative development initiatives, these "problems" would be discussed in terms of "fungibility," accountability, and maybe corruption. While the labels are less harsh in twinning networks, the concerns are very much the same: controlling the flow of resources in ways specified from the north. This is not necessarily wholly problematic, of course. For example, development has a long and sordid history of enriching the global south's elite at the expense of its poor. The legacy of governments borrowing money that benefits the middle and upper classes while accepting structural adjustment programs that disproportionately burden the most impoverished is but one example. The question of how to ensure that the poorest and most vulnerable members of a society are able to practice "liberation" remains unresolved.

The partnership between Our Lady and St. Robert is fraught with many tensions, most notably a lack of trust and mutual respect. These tensions have led, in fact, to real fissures in the relationship. Travels between the parish partners have become infrequent, the priest in Haiti feels compromised and maligned, and those at St. Robert feel exasperated and misunderstood. During an especially emotional and difficult visit that the Haitian priest made at the behest of St. Robert in 2006—under intense pressure from Michigan—the Haiti committee convened a special meeting to "get some answers" about the state of affairs at Our Lady. After many rounds of questioning by the St. Robert Haiti committee, during which Father Yvens reiterated that the relationship was supposed to be a "partnership," Father, through an interpreter, eventually spoke at length about the difficulties of partnership.

> *Father*: Sometimes we don't feel like true partners.
> *Haiti committee member 1*: We want you to be talkative partners.
> *Father*: It's like a song. It's the tone that's used that determines how [communications] are received. You're helping people and channeling through us. You're not helping us, the priests; you're channeling through us. . . . You help people through us. If you want good—let me repeat, good—information, you have to get it through us. That's not happening. You're getting inaccurate information [about what's happening in the programs]. It was very hard for me to come here. But, after many requests, I agreed. I know you're trying to help people going through me. That's how it is. I came here to tell you that I really appreciate the ways you're helping people. We're all humans. I can make mistakes, you can make mistakes. When I tell you this is the way I see it should be done,

because I'm in the field, then you do otherwise, I do not understand. . . . I'm not coming here for myself but for the children you're helping. You have to be very careful about the tone of your conversations. Even two people who are living together married have to watch how they talk with one another.

Committee member 1: If I can respond. We have not been pointed with you. This is how we talk to anyone. If you talk to the people in the countryside about those in Paris [being] rude, they'll say "they're rude to us, too." It's just our style. Then, with the undercurrent of trouble on the committee, when we don't hear from you, it causes problems.

Committee member 2: The amount of involvement, the number of programs, the financial commitment we have is far more than most. We got running with lots of enthusiasm from the parishioners. We're under pressure to keep going to the same degree as we started with.

Father: I definitely understand what you were saying about [the need to come to St. Robert], which is why I came. But, I have the impression that sometimes the committee has coordination problems. For example, let's say I give Dennis a letter, a week later I'll get a letter from Cassie asking for the same information.

Committee member 1: I hope not! Maybe . . .

Committee member 2: When Cassie writes, he doesn't respond. Why?

Father: [Addressing himself to Cassie] You've written before. I don't know what your powers of observation are, but I've never written back.

Committee member 2: We'd like to improve that.

Committee member 1: I don't know if it's you don't like to work with women or what?

Father: No, I'm not macho. I like to work with everyone, but if I don't like the tone, I will not respond.

Committee member 1: In 2003 . . . Father Lou wrote saying that "Cassie represents the committee."

Father: Yes, perhaps the committee is represented by Cassie, but it was the tone.

Committee member 3: Maybe it's a problem of translation. Could we write it in English?

Father: I don't think it's a language problem. No, it's more the personality of the person who writes, the tone that works.

Committee member 2: Understand, all the communication is "cc'd" to the committee. It was group thought [and] Cassie got asked to write the letter.

Father: Yes, it's my understanding. There are 1001 ways of saying something, like there are 1001 ways of disciplining a child. It's how it's expressed. When Cassie writes and I do not answer, it may be a mistake. Forgive me. . . .

Committee member 3: I'd like to say I appreciate Father's coming. These are difficult issues. Aside from fund-raising, it's good to see you. The meetings help to fix difficult issues.

Committee member 1: Or expose them.

Father: When you invited me, I really did not feel comfortable. I postponed it. When I received the invitation, I did not feel like coming. You do not have the right to judge me. These problems run deep. If you use me as a channel, if you want correct information, ask me. I insist, you're helping people, not me. I have a personal life, too. If I start something, if I get involved with something, you do not need to wonder if the work will be done properly or not. A question of

> trust arises. Without trust, there's no hope. There's one thing that really affected me deep down. In 2004, I had to spend 3 months in the U.S. for personal reasons. [I had the blessing and support of] my bishop. If you'd asked me personally [why I went to the U.S.], I'd give you the right information.
>
> *Committee member 1:* Three months is a long time. We'd have like to have known before. We had a trip planned.
>
> *Father:* There are two [priests] in the parish. We work together. We share everything. I'm not holding back anything for myself. Father Salomon can give you information. I can do it, he can do it. My absence or presence would not have changed anything. . . . I'm not the only priest in that parish. You have your private life, and I have mine. I was working with my bishop. . . .
>
> *Committee member 1:* Well, I'm upset by what you said. More than anyone here, I work on Haiti. And, I'm not paid. . . .
>
> *Father:* Frankly, we're interested in helping the parishioners. Everything else is [just] details.

I have quoted this meeting exchange at length because it captures and reveals in startling detail the troubles plaguing these "partnerships." From the outset, the definition of what would make a "good" partnership is raised. "True" partners, Father suggests, are those who communicate in respectful "tones" directly with one another, rather than via proxies, and who trust one another. The Haiti committee says it wants "talkative partners," even when there are disagreements or hurt feelings between them. Because the pairing—despite rhetoric to the contrary—is fundamentally unbalanced, the Haiti committee's preferences can be imposed. Father can be forced to the table in Michigan because, if he does not open himself to communication, the projects St. Robert supports in his parish can be stopped.

Father speaks at length about how he feels that the letters and emails he is receiving disclose a fundamental mistrust and disregard for him on the part of the committee; not only does the committee fail to acknowledge Father's obvious hurt, they dismiss his concerns as unimportant: "We have not been pointed with you. This is how we talk to anyone." While Father eventually apologizes for his lack of communications ["It may have been a mistake. Forgive me"], the committee never extends a similar overture to him. Moreover, one committee member instead focuses on her own hurt feelings ["Well, I'm upset by what you said . . ."] without acknowledging the same "upset" Father himself just expressed as the basis for the behavior the committee dislikes. Perhaps most revealing is the remark, "More than anyone here, I work on Haiti. And, I'm not paid. . . ." The priest should be grateful. It is an option, a choice—and an unremunerated one at that—to be concerned with Haiti, to work toward "helping" people there. While at one level, many Americans might agree with this sentiment—that Haitians should be grateful for the "help" they are receiving—at another level, we instead might consider such help a duty, an obligation, rather than a choice. As liberation theologians contend, those who have more have a moral and/or ethical responsibility to redistribute wealth, to work in solidarity with the powerless, to challenge structures of oppression. Or, we might interrogate the entire notion of "help" itself as something fundamentally problematic, a new modality of "governance" which intends to "discipline" poor subjects (Ferguson and Gupta 2002; Cruikshank 1999; see also Sharp, this volume). Gronemeyer's assertion that "whoever desires help is 'voluntarily' made subject to the watchful gaze of the helper" (Gronemeyer 1992, 54) is an apt description of St. Robert's relationship with Our Lady, where the gaze falls squarely on the Haitian priests. The modern version of help that Gronemeyer (1992, 59) identifies— that which is attached to "overcoming a deficit, a struggle against backwardness"—is likewise expressive of twinning. In any event, the current construction of "helping" tends to cast Haitians as objects of compassion rather than as agents battling to "liberate" themselves from the forces that impoverish them. Drawing on Fogarty's distinction between altruism and solidarity, twinning in this way might be understood best as a "unidirectional" rather than dialogical relationship, one based in charity and philanthropy rather than one rooted in justice and liberation (see Fogarty, this volume).

Conclusion

Clearly twinning encompasses a number of problematic dimensions associated with development initiatives more broadly: depoliticization of poverty, imposition of Western standards, governmentality. I have raised them here not as simple criticisms but to offer starting points for thinking about twinning's possible reworking. The goals and mission of twinning as articulated at the national level suggest twinning could be an alternative *to* development. Yet, its practice at the local level demonstrates instead that it is an alternative form of development, invested in many of development's values, beliefs, and practices. Moreover, it is in these spaces of overlap where the tensions between the two twins emerge: the attempt to "manage" funds from afar, to evaluate program success, to hold the administrators (priests) "accountable" not by relying on trust, "relationships of love," or the bonds of Catholic faith. Instead, St. Robert's Haiti Committee demands the more impersonal and "auditable" mechanisms of ledgers, photographs (e.g., "could you send pictures of the bibles you bought?") and "evidence-based" confirmations that projects are progressing on the ground in Haiti as expected and that funds are flowing for their specified purposes.

Inspired by counterhegemonic visions of development—that is, by liberation theology—twinning ultimately draws on those same hegemonic visions to (re)create a hybrid form of development that invests wholeheartedly in neoliberalism's dominant discourses and practices. Forged and implemented at the grassroots and couched within the language of solidarity, twinning on the surface suggests an alternative way of engaging the world. Yet, beneath the veneer lies an entangled knot of conventional and alternative forms of development that buoy and extend the development machine rather than dismantle it. As this chapter has suggested, however, this new mode of development is not uncontested or uncritically accepted by those who would be its targets. Rather, the fissures characterizing the U.S.-Haiti twinning relationship reveal a continued struggle to reformulate the differing interests, resources, and power positions separating these supposed partners.

Notes

1. Civil society is conceptualized as the "sphere of social relations and institutions that exists between the sphere of government and the sphere of for-profit market oriented organizations" (Wuthnow 2004, 22).

2. See Bretton Alvaré, this volume, for a similar discussion in the context of a Rastafari FBO.

Works Cited

Arce, Alberto, and Norman Long. 1992. The dynamics of local knowledge: Interfaces between bureaucrats and peasants. In *Battlefields of knowledge: The interlocking of theory and practice in social research and development*, ed. Norman Long and Ann Long, 211-46. London, New York: Routledge.

Chambers, Robert. 1993. *Challenging the professions: Frontiers for rural development.* London: Intermediate Technology.

———. 1997. *Whose reality counts? Putting the first last.* London: Intermediate Technology.

———. 2005. *Ideas for development.* London: Earthscan.

Cruikshank, Barbara. 1999. *The will to empower: Democratic citizens and other subjects.* Ithaca, NY: Cornell University Press.

DeWind, Josh, and David H. Kinley III. 1998. *Aiding migration: The impact of international development assistance on Haiti.* Boulder, CO: Westview Press.

Dupuy, Alex. 1989. *Haiti in world economy: Race, class, and underdevelopment since 1700.* Boulder, CO: Westview Press.

———. 1997. *Haiti in the new world order: The limits of democratic revolution.* Boulder, CO: Westview Press.

Escobar, Arturo. 1995a. *Encountering development: The making and unmaking of the third world.* Princeton, NJ: Princeton University Press.

———. 1995b. Imagining a post-development era. In *The power of development*, ed. Jonathan Crush, 211-27. London and New York: Routledge.

———. 2000. "Beyond the search for a paradigm? Post-development and beyond." *Development = Developpement = Desarrollo* 43(4):11-15.

Farmer, Paul. 1992. *AIDS and accusation: Haiti and the geography of blame.* Berkeley: University of California Press.

———. 1994. *The uses of Haiti.* Monroe, ME: Common Courage Press.

———. 2004. What happened in Haiti? Where the past is present. In *Getting Haiti right this time: The U.S. and the coup.* Monroe, ME: Common Courage Press.

Ferguson, James. 1994. *The anti-politics machine: "Development," depoliticization, and bureaucratic power in Lesotho.* Minneapolis: University of Minnesota Press.

Ferguson, James, and Akhil Gupta. 2002. Spatializing states: Toward an ethnography of neoliberal governmentality. *American Ethnologist* 29(4):981-1002.

Gardner, Katy, and David Lewis. 1996. *Anthropology, development and the post-modern challenge.* Chicago: Pluto Press.

Gronemeyer, Marianne. 1992. Helping. In *The development dictionary*, ed. W. Sachs, 53-69. London: Zed Books.

Hefferan, Tara. 2007. *Twinning faith and development: Catholic parish partnering in the U.S. and Haiti.* Bloomfield, CT: Kumarian Press.

Martinussen, John. 1999. *Society, state, and market: A guide to competing theories of development.* London: Zed Books.

Matthews, Sally. 2004. Post-development theory and the question of alternatives: A view from Africa. *Third World Quarterly* 25(2):373-84.

McGlone, Mary M. 1997. *Sharing faith across the hemisphere.* Washington, DC: United States Catholic Conference.

McGovern, Arthur F. 1989. *Liberation theology and its critics: Toward an assessment.* Maryknoll, NY: Orbis Books.

Nederveen Pieterse, Jan. 2000. After post-development. *Third World Quarterly* 21(2):175-91.

Parish Twinning Program of the Americas (PTPA). 2008. PTPA: The Parish Twinning Program of the Americas. http://www.parishprogram.org (last accessed December 2, 2008).

————. n.d. *Building parish to parish relationships: People reaching out to people.* Nashville, TN: PTPA.

Rahnema, M., and V. Bawtree, eds. 1997. *The post-development reader.* London: Zed Books.

Rist, Gilbert. 1997. *The history of development: From Western origins to global faith.* London: Zed Books.

Sachs, Wolfgang. 1992. *The development dictionary.* London: Zed Books.

Salomon, Lester M. 1993. The global associational revolution: The rise of the third sector on the world scene. *Occasional paper 15.* Baltimore, MD: Institute of Policy Studies.

Wuthnow, R. 2004. *Saving America? Faith-based services and the future of civil society.* Princeton, NJ: Princeton University Press.

Zweig, Michael. 1991. Economics and liberation theology. In *Religion and economic justice,* ed. M. Zweig, 3-49. Philadelphia: Temple University Press.

Chapter 5
Searching for Solidarity in Nicaragua: Faith-Based NGOs as Agents of Transcultural Voluntourism
Timothy G. Fogarty

They come here thinking they are going to give something to us, but many discover that instead they receive, from people who have almost nothing, a new experience of hope, faith and love (Dámaris Albuquerque, Executive Director of CEPAD, the Council of Protestant Churches of Nicaragua; quoted in Jeffrey [2001, 6]).

If they come to "help," it won't work. Better that they stay where they are. If they are coming to interact, and to help everyone learn something mutually, then welcome! (Boff 2002, 18).

Introduction

Nearly every airliner that touches down at Augusto Cesar Sandino International Airport in Managua carries at least one group of eager volunteers who have come to help those less fortunate than themselves. They come from North America or Europe with the object of meeting and working alongside some of the most economically marginalized residents of the Western Hemisphere. They do not stay long, usually a week or two. And only about 40 percent return after their initial trip. Some 10 percent become chronic "voluntourists" to Nicaragua, and a few eventually make it their home.

Voluntourism has captured my attention since I first moved to Nicaragua with my family in 1988, where I worked in international development until 1990. I returned to Nicaragua to begin my academic field research in 1999 and had subsequent fieldwork experiences in 2003 and 2004 for a total of eighteen months.[1] My initial focus was on how middle-class North Americans and popular-class Nicaraguans forge—or fail to forge—bonds of cross-cultural solidarity within the short voluntourism encounters. As there were few unmediated encounters between Nicaraguans and North Americans on these trips, my focus shifted to how the faith-based non-governmental organizations (NGOs) serve as the in-country hosts, intermediaries, and interlocutors.

By voluntourism, I mean a short (one week to one month) trip to a destination that is culturally different from the sending community. The sending regions are always in the one-third (developed) world and the receiving regions are in the two-thirds (developing) world. The groups of voluntourists are usually organized by sending organizations such as churches, educational institutions, or civic associations, and the experiences are organized by transnational or national NGOs. These NGOs serve as the voluntourists' hosts, guides, translators, and work supervisors on a round-the-clock basis, from the visitors' arrival until their departure. The purpose of the experience for the voluntourist often includes elements of altruism and adventure. From the NGO's point of view these experiences can lead to increased program support from and conscientization of the visitors. I do not include within this study those groups that are organized for the purpose of proselytizing, and I do not claim that my findings apply to such groups.

In this chapter I show that faith-based NGOs that bring short-term volunteers to Nicaragua have a responsibility to decide what place solidarity formation[2] has among their priorities and to design their programs accordingly. While solidarity formation by means of voluntourism is a complex endeavor, it has identifiable components that can be enhanced or hindered by NGO praxis. I explain how voluntourism has become a significant global social movement. Then I show how this practice has particular importance in Nicaragua because of its history of revolution and its plethora of NGOs. Next I describe how the crucial choice for NGOs of whether they will follow a praxis of solidarity or of altruism has profound implications for their short-term volunteers, though all NGOs will inevitably incorporate elements of each. I conclude with a description of six NGO practices that can foster solidarity between voluntourists and Nicaraguans.[3]

The Significance of Voluntourism

The significance of voluntourism is severalfold. First, this social practice is a growing phenomenon that started as a rather exceptional experience in the lifestyles of one-third world citizens but now is becoming almost commonplace. The widespread growth of voluntourism has been possible through the growth of commercial air travel. Though not all parts of the world are equally accessible or exotic, few regions of economic need today do not receive delegations of international helpers.[4] Few two-thirds world countries do not have some civil society organization inviting groups to come and participate in its work (Salazar 2004). In Nicaragua voluntourism has proliferated from the church-sponsored or politically motivated voluntourism of the 1980s to the commercial voluntourism offered by a multitude of travel agencies today.

Voluntourism has become an important organizational development strategy for transnational and national NGOs that need international support to maintain their humanitarian assistance and development work in the two-thirds world. This is particularly true of faith-based NGOs whose smaller size and denominational funding base have kept them from relying heavily on bilateral government or multilateral agency funds that have increasingly been channeled through secular NGOs. These faith-based NGOs are learning that their most loyal donors are those with direct experience with their international programs. Program participants become the NGO's most enthusiastic ambassadors and the backbone of its organizational leadership.

Additionally, voluntourism has become an important form of "deprivation education" for one-third world citizens, introducing them to abject poverty. As forces of globalization become ever more pervasive and influential, there is a dawning awareness that the global problems we confront as a species and even as a planet require transnational solutions. No nation or ethnic group is an island, and our collective problems can only be solved by those who see that the micro-, meso-, and macrolevels of social interaction are interrelated. As "multilaterals" (e.g., the United Nations, the World Bank, the International Monetary Fund, the World Trade Organization) and regional alliances (e.g., the European Union) have come to dominate our global political economy, it has become critical to understand how planetary policies affect each of the different regions of the world and the localities within those regions. Those who have been acculturated in relatively affluent and politically powerful regions have a need (sometimes unfelt) to learn how the other two-thirds of the world lives,[5] and it is clear that mass media in the "developed" world have not been wholly effective in accomplishing the task of cross-cultural understanding.

The faith-based NGO sector has a rich social gospel and liberation theology tradition from which to address the social injustice that typifies the political economy of the planet. The ecclesial practices of preaching and teaching often include topics of global injustice and can provide believers with social analysis skills.[6] Visiting marginalized populations has become a common "outreach" activity of churches of the global north. Voluntourism (often called "short term mission" by faith-based organizations) has become a mark of devotional dedication in many faith communities. NGOs that sponsor these encounters often cite religious or spiritual motivations for doing so.[7]

Voluntourism has become an effective strategy for strengthening civil society as distinct from state and market sectors. It has arisen from the transnational reach of churches, unions, and humanitarian organizations. These institutions are among those that constitute civil society and that currently vie for political power to offset that of nation-states and commercial businesses. Currently voluntourism serves as a chance to learn both resistance and accommodation to transnational corporate capitalism. It is a practice in which the personal becomes political and empowers global citizens in their struggles for social justice or channels them into works of charity.

If transcultural solidarity is an important value to instill in global citizens, then voluntourism is a singularly effective strategy for accomplishing that task. From an educational point of view, cross-cultural exposure through somatic as well as cognitive and affective involvement in the lives of cultural "others" is one of the most important ways of changing people's lifestyle decisions. Research suggests that culture shock is necessary to move to an intercultural frame of reference (Kim 1988), that cross-cultural participation is necessary for planetary consciousness (Hanvey 1982), that students involved in international service show increased levels of global concern (Crabtree 1998; Myers-Lipton 1998), and that physical labor and intellectual endeavor are both essential components in international service learning and participatory development (Crabtree 1998). In short, voluntourism is a powerful laboratory for conscientization (Freire 2002[1970]).

The NGO-ization of Nicaragua—A Historical Context

Besides the importance of voluntourism to society as a whole, we need to consider its connection to and dependence on the NGO sector. My research sites are in Nicaragua, one of the most NGO-ized nations in the world (O'Neill 2004), with more than 4000 legally recognized NGOs in a country of five million people (Briones 2004). Over a quarter of the national GDP is generated by the NGO sector, which distributes 75 percent of the foreign aid that comes into the country (CAPRI 1996). Perhaps no other country, with the possible exception of Mozambique (O'Neill 2004), is as affected by its NGO sector. So while the prominence of the NGO sector in Nicaragua may be atypical, it provides a rich laboratory for understanding how voluntourism aids in the growth of the NGO sector and how voluntourism might provide the conditions for forging a solidarity consciousness among its participants.

Because of the number and economic importance of NGOs in Nicaragua, it is critical to understand how they influence both the private and public lives of its citizens. Indeed, NGOs have become part of the historical cultural consciousness of the Nicaraguan people. As one young Nicaraguan told me enthusiastically in the context of discussing the virtues of NGOs over the government, "The people here say, 'Una ONG es un tiro seguro!'" (An NGO is a sure bet!). During the Somoza era (1930s through 1970s) few NGOs existed in Nicaragua; their advent began with the 1972 earthquake that leveled the capital city of Managua and killed more than ten thousand people. When it became apparent that Somoza's clan and cronies were pocketing much of the relief money arriving through governmental channels, the international humanitarian community began fostering the growth of non-governmental networks that could serve as conduits of emergency assistance and later of development aid to urban and rural communities throughout the country. Many of these agencies were church affiliated or faith-based.[8]

When the Sandinista-led insurrection triumphed and Somoza and his National Guard fled the country, the new (penniless) government and war-torn society received an influx of international visitors wishing to support the revolutionary "project" of the Nicaraguan people. Christians arrived from various parts of the world to support a revolution they saw to be inspired by both Christ the liberator and class struggle. Once there, they found ample support for their convictions in a country where three key cabinet positions were held by Catholic priests[9] and the numerous base communities had become integrated into the mass organizations of the revolution (Lancaster 1988; Randall 1983; Cardenal 1977). The unique historical conjunction of forces in Nicaragua at that time resulted in a deeply religious revolutionary consciousness on the part of many, perhaps the majority of those in the popular classes (Nepstad 1996).[10]

Foreigners arrived to show their solidarity with the revolution by working, bringing material aid and learning about the revolution from its leaders and participants. Tens of thousands of sympathetic citizens arrived from Europe and North America during the 1980s. As U.S. government support for the counterrevolutionaries increased, a countervailing group of U.S. citizens, Witness for Peace (Acción Permanente Por la Paz) who had ties to U.S. churches, came to investigate the atrocities and human rights violations being financed with their tax dollars (McGinnis 1985). By the end of the 1990s, ten thousand U.S. citizens had come specifically for that purpose. While in Nicaragua, they would provide a North American or European presence in zones of danger for Nicaraguan civilians, and they would assist in the coffee harvest or other economic activity in the rural communities they visited (Fogarty 2002).[11] In this era, *internationalistas* were seen by poor Nicaraguans as personal emissaries of solidarity from around the world. Thus was coined the revolutionary slogan, "La Solidaridad es la Ternura de los Pueblos" (Solidarity Is the Tenderness of the Peoples).

Voluntourism, in sum, began in Nicaragua in prerevolutionary times as a form of disaster relief, then became an ongoing form of political support for the revolutionary regime and/or of resistance against the counterrevolution funded by the U.S. government.[12] For the last 16 years, in a neoliberal Nicaragua, voluntourism has been a tactic for building up civil society (Núñez Soto 1999) and for fomenting citizen-to-citizen contact that bypasses both the market and the nation-state. Many social-justice-oriented leaders who entered the government under the revolutionary regime migrated to civil society organizations and NGOs when they lost their positions after the 1990 electoral defeat of the FSLN (The Sandinista Political Party). They often had connections to international solidarity organizations that were willing to shift their support from state agencies to NGOs in order to avoid assisting the counterrevolutionary government.

I heard several post-Sandinista mayors complain that they lacked the international aid their FSLN predecessors had siphoned off to the NGOs.

Both the commercial forces that had resisted the revolutionary government internally and their allies returning from Miami after a decade away proceeded to construct a quintessentially neoliberal regime. During the 1990s all state en- terprises were sold at bargain prices to transnational or national corporations. Utilities were privatized, and many social services ceased to exist. The national development bank was closed. Credit to small agricultural producers dried up (Jonakin 1996). The scene was set for the hyper-NGO-ization of Nicaraguan society. NGOs that had been involved in development efforts found themselves more and more relegated to being social service providers in the absence of any government providers. In a series of radical structural adjustment programs dic- tated by the International Monetary Fund, the award-winning education and health services developed under the Sandinistas became nominal agencies with- out sufficient budgets to maintain program quality. NGOs were called on to fill the breach.

Today, understanding solidarity between Nicaraguans of the popular classes and North Americans of the middle class requires a comprehension of the unique bilateral relationship between the peoples and governments of the two countries over the last 160 years. As U.S. hegemony over Nicaragua has been constant and at times brutal, any attempt at securing true solidarity must rely on analysis of the historical collective consciousness of citizens from both nations. Yet it would be a mistake to consider the issues of social justice as served by an exclusively nationalist analysis. William Robinson (1998) has argued that the Central American revolutions of the 1970s and '80s were inadvertently instru- mental in clearing the way for the neoliberal hegemony of the '90s and beyond. Those that are seeking now to jettison the small-holder agriculture that consti- tutes half of the current economy of Nicaragua in favor of export-oriented indus- trial and tourist development are members of what Sklair (2002) calls the trans- national capitalist class.[13] It is important that voluntourists understand the macrocontext of their efforts in order to make informed choices about their participation.

Orlando Núñez Soto (1999) observes that NGOs in Nicaragua (and so by implication their voluntourists) are faced with a dilemma. They can opt for the economic and political security of aligning themselves with a neoliberal state, its multilateral backers (the International Monetary Fund or World Bank) and the transnational capitalist market sector (CAFTA). Doing so will distance them from the popular social movements that are struggling to preserve political and economic space for the majority of Nicaraguans and to preserve agrarian lifeways. NGOs that take this stance will lose their moral authority among the strata of society from which their program beneficiaries come. Or they can choose to stand with popular social movements and challenge the transnational forces that seek to continue exploitation of the majority of Nicaraguans as low-paid service and manufacturing workers for foreign investors and international clients. This choice for NGOs in Nicaragua is isomorphic with those that Occhipinti (in this volume) identifies among the liberation-theology-inspired Argentine NGOs. In Nicaragua the myth of *mestizaje* has obscured many of the indigenous dimensions of peasant lifeways, but the issues of articulation with international markets are similar (Gould 1998; Hale 1996; Téllez 1999).

The typical voluntourist is oblivious to the evolution of NGO involvement in Nicaraguan society. Nonetheless, this history continues to inform NGO praxis. Those NGOs that challenge their volunteers to engage in analysis of the current social context must take stances on development models (favoring the transnational capitalist sector or favoring the small-holder agriculturalist and informal commercial sector) (Núñez Soto 2003). Those who believe, because of religion or political theory, that "another world is possible" may find ways to reforge an international solidarity similar to that which helped sustain the revolutionary morale of the 1980s.

Solidarity is more complicated to achieve in a postsocialist, postmodern, neoliberal era. My research indicates that certain NGO practices can sustain solidarity while others will devolve into an altruism that has little or no prophetic value in the face of capitalist exploitation of the marginalized populations of Nicaragua. But practices of altruism (charity) and practices of social justice (conscientization) are not exclusive. Every NGO and its volunteers will partake in both practices and both discourses. The crucial issue is whether they are engaging in a critical and reflexive praxis. We now turn to the concepts of solidarity and altruism, and how each might be operationalized by faith-based NGOs.

Solidarity Formation

Solidarity is a difficult idea to get across to voluntourists when they arrive seeking to "help". Some NGOs are blunt in confronting the misconceptions that voluntourists have of their capabilities to solve the problems of Nicaraguans:

> All the people who think they are going to save Nicaragua by taking two weeks of their vacation coming down here and building a health center or whatever, they really ought to just not waste their time. Other people see a whole lot of value in that kind of work. But my own personal perspective is that you need to be here not because of what you can *do*, not because *people here* need you to be here. You need to be here because *you* need to be here. This is something other than what you know. It is a full sensory experience. You cannot have the same experience, gain the same understanding or insight by reading a book, or watching a broadcast or a documentary. You have to *be here*, you have to smell it and taste it and touch it and see it and feel it. No one can describe it. You have to live it (Director of a Nicaraguan faith-based NGO).

Solidarity must begin with lived experience, *and* must lead to a change in personal orientation from doing for Nicaraguans to being in relationship with them.

> Many team members are changed by the experience. Although they have volunteered in order to do something for the poor, their paternalism comes apart when they meet articulate poor people who often believe in God more than they do and who want a world where North–South relations are characterized by justice rather than charity. . . . A good start is to help volunteers overcome the "edifice complex" by downplaying the notion that what's most important for the group is the classroom, clinic or house they are going to build, and emphasizing that the real purpose is accompaniment (Jeffrey 2001).

Solidarity as Virtue

The issue of human solidarity bears on the continued survival of the species *Homo sapiens.* The frequency and savagery of wars and oppressions in our age correspond to an extreme and intensifying inequity in access to global resources, more acute than at any time in history. When coupled with rapid population growth, unsustainable levels of consumption, and environmental degradation, the material conditions for genocide and even species extinction exist. No longer can we afford the illusion of believing that our future lies in our ability to compete with other members of our species. The terms and technology of competition have outstripped our ability not only to find win/win solutions but even to find win/lose solutions. Global competition is yielding a lose/lose scenario of apocalyptic proportions. As Martin Luther King, Jr., so succinctly observed, we have a choice between coexistence or nonexistence. In the present global political economy, ways must be found to achieve distributive justice or face mutual annihilation.

One of the forces undergirding the sense of solidarity that may help prevent global self-destruction is the conviction of the universal siblinghood of humanity that is an element of many religious faiths. One eloquent expression of the need for this new conspecific solidarity came from Pope John Paul II (1987):

> We have to be converted. We have to change our spiritual relationship with self, with neighbor, with even the remotest human communities, and with nature itself, in view of the common good of the whole individual and of all people. *This felt interdependence is a new moral category, and the response to it is the "virtue" of solidarity.* Solidarity is not a feeling of vague compassion or a shallow sadness but a firm and persevering determination to commit oneself to the common good. It is in attitude squarely opposed to greed and the thirst for power (*Sollicitudo rei socialis,* section 38; emphasis mine).

Solidarity as Habitus

Virtue is a useful metonym for solidarity in a religious context, since it connotes both an individual and interior dimension and a social consequence. For the purposes of social science, we can find isomorphic concepts that have been adequately theorized, such as Pierre Bourdieu's *habitus*. Bourdieu (1977) observed that even though individual humans have agency, they tend to act in similar ways. He attributed this to the internalization of learned social structures. Habitus is not just the repetition of behaviors imposed by external reality, because human behavior is always performed with an element of improvisation given the exigencies of the moment and the particularities of any given historical context. Habitus enables us to live according to social rules in continuity and predictability while enabling us to innovate as needed in playing the game of life. This interior principle is prerational and subconscious; it is also collective rather than individual and is formed within social institutions. This concept is helpful in understanding how voluntourists acquire the practice of solidarity and how institutional cultural logics coalesce within the context of an NGO.

Bourdieu also alerts us to the tendency to "mis-recognize" the power structure that oppresses the many in favor of the few. The symbolic violence that comes from institutionalized injustice and the self-interest that generates a stratified society are rendered invisible by the discourse of institutions that purport to offer their services for the public welfare or some other magnanimous objective. The actual agendas of institutions flow from a subconscious habitus that is quite distinct from the overt and rational goals of their mission statement (Bourdieu 1977). Solidarity has a different valence than misrecognition. Solidarity between culturally distinct groups requires rethinking the issue of power and understanding it as something that, like material resources, must be shared in order to function. In solidarity, power is redistributed intentionally as the powerful divest themselves and the powerless invest themselves with it, but with an eye to transforming power relationships rather than reversing them.[14]

Solidarity or Altruism?[15]

It is important to distinguish between two related but fundamentally distinct types of relationships that are fostered by faith-based NGOs, those of solidarity and those of altruism. Altruism is fundamentally a unidirectional impetus of the human spirit to reach out and help other human beings by supplying all or part of their necessities out of one's surplus. The interior disposition of altruistic givers is often one of gratitude to some higher power for their own prosperity and sympathy for their fellow humans' plight. Altruism is the orientation for practices of charity and philanthropy. Altruism is a virtue in the sense described above, and it becomes a part of social habitus.

Solidarity, in contrast, is fundamentally dialogical. It is an impetus of the human spirit to reach out and establish a relationship with another human for mutual benefit that will result in a sharing of material and spiritual resources. Friendship and cooperative relationships such as teamwork are largely solidarity. Solidarity is an effective orientation for practices of justice and liberation. Solidarity is also a virtue which may inform the habitus of an individual or organization.

Altruism implies a less radical stance in that it does not require resistance to structural injustice. In fact it becomes all the more prominent and beneficial to the giver as inequity increases. The less equitable the distribution of resources, the more virtuous appears the altruist who would share his or her surplus with those less "fortunate." But a common form of altruism is ultimately based on the half-truth that it is good to share one's surplus, without asking whence it came. "For them to *be* is to *have*, and to be the class of the 'haves' . . . The oppressors do not perceive their monopoly on having more as a privilege which dehumanizes others and themselves" (Freire 2002[1970], 59).

Another common practice in the habitus of altruism is to attribute one's surplus to individual industry or divine providence without recognizing the role played by the toil of one's fellow human beings in generating that wealth and the role of the socio-economic system in redistributing it in unequal portions.

> If others do not have more it is because they are incompetent and lazy, and worst of all is their unjustifiable ingratitude toward the "generous gestures" of the dominant class. Precisely because they are "ungrateful" and "envious," the oppressed are regarded as potential enemies who must be watched (Freire 2002[1970], 59).

Solidarity, which recognizes the ontological unity of all human beings, is moved to establish a relationship of mutual exchange out of the realization that neither party to the exchange can endure in their humanity when there is a social relation of structural injustice, one which deprives one of the partners of the necessities for a satisfying life while providing the other with a surplus. Solidarity recognizes the surplus of the one partner not as an evidence of prosperity but as evidence of maldistribution and lack of justice.

> An unjust social order is the permanent fount of this "generosity" of the oppressor. . . . True generosity consists precisely in fighting to destroy the causes which nourish false charity. This lesson . . . must come from the oppressed themselves and from those who are in solidarity with them (Freire 2002[1970], 45).

Altruism is easier to operationalize than solidarity. Because it is less radical, it is less controversial and more people are open to it. It is faster, more tangible, more orderly and hence more predictable, and less socially disruptive of a stratified society than solidarity. Perhaps its most attractive quality is that it does not require the givers and the receivers to reverse dynamics. One can learn to be either a giver or a receiver and become comfortable in that role. In some types of altruism, human relationships can be objectified and even commodified, resulting in more alienation rather than less—because, as Henri Nouwen observes, "All forms of help become forms of violence when giving does not presuppose receiving."[16] As Marcel Mauss (1996[1924]) reminds us, at some level giving always presupposes receiving.

There are theologies of social service, international development models, and practices of faith-based NGOs based on altruism and others based on solidarity. The habitus of most NGOs is a mixture and often a conflation of the two. It is not unusual to find within the same document or on an organization's web page tropes of both altruism and solidarity. This indicates that NGOs, because of their location in the social matrix, and because of their habitus, are involved in practices of altruism and solidarity simultaneously. While they may be logically contradictory practices at various levels of analysis, they function among NGOs and their volunteers in a compartmentalized fashion analogous to the way June Nash (1979) describes the composite religious cosmology of the indigenous Bolivian tin miners she researched. For them certain realms are amenable to Christian supernatural and preternatural forces while other realms (deep in the mines) are amenable only to indigenous demons and divinities. There is complementarity without contradiction, until those who seek religious conformity and consistency (Westerners) exert pressure on the indigenes to choose and exclude. It is possible that choosing either altruism or solidarity to the exclusion of the other is to erroneously bifurcate and misunderstand the holism of the pastoral/prophetic vocation of faith-based organizations.

It is my bias that solidarity is the more equitable and effective paradigm for transnational cross-cultural quests for social justice. In the final section I share the program components prominent among faith-based NGOs that seek to foster solidarity between North Americans and Nicaraguans through short-term voluntourist experiences. This is not to claim that durable solidarity relationships can be forged in a seven- to fourteen-day excursion to a foreign country. But ethnographic data make clear that such bonds can begin even in such a cursory encounter and that they do deepen over time.

Solidarity is not inevitable. Few NGOs provide all six of the conditions I find crucial to the formation of cross-cultural solidarity, and most provide only one or two to the fullest degree. NGO organizational energies are more often directed to accomplishing proximate institutional objectives, such as serving their program participants, developing their donor base, and maintaining or expanding their own program capacities. Specific and intentional solidarity formation, while not necessarily an afterthought, is rarely a central priority.

Program Components of Solidarity-Nurturing NGOs

Six important NGO practices create the conditions for cross-cultural solidarity between middle-class North Americans and popular-class Nicaraguans. In my study of a dozen NGOs that bring short-term voluntourists to Nicaragua, I found that many of them have elements of one or more of the six practices, in differing degrees of prominence, in their organizational habitus. Some of the NGOs do not include solidarity in their discourses or practices. Others are happy to include solidarity in their discourses but find altruism more practicable. Still others combine both simultaneously in various ratios.

An Articulated Transnational Development Model

Just as every budget of a faith-based organization is a theological statement, so too is every development model. If an NGO's model is one of alternative development rather than an alternative *to* development, as Hefferan (this volume) distinguishes, then it may find itself poorly equipped to operationalize solidarity. It may devolve back into practices of paternalistic altruism motivated in part by what Quijano (2000) terms the "coloniality of power," which, at its root, is racism. Some small faith-based NGOs do not articulate their development models, but each has an implicit one, or contending ones, which motivate and guide its practice. Critical discourse analysis (Fairclough 1995) of oral and written discourse formations reveals the elements of the models, and participant observation reveals the congruency or lack thereof between discourse and practice. My research showed great variance among NGO development models.

Bicultural Competency

A factor in solidarity formation is the degree of bicultural competency within the organization. This depends most directly on both the intrapersonal and interpersonal characteristics of the NGO staff. NGOs with biculturally competent individuals in key positions dealing directly with volunteers had a much higher likelihood of fostering solidarity, since these individuals often were demonstrating solidarity in their various relationships with Nicaraguans and North Americans. NGOs that had solidarity relationships between members of bicultural teams likewise kept solidarity constantly in front of the volunteers. NGOs that had bicultural staff in which North Americans were the superiors of their Nicaraguan employees offered a counter-solidarity model of relationships that had to be overcome in order to achieve solidarity with Nicaraguans.

Sometimes NGOs would obfuscate the power relationships by asserting partnership and coresponsibility when the dynamics were clearly not equal. I never encountered a Nicaraguan on the boards of directors of transnational

NGOs, except the ones that were national offices of NGOs affiliated with an international network; for instance, World Vision Nicaragua or Habitat for Humanity Nicaragua. By contrast autochthonous Nicaraguan NGOs have international funding sources but are staffed by nationals. As Alvaré and Hefferan (this volume) indicate, local NGO leadership may not preserve local sovereignty of the development enterprise in a stratified global context. Relationships between NGOs and their donors can devolve into a clientism that precludes solidarity in favor of altruism.

Relationship with Popular Social Movements

As Núñez Soto (1999) states, the litmus test for NGO solidarity with the Nicaraguan popular classes is whether an NGO stands in solidarity with local popular organizations. Bypassing questions of which social movements are most representative and acknowledging contradictions among them, coalitions, alliances, and coordinating bodies do exist and are able to mobilize people to resist the most egregious violations of their human rights. NGOs that consider their work separate from that of the social movements do so at the risk of losing moral legitimacy.

I once encountered a roadblock set up by landless campesinos who had lost their farms and their livelihoods in the coffee price collapse of 2000.[17] Five thousand of them (men, women, and children) had been traveling throughout Nicaragua for months, camping on the side of the road under black plastic shelters, demonstrating to show that the government that had guaranteed them land and production inputs had reneged on its promises. This day they were blocking the Pan American Highway, the main route between Honduras and Costa Rica, stopping all vehicles and requiring passengers to walk six kilometers of highway to get to the other side. I met the ex-coffee growers in the presence of the director of a faith-based NGO whose central office was located two kilometers from the roadblock and was at that time housing a group of North American volunteers. I suggested it might be educational for the North Americans to be brought to the roadblock to talk with representatives of the *campesinos*. He responded casually that it might be a good idea. But it never happened. The North Americans returned to the States without ever having been informed about the demonstrators' pilgrimage. In contrast, the director of a transnational NGO that focuses on U.S. policy toward Nicaragua said to me, "We work on whatever the popular social movements want us to work on. If it's not on their agenda, then it's not on ours either." Most NGOs fall on a continuum between these two examples. Many NGOs take their volunteers to hear speakers from social movements, but they do not necessarily actively cooperate with the work of these movements.

Intercultural Interpersonal Contact

For solidarity to take hold one needs to understand the life struggles of those with whom one is to be in solidarity. Or as Paulo Freire puts it, "Solidarity requires that one enter into the situation of those with whom one is solidary; it is a radical posture" (2002[1970], 49). It is possible for North Americans to volunteer with a faith-based NGO in Nicaragua for two weeks and never meet a Nicaraguan who is not a paid staff member of that organization. It is possible to depart without ever having had a conversation with a program participant, much less a random member of the community. NGOs that do not initiate *convivencias,* or accompaniment experiences, for their short-term volunteers significantly reduce the chances that these people will enter into a solidary relationship with Nicaraguans. A common form of pseudosolidarity is promoted when the NGO equates the visitor's support for the NGO itself as solidary with the Nicaraguan popular classes. While there ought to be a relationship between the mission and practice of the NGO and marginalized populations in its service area, it is not a direct relationship, and the NGO has not been elected to represent them. Relationships with a transnational NGO staff cannot substitute for relationships with persons of marginalized communities.

Social Analysis

NGOs that are serious about fostering solidarity between North Americans and Nicaraguans must become involved in the conscientization of the North Americans. Most North Americans who come to Nicaragua are surprised to learn of 150 years of domination by the U.S., including half a dozen invasions by U.S. armed forces. They have no idea what is at stake for the peasants as a result of CAFTA or the Plan Puebla Panama. They have no inkling of the degree of involvement the U.S. ambassador has in the internal politics of the sovereign nation of Nicaragua. For instance, when I informed my students from Florida that their own governor had purchased full-page advertisements in one of the largest newspapers in Nicaragua recommending that Nicaraguans vote for the candidate he endorsed and against the candidate of the FSLN, they were indignant.

Some NGOs have one session of sociopolitical orientation for their visitors; others have a series of sessions; but by far the most effective method of social analysis is when all of the NGO staff constantly stress the causes and consequences of the poverty that is assaulting their visitors' senses at every turn. Most North American visitors do not yet understand the relationship between the poverty they see in front of them and the prosperity they experience daily at home. It is a waste of everyone's resources not to help volunteers make those connections. Otherwise the suffering they witness, as well as the Nicaraguan people's valiant will to survive, does not hit home. Poverty becomes objectified rather than subjectively (if vicariously) experienced. When volunteers return to the States and they sum up the significance of their trip with the statement, "It made me so thankful for what I have as an American," a great opportunity has been lost.

Long-Term Mutual Involvement

NGOs that seek to foster solidarity can more effectively do so when they provide the opportunity for volunteers to return, to deepen their involvement through longer and more challenging cross-cultural experiences. About 40 percent of first-time visitors return again. Some return annually; a few, multiple times in the same year. Some NGOs offer three-, six-, or twelve-month placements for trip graduates who have shown a high degree of cultural competency and personal maturity. One potential improvement of solidarity formation programming that has not been tried is setting up a graduated curriculum. NGOs do not have distinct first-, second-, and third-time itineraries, so returning volunteers have basically the same experiences multiple times. Since NGOs rely on veteran volunteers to act as culture brokers and group leaders for their first-time peers, total segregation according to experience is probably not advisable, but a graduated curriculum could accelerate acculturation of volunteers and deepen levels of solidarity.

Volunteer Activism Opportunities

Volunteers need to understand from early on that the amount of good they can do for Nicaraguans in Nicaragua pales by comparison to what they might accomplish by education, publicity, and policy work once they return to the U.S. In ecclesial parlance, the reverse mission is more important than the mission. As one NGO director says to each of his visiting group members, "If you go back to the States and don't share about what you've learned here about material and political inequality, then you have cheated the Nicaraguans who have shared their lives with you this week." Some faith-based NGOs, such as Witness for Peace, have participants sign covenants at the end of their trip, which state in some detail what they are planning to do on their return. One of the difficulties is that small NGOs do not have adequate staff in the States to organize networks of returned volunteers; hence, follow-up efforts are rare, though this may vary greatly depending on the history of organizing within the sending institution. Usually when a former volunteer is contacted, it is to ask them to recruit voluntourists for next year's trip. The rapid expansion in numbers of voluntourists indicates there is no shortage of potential visitors. Perhaps faith-based NGOs would do well to concentrate more on how to deepen the solidarity experience for their many graduates in ways that will affect vocational choices and political policy in the U.S. The quality of progressive experiences of solidarity travelers seems as important in the struggle for social justice as does signing up more people for an initial experience.

Conclusion

Thousands of U.S. citizens go to Nicaragua each year with faith-based NGOs, seeking adventure and altruistic outlets for their goodwill. Many can potentially live in life-long solidarity with the people of Nicaragua and other two-thirds world peoples. They will joyfully make the many sacrifices necessary to do so, if the NGOs develop a habitus of solidarity with the Nicaraguans of the popular classes, which can be communicated readily to their short-term volunteers. Effective organizational strategies for fostering solidarity include specific practices like carefully articulating a well-thought-out "alternative-to-development" model, one which advocates the interests of marginalized segments of the population, making a preferential option for the poor. Another NGO strategy is to ensure that its staff has bicultural competency and can introduce voluntourists to Nicaraguan culture effectively.

NGOs must decide their standpoint in relation to the various popular social movements. These movements can instruct solidarity travelers about what issues matter to the Nicaraguans they represent. Faith-based NGOs would do well to structure opportunities for their short-term volunteers to get to know Nicaraguans face-to-face, offering home stays and other forms of *convivencia* that allow for interpersonal bonding. Yet friendship is only one dimension of solidarity: social analysis skills are essential for being able to discern how we are all interrelated. Tools are necessary to see the structural connections between poverty and wealth at micro-, meso-, and macrolevels of analysis.

Finally, NGOs that want to take solidarity to the next level must offer graduated experiences in Nicaragua and activist networks for returning volunteers. NGOs have a mission, and to the extent that they seek to foster cross-cultural solidarity, face-to-face interactions, connections to popular social movements, and social analysis skills are some of the specific practices that will enable them to fulfill it.

As Anna Tsing observes:

> Emergent cultural forms are persistent but unpredictable effects of global encounters across difference. . . . Interactions I call "friction," awkward, unequal, unstable, and creative qualities of interconnection across difference . . . remind us that heterogeneous and unequal encounters can lead to new arrangements of culture and power. . . . The effects of encounters across difference can be compromising or empowering (2005,5).

The phenomenon of NGO-mediated voluntourism is a transnational social movement that can "lead to new arrangements of culture and power." Whether these new arrangements will yield mutual empowering solidarity will depend on the specific character of those human relationships across difference.

Notes

1. My research was supported by grants from the Interamerican Foundation, the Center for Latin American Studies at the University of Florida, and the Fulbright-Hays Foundation, for all of which I am appreciative.

2. By solidarity formation I mean the process of fostering the interpersonal capacity for cross-cultural relationships of a solidary nature, in this case between North Americans and Nicaraguans.

3. Limitations of space and the nature of this essay compel me to offer my findings rather than methodology and description of field data, which can be accessed in my dissertation at www.ufl.edu.

4. Among the NGOs I studied, in addition to the brigades to various countries in Central America, they sponsored trips to South America, Africa, South Asia, Central Asia, South East Asia, Oceania, the Philippines, and Eastern Europe.

5. This is true whether their objective is to work toward a more equitable global political economy or to maintain the status quo.

6. Social analysis was the second of the three aspects of the Catholic Action process (observe, judge, act) of the 1950s Spanish movement referred to by Occhipinti in this volume.

7. Perhaps it would be more accurate to use Smith and Sosin's (2001) term "faith-related" rather than faith-based since many of the NGOs do not have formal ties to religious organizations. (See Peters in this volume for a discussion). But for purposes of simplicity, I will use "faith-based" here in a very generic sense.

8. One of the most important of these was, and still is, CEPAD (Consejo de Iglesias Evangélicas Pro-Alianza Denominacional), the Council of Protestant Churches of Nicaragua, which represents eighty different church entities (Christian Protestant) throughout the country.

9. Padre Miguel D'Escoto Brockmann served as Foreign Minister, Fernando Cardenal as Minister of Education, and Ernesto Cardenal as Minister of Culture.

10. Nepstad (1996) identifies five key factors leading to religious revolutionary action in Nicaragua and El Salvador: (1) peasants converted key clergy and religious to their cause, (2) the egalitarian structure of the popular church and the conversion of a cohort of clergy and religious, (3) a shortage of clergy in the church which led to the development of training programs for laity, (4) structures of ritual and institutional support such as the *Missa Campesina*, lay training institutes, written materials, and the declarations of Vatican II and Medellin, (5) the presence of established resistance movements, the Frente Sandinista de Liberación Nacional (FSLN) and the Frente Farabundo Marti de Liberación Nacional (FMLN).

11. The organization that served as the coordinator of hundreds of voluntourism brigades (although they themselves downplayed the volunteering aspect of the experience in favor of the fact-finding and accompaniment aspects) was Witness for Peace.

12. This was assisted by illegal covert sales of weapons and drugs by U.S. government employees in defiance of a congressional ban, the discovery of which became known as Contragate.

13. This is a policy actively endorsed by the multilateral lending agencies.

14. See Hefferan in this volume for a classic case of misrecognition on the part of those who would "help."

15. For a detailed analysis of the subjective and structural dimensions of solidarity, as well as the process of solidarity formation within the subjectivity of the voluntourist, see Fogarty (2005).

16. America, April 21, 1984 cited in McGinnis (1985).

17. Coffee lost over 50 percent of its wholesale value practically overnight as a result of the first harvest from Vietnam, which had been extensively planted in coffee with World Bank financing some six years prior. Vietnam went from a non-coffee-producing state to one of the top world producers in one year. Meanwhile, children died of hunger throughout Central America as a result while global coffee retailers reaped record profits.

Works Cited

Boff, Leonardo. 2002. Reflections about the North from the South: Volunteering for solidarity implies both interchange and a common future ideal. *Alternativas* 9(22/23):177-84.

Bourdieu, Pierre. 1977. *Outline of a theory of practice.* Cambridge: Cambridge University Press.

Briones, William. 2004. Preocupación por "industria de ONGs." *El Nuevo Diario* (Managua), February 10.

CAPRI, Centro de Apoyo a Programas y Proyectos. 1996. Directorio ONG de Nicaragua 1996-1998. Managua: CAPRI.

Cardenal, Ernesto. 1997. *El evangelio in Solentiname.* Salamanca: Ediciones Sigueme.

Crabtree, Robbin D. 1998. Mutual empowerment in cross-cultural participatory development and service learning: Lessons in communication and social justice from projects in El Salvador and Nicaragua. *Journal of Applied Communication Research* 26(2):182-209.

Fairclough. Norman. 1995. *Critical discourse analysis: The critical study of language.* London: Longman.

Fogarty, Timothy. 2002. Effects of short-term work-camp delegations as strategies of solidarity travel to rural Nicaragua. Unpublished report. Gainesville: University of Florida.

———. 2005. From volunteer vacationing to solidarity travel in Nicaragua: An NGO mediated rural development strategy. Ph.D. diss., University of Florida.

Freire, Paulo. 2002[1970]. *Pedagogy of the oppressed.* Trans. M. B. Ramos. New York: Continuum Publishing.

Gould, Jeffrey L. 1998. *To die in this way: Nicaraguan Indians and the myth of* mestizaje *1880-1965.* Durham, NC: Duke University Press.

Hale, Charles R. 1996. *Mestizaje,* hybridity, and the cultural politics of difference in postrevolutionary Central America. *Journal of Latin American Anthropology* 2(1):34-61.

Hanvey, Robert G. 1982. *An attainable global perspective.* New York: Global Perspectives in Education.

Jeffrey, Paul. 2001. Short term mission trips. *Christian Century* 118(34):5-7.

Jonakin, Jon. 1996. The impact of structural adjustment and property rights conflicts on Nicaraguan agrarian reform beneficiaries. *World Development* 24(7):1179-91.

John Paul II. 1987. *Sollicitudo rei socialis.* Rome: The Vatican.

Kim, Y. Y. 1988. *Communication and cross-cultural adaptation.* Philadelphia: Multilingual Matters.

Lancaster, Roger. 1988. *Thanks to God and the revolution: Popular religion and class consciousness in the new Nicaragua.* New York: Columbia University Press.

Mauss, Marcel. 1996[1924]. Excerpts from *The gift.* In *Anthropological theory: An introductory history,* ed. R. J. McGee and R. L. Warms, 103-115. Mountain View, CA: Mayfield.

McGinnis, James. 1985. *Solidarity with the people of Nicaragua.* Maryknoll, NY: Orbis Books.

Myers-Lipton, S. J. 1998. Effects of a comprehensive service-learning program on college students' civic responsibility. *Teaching Sociology* 26(4):243-58.

Nash, June. 1979. *We eat the mines and the mines eat us: Dependency and exploitation in Bolivian tin mines.* New York: Columbia University Press.

Nepstad, Sharon Erickson. 1996. Popular religion, protest and revolt: The emergence of political insurgency in the Nicaraguan and Salvadoran churches of the 1960s-80s. In *Disruptive religions: The force of faith in social movement activism*, ed. Christian S. Smith, 105-124. London: Routledge.

Núñez Soto, Orlando. 1999. NGOs, 20 years after: Assistance or resistance to neoliberalism. *El Nueva Diario* (Managua), July 22

———. 2003. *La otra estrategia.* Managua: CIPRES (Centro para la Promoción, la Investigación y el Desarrollo Rural y Social).

O'Neill, Sally. 2004. The ever-changing face of non-governmental cooperation. *Envío* 23(276):39-47.

Quijano, Anibal. 2000. Coloniality of power, Eurocentrism, and Latin America. *Nepantla: Voices from the South* 1(3):533.

Randall, Margaret. 1983. *Christians in the Nicaraguan revolution.* Trans. Mariana Valverde. Vancouver: New Star Books.

Robinson, William I. 1998. (Mal)development in Central America: Globalization and social change. *Development and Change* 29:467-97.

Sklair, Leslie. 2002. The transnational capitalist class and global politics: Deconstructing the corporate-state connection. *International Political Science Review* 23(2):159-74.

Salazar, Noel B. 2004. Development tourists vs. development tourism: A case study. In *Tourist behavior: A psychological perspective*, ed. A. Raj, 85-107. New Delhi: Kanishka Publishers.

Smith, Steven R., and Michael R. Sosin. 2001. The varieties of faith-related agencies. *Public Administration Review* 61(6):651-70.

Téllez, Dora María. 1999. *Muera la gobierna! Colonización en Matagalpa y Jinotega (1820-1890).* Managua: Universidad de las Regiones Autónomas de la Costa Caribe Nicaragüense (URACCAN).

Tsing, Anna Lowenhaupt. 2005. *Friction: An ethnography of global connections.* Princeton, NJ: Princeton University Press.

Chapter 6
Beyond Development and "Projects":
The Globalization of Solidarity
Julie Adkins

Prologue

It began simply enough, as the outgrowth of one woman's curiosity and commitment. Susan, a nurse anesthetist and a deacon in her local Presbyterian church,[1] let herself be talked into making a "medical mission trip" to Guatemala with a team of doctors, nurses, and other medical personnel under the auspices of HELPS International, a U.S.-based, Christian nonprofit organization. Focusing its attention exclusively in Guatemala (until November of 2007, when it expanded into Mexico), this faith-based NGO organizes and provides not only medical care in remote regions of the country, but also education for grades K-6, community development, improved cooking technology, agricultural assistance, safe drinking water, microcredit, and marketing for Guatemalan products from coffee to crafts (see http://www.helpsintl.org/). For several years, Susan has returned to the highlands of Guatemala with HELPS International once or twice a year, and has also persuaded the doctor with whom she works in the U.S. to join the team and perform cataract surgeries.

Three years into her activities with this nondenominational Christian group, Susan became curious about "what the Presbyterians in Guatemala are doing." She pursued contacts in both the U.S. and Guatemala, and, two years later, not only brought four additional members of her church on the medical mission trip, but also persuaded them to spend their "R & R" time afterwards meeting U.S. Presbyterian mission coworkers, becoming acquainted with leaders of the Iglesia Evangélica Nacional Presbiteriana de Guatemala (IENPG), and touring churches in one region of the country.

Susan returned home, filled with enthusiasm, and reported to her pastor all that she had learned. He in turn encouraged her to become involved at the next higher level above the congregation, the East Dallas (Texas) regional cluster of Presbyterian churches of which they are a part.[2] "[He] asked me if I would serve on the mission committee . . . and when I got there I found out I *was* the mission committee!" (Interview, October 7, 2004). Thus, when the cluster determined that it wanted to plan and carry out a mission trip, Susan was well positioned to suggest Guatemala based on the contacts she had already made.

Presbyterians in Guatemala

The latter part of the twentieth century saw a dramatic increase in the number of Protestants/Evangelicals[3] in Guatemala, particularly in the aftermath of the 1976 earthquake which devastated great portions of the country. The Protestant presence had its beginnings, however, almost a century earlier. In the early 1880s, Liberal Guatemalan President Justo Rufino Barrios let it be known that he was open to receiving Protestant missionaries into Guatemala.[4] Barrios met with the Presbyterian Board of Foreign Missions in 1882 while on a trip to New York, and as a consequence of that meeting invited the Presbyterian Church in the United States of America to send missionaries. His motives appear to have been far more political than religious in nature. As part of the Liberals' program to "modernize" Guatemala, they were determined to challenge the long-held power of the Catholic Church. At one level, this was nothing more than political revenge: the Church had consistently supported the Conservative agenda and the Guatemalan "aristocracy" over against Liberal notions of broadening access to power. Some of this spirit of vengeance could be seen in the confiscation of Church lands for other uses. All considerations of retribution aside, however, Liberals were convinced that the Church was contributing to Guatemala's "backwardness" by encouraging a fatalistic, otherworld-centered worldview among its adherents. Consequently, one of the first tasks which Barrios set for the Presbyterian missionaries was the founding of schools, so that they might provide an alternative to the Catholic Church's existing monopoly on education. The Liberals' mixed motives became clear when Barrios and his Cabinet ministers elected to send their sons to the Presbyterians' school but did not themselves choose to participate in the congregation that missionary John Clark Hill was attempting to form.

American Presbyterians of the time shared the Liberal Guatemalan belief that economic development/modernization was a worthwhile goal, and believed that they had the resources to contribute to such a project. However, they also shared the Liberals' ethnocentrism in assuming that assimilation of the indigenous population was the only way in which modernization could move forward. To this end, the early missionaries taught only English in their schools and carried out their evangelistic work only in Spanish. A few learned indigenous languages, but they were not permitted to found indigenous-language congregations. U. S. missionaries in Guatemala after Hill argued this point with their superiors at the Board of Foreign Missions, but to no avail. The policy did not change until 1922 (Koll 2003).

In addition to schools, the Presbyterians—the only nonfundamentalist Protestant group active in Guatemala at the time—founded a number of other secular institutions. A hospital in Guatemala City became the nation's first modern medical facility, and soon there were permanent medical clinics scattered throughout the highlands. Presbyterians also operated two printing presses, from which they published journals, books both religious and secular, and a variety of smaller projects such as tracts (Garrard-Burnett 1998, 33).

For the first sixty-plus years of Presbyterian presence in Guatemala, the North Americans remained firmly in charge of operations. There were no Guatemalans in positions of leadership, and funds were controlled entirely by missionaries and the Presbyterian Church, USA Board of Foreign Missions. Only in 1923 and 1929 were the first two Guatemalan presbyteries (regional governing bodies) organized; it was in 1925 that the first non-missionary pastor was ordained. This paternalistic model of oversight remained in place until after the Second World War (Koll 2003).

During Guatemala's "revolutionary years," American and Guatemalan Presbyterians largely supported the reforms instituted by democratically elected presidents Juan José Arévalo (1945-1950) and Jacobo Arbenz (1950-1954). Arévalo, in particular, welcomed the support of Protestant missionaries in his efforts to strengthen labor unions, promote social justice, and uplift the poor through education. Arbenz—though himself baptized by a Presbyterian missionary—was far more suspicious of the churches' motives; the churches, in turn, often reacted against what they perceived as Arbenz's too-cozy embrace of Communist principles, particularly his suspicions about private property (Garrard-Burnett 1998). Sermons were preached, and pronouncements sent from the Board of Foreign Missions, that argued both for and against some of Arbenz's more radical policy proposals.

Garrard-Burnett (1998) notes that the Presbyterians were the only Protestant denomination that was consistently supportive of popular movements during the time of Guatemala's civil unrest (referred to as a civil war or as guerrilla uprisings, depending on one's social and political location) in the 1980s and 1990s. She attributes this in part to the presence of numerous indigenous congregations and presbyteries in the IENPG and in part to theological understandings about the need for justice in the present world and not just the world to come, similar to the beliefs of Catholic liberation theology. Koll, however, argues that the IENPG was divided during this period in much the same manner as the society as a whole: Mayan presbyteries were largely supportive of the popular movements and advocated for human rights—indeed, at least one Mayan Presbyterian pastor was assassinated during this period—but the denomination as a whole remained largely silent (personal communication, March 22, 2008).

The Presbyterian presence is small, however—in Guatemala as in the U.S.—and its influence is not broadly felt. Many scholars of religion in Guatemala give the IENPG little to no mention, even in book-length treatments of Protestantism (see, for example, Sherman 1997 and Gooren 1999).

Development and Neoliberalism in
U.S. Presbyterian Discourse and Action

Since the coming of "independence" for the Presbyterian Church in Guatemala
and other nations with a similar missionary history, Presbyterians and other denominations in the U.S. have come to recognize that their missionary presence,
despite the benefits it provided in many instances, had certain unintended consequences. A study paper adopted by the Presbyterian General Assembly in 1969
noted that institutions founded by missionaries had often inappropriately imposed middle-class U.S. norms, and had inadvertently served the privileged at
the expense of the poor. In consequence, the church had at times contributed to
social injustice rather than confronting it, and had helped certain sectors of the
population to "develop" at the expense of others. As Presbyterians in the U.S.
helped birth the IENPG (and new national Presbyterian churches in other countries as well), they began to revisit not only their models of missionary activity
and behavior, but also the cultural assumptions that had led them to impose their
ideas about "development" on other peoples in other places (Koll 2003).

At the same time, the denomination's long-term commitment to social justice made U.S. Presbyterians reluctant to abandon the idea of development altogether. A 1996 policy statement suggested that development must be reframed
in ways that are both just and sustainable:

> The term "human development" highlights the claim that the goals of development
> ought to be focused on advancing human well-being. It is more—much more—than
> economic growth. In its economic dimension, it is best described as just and sustain-
> able sufficiency for all. "Justice" is required in order to ensure fair treatment for
> nonhuman as well as human life. "Sustainability" implies living within the carrying
> capacities of the planet. And just and sustainable human development suggests a just
> distribution of well-being between present and future generations by following poli-
> cies that ensure the ecological conditions necessary for thriving in both the present
> and the future (Advisory Committee on Social Witness Policy [henceforward
> ACSWP] 1996, 12).

Thus, the Presbyterian Church (USA) echoes in many ways anthropologists' insistence on "putting people first" (Cernea 1985). In connection with
such internal policy statements, the Presbyterian Church has also passed resolu-
tions calling upon the World Bank and International Monetary Fund to replace
"structural adjustment" with policies and programs that meet the needs of the
poor, to cancel and/or substantially reduce multilateral debt, and to restructure
themselves in order to provide greater accountability and transparency (ACSWP
1996, 131).

In a more recent statement, the Presbyterian Church (USA) has also made
clear its rejection of the ideology of neoliberalism and its consequences:

Neoliberalism . . . seeks to make the whole world an integrated mechanism of production and consumption where the self-interest of economic actors is granted free rein in the assumption that competition will make everything work out well in the end. The real intention is to make a world freely accessible to those who already have the most power—a handful of countries, a few hundred thousand wealthy individuals, and the few hundred large corporations and financial institutions they control. The result of more than a quarter century of neoliberalism has been to increase the economic disparity between rich and poor within countries and between them. The poorest are simply being left behind at an increasing rate (ACSWP 2006, 48).

As is often the case with multilevel institutions, it is unclear whether policies and pronouncements that issue from the highest levels within the Church are influential at the grassroots. Nevertheless, the interest and commitment demonstrated by Susan and her friends from church suggest that there are many American Presbyterians with an active interest not only in learning about other parts of the world, but also in exploring ways that their lives can and should intersect with sisters and brothers far away. As with Susan, the original impulse is often altruistic: to go somewhere and "do good" in the lives of people known to be suffering and lacking in material wealth. For some, the altruistic impulse is as far as it goes. But for others, those first contacts lead in directions that are far more interesting . . . and, ultimately, more demanding.

Mediating the Relationship: PRESGOV

As Tim Fogarty has noted (2005 and this volume), the rapid increase in volunteer tourism in recent years has created a demand for organizations that have the capacity to mediate relationships between first-world "guests" and their two-thirds-world "hosts." These organizations are most often responsible for making logistical arrangements for the travelers—accommodations, vehicles and drivers, competent translation, handling money, a schedule of activities—and for ensuring their safety. Generally, at least one person from the mediating organization will travel with the guest group for the entire duration of their journey. In addition, they bear the (sometimes self-imposed) responsibility for quickly educating newly arrived guests into the host country and culture. This process often begins even before the commencement of the trip, with guidelines provided to travelers about what kind of clothing to pack in terms of both the weather and the host culture's view of appropriate dress, reminders to bring and to use hand sanitizer, instructions about necessary travel documents and fees, etc. Mediating organizations normally also provide a "crash course" for participants on the history of the host country, the current political and economic situation, relationships with the U.S. and the rest of the world, and nearly anything else that seems important in terms of framing the visitors' relationship with the people they are preparing to meet. These briefing sessions may be part of a group's scheduled activities, or they may occur informally as a way of passing time on long drives in-country . . . or both.

For Presbyterians in Guatemala and the U.S., that mediating organization is called PRESGOV; i.e., Presbyterian *Grupos, Obreros, y Voluntarios* (groups, workers, and volunteers). PRESGOV is a hybrid agency: it is part of the structure of, and accountable to, the IENPG, but it has historically been staffed by U.S. Presbyterian missionaries. These range from Young Adult Volunteers (YAVs)—recent college graduates who volunteer a year of their time at a variety of projects directed by the IENPG—to career missionaries whose terms of service may be anywhere from a few years to a lifetime. The purpose of creating PRESGOV, at least in part, was to give the Guatemalan Presbyterian Church a measure of authority over North Americans working in-country. And one of the tasks at which PRESGOV spends a significant portion of its time is "help[ing] organize and support PC(USA) study and work group trips to Guatemala" (Van Marter 2007). In addition, where there are longer-term relationships such as the one described here, PRESGOV remains involved between visits on an as-needed basis for tasks such as the negotiation of expectations between partners and offering suggestions on how to strengthen the relationship.

Evolution and Development of the Covenant Partnership

It was on the basis of recommendations from PRESGOV—recommendations based primarily on their experience with widespread corruption and financial shenanigans in a majority of presbyteries of the IENPG—that Susan and the cluster narrowed their choices for a partner to two. The first cluster trip to Guatemala, then, took place primarily for the purpose of visiting those two regions of the country and meeting representatives from each of the presbyteries. PRESGOV arranged travel and introductions, and brokered the discussions in each location. On the basis of the interactions that took place during this trip, the cluster chose to cast its lot with the Presbiterio del Norte, made up of sixteen churches in the easternmost region of Guatemala.[5]

As it has taken shape in the past seven to eight years, the relationship between the East Dallas Cluster and the Presbiterio del Norte bears a great deal of resemblance to the "twinning" relationships described by Tara Hefferan (2007 and this volume), but on a slightly larger scale. A partnership has been created, with the assistance and mediation of PRESGOV, between a cluster of nine churches in the U.S. and a presbytery of sixteen churches in eastern Guatemala. This "inequality" at the structural level at first caused great consternation in various parts of the Presbyterian Church (USA).[6] The East Dallas group was told that under no circumstances would they be permitted to create a partnership between two unlike structures; that is, a congregation could partner with another congregation, or a presbytery could partner with a presbytery; but a "cluster" representing only part of a presbytery could not partner with an entire presbytery. Susan and her group pointed out that the inequality would be far greater if they asked the small Guatemalan presbytery to be a partner with the huge (~180 churches) presbytery in the Dallas area. Nevertheless, ecclesiastical bureaucrats were firm: the two groups could not be "unequally yoked" in an officially recognized partnership. The impasse was not broken until one of the U.S. pastors realized that the issue could be solved with semantic creativity. Once the cluster and the Guatemalans agreed that they would embark upon a "covenant of friendship" rather than a "partnership," previous objections vanished. Ironically, higher-ups in the national office of the PC(USA) now cite this particular cluster-to-presbytery relationship as being one of the most successful in existence denomination-wide, and lift it up as an example for others to emulate.

The cluster's first "mission trip" to Guatemala took the form of a work project in which they spent the better part of a week building a house for an impoverished member of one of the partnering congregations. Subsequent trips over several years involved some kind of work at one of the presbytery's churches: putting on a new roof, painting the inside and outside of the building, and the like. These proved to be less satisfying than both sides had hoped, however. Many of the Guatemalan men were not able to take time off from their usual jobs to volunteer their time on a weekday to labor alongside their visitors. And the gendered division of labor meant that the Guatemalan women were committed to spending their time in the kitchen, preparing meals for those who were working. Thus, there was very little interaction between hosts and guests. Since the building of relationships was one of the stated goals on both sides, clearly, something was going to have to change.

Recognizing that a weekday presence meant the opportunity to interact in more depth with women and children, the Guatemalans asked whether the cluster would consider putting together a vacation Bible school for children rather than doing a "work" project. This, along with craft activities and a women's Bible study, formed the activities for the first week-long trip that I made with the group in 2005. In addition, since one of the "regulars" from the Dallas group is a certified Christian educator, she has been asked on several occasions to provide Saturday teacher-training workshops.

The most recent development in the evolution of these week-long trips is that they have begun to include recreational adventures in which the *norteamericanos* and the Guatemalans participate together. Recent years have seen the groups climbing Mayan ruins at Quirigua and Iximche, and exploring a Spanish fort left from the colonial era. Cluster visitors found these activities disconcerting at first, as though they were not making the best investment of their time being "useful" while in-country. PRESGOV has helped the group to understand how important it is for the Guatemalans, first, to have the opportunity to do something for their guests; and second, to take time for recreation themselves. "Their lives are hard," wrote one former PRESGOV staffer in a 2006 e-mail, "with no relief from the pressure to produce the next meal and to cover the next medical expense, or to provide education for their children."

In addition to the "work" trips, study trips have also taken place on several occasions, once in the U.S. and at least twice in Guatemala. Guatemalan and U.S. church leaders travel together to a retreat setting and meet as equals, as they are led in study and reflection. The most recent study-retreats have considered the topic of Mayan spirituality, inviting both groups to learn from a tradition they have in the past scorned and rejected. Given the quasi-fundamentalist history of the Presbyterian church in Guatemala, it is astonishing that such encounters are happening.

Beyond the once- or twice-yearly trips, however, the Dallas cluster group has wanted to share of its resources in more significant and long-term ways. Guided again by PRESGOV, they initiated conversations with the leadership team of the Presbiterio del Norte about ongoing needs that these church leaders perceived in their communities and churches. What new projects would they undertake, what old projects might they do differently, if they had funding available? Over a period of several years, two projects have arisen out of these discussions. The first was suggested by the leadership team itself: The presbytery has many small churches and cannot afford to send pastors to all of them.[7] Would the cluster consider helping with half the cost to provide a pastor for one small congregation if the presbytery could come up with the rest of the money? The dollar amount for such a salary was remarkably small by U.S. standards, and the cluster readily agreed to this proposal. It proved difficult to implement, however, due in large part to the educational requirements for Presbyterian clergy.[8] After a couple of years with no viable candidates for the funds, both sides agreed that the money could instead be used to support an *obrero*, a lay pastor, to serve one or more of the small congregations.

The second project—a nutrition project aimed at children communitywide—drew special enthusiasm from members of the Texas cluster for two reasons. In the first place, it focused not only on the needs of the Presbyterian churches but also of the communities in which they are situated. Secondly, though, cluster members were thrilled because this project was the brainchild of the *women* of the Presbiterio, who persuaded the leadership team that it was worthy to present for the cluster's consideration.[9] Funded at the same level as the pastor-support project, this small-scale effort focuses on one community at a time, for a period of approximately six months at a time. Children in the program come to the church two days a week for a morning's activities which include a nutritious breakfast and lunch. Parent education about nutrition is part of the program, as is the provision of vitamins and antiparasitic medicines to participating families. The nurse who oversees the project—a member of one of the Presbyterian churches—weighs and measures each child at entry into the program, and again at the halfway point. Those who have reached the desired weight for their age are "graduated" from the program in order to make room for other community children in need. Those who are still underweight remain for the rest of the program's duration in the community. Thus far, the nutrition program has rotated to four different communities within the presbytery; in fact, it is a matter of no small competition among the clergy leaders as to whose small town will be the next to benefit.[10]

Promise and Problems of a "Solidarity" Model

What Seems to Be Working Well

The persons I interviewed as I began this study were self-selected—that is, not everyone chose to respond to an e-mail request for interviews that was sent to all prior trip participants. Thus, they may not be entirely representative of all those who have visited Guatemala with the cluster over the years; and they certainly cannot be taken as representing the opinion of every church member in the cluster. Nevertheless, I was struck by interviewees' unanimous emphasis that the most important piece of the work they do in Guatemala is the building of relationships. This remained true despite my very specific queries about the particular work projects they had undertaken in different years. Interviewees responded to the question willingly enough, but consistently steered me back to their primary concern with knowing people and learning about their lives. Experienced participants, in particular, note that "work projects" have great potential for causing more problems than they might solve. Construction and repair projects performed by volunteers may take the opportunity for paying jobs away from Guatemalans who need them. Completing a project in one community may lead to jealousy on the part of neighboring communities. If the point of a work project is to have North Americans and Guatemalans build friendship by working alongside one another, then the Guatemalan partners have to take valuable time away from their own paid work in order to volunteer with their guests.

I heard this emphasis as well in the debriefing time at the end of each of the two trips I have made with the group. Regardless of what participants thought about the meaning and purpose of the trip when they first signed up, they talk most about the new friends they have made. Only later does the group refer back to the roof they nailed on, or the Vacation Bible School they led, or the supplies they distributed. Jane,[11] a participant who has made the trip multiple times, summarized her experience by saying, "It's all about couches!" (Interview, October 19, 2004). That is, participants sit alongside their hosts; they share meals together; they spend time talking about their lives . . . even across the barriers of language. And there is sadness that, due to both financial limitations and immigration fears, very few of their Guatemalan friends will ever be able to visit the U.S. and sit on *their* couches.

The downside to this emphasis on relationship and solidarity, however, is that there are some members in the Dallas churches who have stated clearly that they are not interested in making a "mission trip" that doesn't involve them in tangible, physical labor. Long-term participants note the need to include some kind of work component in the annual trips so that those who feel that they must *do* something can be included and gradually eased into the understanding that the work is less important than they had thought.

The level of trust between the groups has grown fairly high, suggesting a move toward greater solidarity. During the most recent visit in which I participated (July 2007), we discussed at length political matters such as the upcoming Guatemalan presidential election and U.S immigration policy, and sensitive historical issues such as U.S. intervention in Guatemalan politics and governance, and the lengthy Guatemalan civil war. We have also had interesting and sometimes humorous discussions on touchy (to us!) theological matters such as the baptism of infants and the role of women in church leadership. In the process, North Americans learn about Guatemala from its own citizens, and about North America from an outsider's point of view.

The U.S. group is fairly consistent about allowing the Guatemalans to set the agenda for their time together, although negotiation also takes place frequently. When money is given, it goes to those projects and needs that the Guatemalans have identified as their priorities, not to what their U.S. partners might believe is most important. The week-long trip schedule and itinerary are set by PRESGOV in consultation with the Guatemalan Presbyterians, and sometimes come as a surprise to the U.S. group when it arrives. Indeed, last summer's group learned only after arriving that we were scheduled to climb a volcano with our Guatemalan friends during the week, an adventure for which few of us had brought appropriate footwear!

Relationships do not cease when the *norteamericanos* return home at the end of their week's travel, but continue in a less intensive form through e-mail and other electronic forms of communication. In particular, the Presbiterio del Norte's executive committee sends occasional prayer requests for various congregations in need or pastors in ill health. Photographs are sent back and forth electronically as well. In addition, there are times when it is clear that the Guatemalans are offering care and concern to their friends in the U.S., not the reverse:

> *Con profundo pena, por los medios de comunicación, hemos seguido los aconteci-*
> *mientos sufridos por los habitantes de las áreas afectadas por el huracán Katrina.*
> *Expresamos nuestra solidaridad con el pueblo de los Estados Unidos, especialmente*
> *con la gente que está sufriendo en este momento . . .*
> With deep grief, we have followed through the media the sufferings of the inhabi-
> tants of those areas affected by Hurricane Katrina. We express our solidarity with
> the people of the United States, especially with the people who are suffering at this
> time . . . (E-mail message sent September 4, 2005)

A similar message was sent in the days after September 11, 2001. For North Americans who are accustomed to thinking of themselves as privileged and the rest of the world as places of suffering, these expressions of care from friends hundreds of miles distant were powerful expressions of unity and solidarity.

Finally, another encouraging piece of the puzzle is that some individuals on the U.S. side are making solidarity-inspired choices about how they will live their lives in their own setting. Susan, whose commitment and curiosity initiated this partnership, eventually quit one of her contract positions as nurse anesthetist for a prestigious plastic surgeon: "I decided I didn't have that value any longer. I couldn't just be working on something that was really just an ego thing, cosmetic surgery . . . So, after thirteen years of being with him, I quit." Jane, who envisions her friendships as being "about couches," described what happened when she and her husband Beavan retired and built their dream house. "You work thirty-five years, scratch all your money together, and build what you've been waiting all your life to build. And the first night in that house, I looked around our bedroom, and I said, Beavan, our bedroom is bigger than a house in Guatemala. And I have felt uncomfortable in that house, and I realize this house is too big, and so we're moving out." As of this writing, Jane is in Mississippi on a several-month assignment with the Presbyterian Church (USA), coordinating work teams that have come to help rebuild communities still suffering the aftermath of Hurricane Katrina.

Areas of (Possible) Concern

Presbyterians—particularly the clergy—are among the most highly educated persons in Guatemala. While this does not necessarily guarantee them well-paying jobs in the current economic climate, it does mean that most of the church leaders whom the Americans meet are solidly middle-class by Guatemalan standards. Yet even these appear relatively impoverished in comparison to their U.S. visitors . . . persons who can comfortably afford $1300-1500 to make an international journey of a week's duration. It can and should be questioned whether the resource-sharing and transfer of wealth that does occur between these American and Guatemalan churches is able to make any impact at all on the lives of Guatemala's most needy, or whether it is (ironically) helping to create an even greater divide between that country's have-nots and have-mores. (For a prescient discussion of similar concerns in Peru, see Michenfelder 1969.)

Not unrelated to the prior concern is that Guatemalan Presbyterians in this particular relationship are largely Ladino in ethnicity and outlook. There is a significant indigenous presence in the IENPG that is not reflected in the region of the Presbiterio del Norte. The majority of presbyteries within the IENPG, and the majority of its members, are indigenous, worshipping and conducting their ecclesiastical business in a variety of Mayan languages. But, according to reports from long-term group members and PRESGOV contacts, indigenous members are often treated like second-class citizens even within the churches. Ladinos preach; Mayans sweep the floors. Ladinos hold all significant leadership positions within the denomination, and are occasionally willing to maintain their position of privilege by playing different indigenous groups against each other (Koll, personal communication, March 22, 2008). At times, the Presbyterian Church (USA) has inadvertently exacerbated such divisions. By insisting that it will work only with the organized church (i.e., the denomination) and its leadership, the U.S. church has in effect sided with the Ladinos against indigenous groups seeking greater inclusion and justice.

No degree of solidarity or depth of friendship can erase the differences in wealth and power between the North American and the Guatemalan partners in this relationship. Money remains an awkward topic, although there has been some improvement over the years. Jane, who was cluster treasurer at the time, recalled an early disagreement that arose when the cluster discovered that the money sent to help support a pastor had not in fact been spent. "[T]o me, stewardship means getting Jesus's [sic] money out there to Jesus's people where Jesus wants the money. To [the] Guatemalans, on the other hand, stewardship means keeping Jesus's money safe in the bank where nobody else can hurt it" (Interview, October 19, 2004). As mentioned above, the Guatemalans had encountered difficulty in finding pastors willing or available to come to some of the smaller and more remote churches in their presbytery . . . and so, having not found an appropriate person, they had not spent the money. Both sides felt unappreciated: the North Americans because their gift was not being used, the Guatemalans because their management of it was being questioned. It has taken time for the groups to understand one another's desires and expectations. In this respect, the long-term nature and ongoing commitment of this relationship have been important in providing the space in which to negotiate conflicting understandings and misunderstandings. Even so, the subject remains awkward. It is often unclear, for example, when Guatemalan leaders describe for their visitors a new project they are hoping to begin, whether they are merely sharing their plans or are politely hinting that outside financial help will be needed. Certainly, some of this difficulty arises because of having to work through a translator for key points of the conversations, which highlights the difficulty also of creating lasting solidarity across the boundary of language difference. Were it not for the services provided by PRESGOV, this might well be insurmountable.

As these cross-boundary relationships develop and deepen over time, it becomes increasingly difficult to maintain other boundaries that the groups have covenanted to honor. One such is that the U.S. participants will not offer financial assistance—either as a group or as individuals—to *individual* persons within the Guatemalan presbytery or its churches. All such gifts are to be directed through the presbytery, to the agreed-upon projects. This has caused misunderstanding at times and heartache at others. Not a year passes that the group, as it travels and visits different congregations, does not receive an urgent request from someone soliciting help with medical bills for an ailing parent, or from an individual desperate to obtain a visa to work in the U.S. Shortly after the trip in July 2007, I personally received a frantic e-mail from one of the young women who has been connected with the group for most of its existence: she had just been laid off from her job, which was going to force her to drop out of college for financial reasons . . . and she happened to still have a tourist visa to come to the U.S. and wanted to know if she could come and live with me. There was (and is) no completely satisfactory answer to the dilemma created by such a situation. Solidarity with the group means denying the wishes of the individual in hurtful ways. Solidarity and friendship with the individual means contravening the commitments made in solidarity with the group.

For all its strengths, this is an incredibly small effort, influencing few people on either side. No more than five percent of the membership of the churches on the U.S. side has ever participated in traveling to Guatemala, though many more than this are aware of the partnership and its various aspects and help support it financially. Because it is so difficult for Guatemalans to travel to the U.S., there has been little opportunity for the nontravelers on the U.S. side to meet their covenant partners in person. To give some additional perspective: even if every Presbyterian in both countries were somehow able to become involved in partnering relationships such as the one described here, it would still involve only about 1 percent of the U.S. population and less than one-half of 1 percent of Guatemala's.

The deepening sense of solidarity which has arisen can and often does lead to feelings of frustration and impotence on the part of the North Americans: visiting friends and hearing their stories, we realize that the largest concerns impinging on their lives are issues over which we have no control, even from our position of relative privilege. It is noble to provide a nutrition program for undernourished children, to be sure, but cluster members have no sense that they have any power to change neoliberal trade policies that lead to family poverty and child hunger in the first place. It is worthwhile to purchase fair-trade coffee and handicrafts, but far more useful would be a complete rewrite of CAFTA and its broad "free" trade policies. It remains to be seen how, and whether, the U.S. Presbyterians in this relationship will find ways to demonstrate their solidarity beyond the choices they have made for their individual lives.

"Solidarity": An Alternative to "Development"?

The old proverb stating that "the road to hell is paved with good intentions" seems particularly appropriate for analyzing and evaluating the efforts of faith-based organizations. Those who enter into "development" activities from religious motives, even if their intentions are entirely noble, are still the products of their own culture and its assumptions about what a "good life" should look like. For American Christians in particular, the mere fact of living in the wealthiest nation in the world often leads to a sense of obligation to share. After all, they have heard countless sermons on the gospel of Matthew, chapter 25: "For I was hungry, and you gave me food; thirsty, and you gave me drink; I was a stranger, and you welcomed me; naked, and you clothed me; sick, and in prison, and you visited me . . . Inasmuch as you have done it to the least of these who are my brothers and sisters, you have done it to me." For persons and organizations operating from a faith stance, offering help and service to other human beings is not merely kind or reasonable, but carries meaning and consequences in another realm as well.

And yet, faith-based organizations are learning that they must ask the question *"Are* you hungry?" rather than assuming that a recipient is hungry. They must also ask "What do you like to eat?" and "Can this be grown here?" and, perhaps most important, "Why don't we share this meal together?" For the North American group described in this chapter, this insight might never have arisen without the mediating influence of PRESGOV. It is impossible to overstate the importance of such a cultural and religious broker in the creation of solidarity relationships across boundaries of wealth and language in particular.

For this group of travelers, and for American Presbyterians in general (insofar as official policy statements can reflect their position), solidarity seems not so much an alternative to development as it is a lens through which development must be viewed. They are not prepared to give up offering assistance from their position of relative privilege; however, they do seem prepared to give up control over much of the conversation. Without the establishment and nurture of ongoing relationships, the sending of money is just a salve to an uneasy conscience. But without a willingness to share one's resources generously, transnational friendships may become just one more luxury among many.

Notes

Many thanks to Karla Ann Koll for her helpful critique of an earlier draft of this chapter, to Robert V. Kemper for his thorough editorial assistance, and to Jane and "Susan" for their feedback and suggested revisions.

1. *Deacons* are elected and ordained lay leaders in the Presbyterian Church (USA), with their primary attention given to ministries of compassion both within the church and outside its membership. *Elders*, also elected and ordained, have the role of governing the church together with the clergy.

2. Officially, in the PC(USA) the next structural level above the congregation is the presbytery. "Clusters" are created in some areas where a presbytery is so large, geographically or numerically or both, that churches within a smaller region band together to pursue particular interests or projects that they cannot undertake alone. Grace Presbytery, to which Susan's church belongs, consists of approximately 180 congregations spread over fifty-three counties in northeast Texas; in contrast, the Presbiterio del Norte in Guatemala, with which the East Dallas cluster is partnered, includes only sixteen congregations. Clusters have no governing authority within the PC(USA), but have proven to be a useful mediating structure for many small to mid-sized congregations, especially in large presbyteries. The East Dallas cluster of Grace Presbytery is comprised of nine congregations in eastern Dallas County.

3. "Protestant" and "evangelical" are essentially synonymous in Guatemala, as in most of Latin America, and unlike in the U.S., where the former tends to refer to mainline Protestant denominations and the latter to more conservative groups. Protestants in Guatemala, even those in denominations that parallel the U.S. mainline, are generally far more conservative theologically, politically, and socially than their U.S. counterparts. Garrard-Burnett (1998) offers a thorough explanation of why this is so in the Guatemalan context.

4. I am particularly indebted to Karla Koll for her careful dissertation research on the history of Protestant missions in Central America (Koll 2003). Unless otherwise cited, her work is the source for the historical information in this section.

5. Guatemala's northeastern lowlands contain only a relatively small indigenous population. This is reflected in the membership of the Presbiterio del Norte, which is made up of mostly Ladino, Spanish-speaking congregations. As such, they represent a middle-class, privileged sector within both Guatemala and the IENPG.

6. This "unequal" partnership may well have raised concerns in the IENPG as well, since the agreement worked out between the two denominations (U.S. and Guatemalan) provided only for partnerships at the presbytery level. The U.S. cluster, however, was not apprised of such concerns, if indeed they did arise.

7. Unlike the model of church financing to which most North Americans are accustomed, in many presbyteries of the IENPG the pastors receive their salary not from the congregation that they serve, but from the presbytery.

8. Educational requirements for pastors in the Presbiterio del Norte are similar to those for U.S. Presbyterian pastors: a four-year university degree plus three years of seminary. This is not the case throughout the IENPG, however; in particular, the indigenous presbyteries tend to have much lower educational requirements.

9. Although official policy of the IENPG is that women may be ordained to the offices of pastor, elder, and deacon, this is quite rare so far. As of this writing, there is only one woman elder in the Presbiterio del Norte, and no female clergy. There *are* women in college and seminary, waiting for their opportunity. When I have made trips with the East Dallas cluster, one of my joys is watching the Guatemalan women's (and a few of the men's!) faces light up when I introduce myself as a Presbyterian pastor.

10. Unfortunately, there are no resources available for follow-up so that one might ascertain whether children in communities previously served have been able to maintain a higher standard of health, or whether they have returned to being underweight and undernourished once the program has moved on.

11. Jane agreed to the use of her real name in order that readers might be referred to her website and blog, in which she frequently (and with great insight) comments about her journeys in mission: www.JaneEls.com. She is in process of turning these reflections into a book.

Works Cited

Advisory Committee on Social Witness Policy (ACSWP), Presbyterian Church (USA).
　　1996. Hope for a global future: Toward just and sustainable human development.
　　Louisville, KY: Presbyterian Distribution Services.
　　———. 2006. Resolution on just globalization: Justice, ownership, and accountability.
　　Louisville, KY: Office of the General Assembly.
Cernea, Michael M., ed. 1985. *Putting people first: Sociological variables in rural devel-*
　　opment. New York: Published for the World Bank by Oxford University Press.
Fogarty, Timothy. 2005. From volunteer vacationing to solidarity travel in Nicaragua: An
　　NGO mediated rural development strategy. Ph.D. diss., University of Florida.
Garrard-Burnett, Virginia. 1998. *Protestantism in Guatemala: Living in the new Jerusa-*
　　lem. Austin: University of Texas Press.
Gooren, Henri. 1999. *Rich among the poor: Church, firm, and household among small-*
　　scale entrepreneurs in Guatemala City. Austin: University of Texas Press.
Hefferan, Tara. 2007. *Twinning faith and development: Catholic parish partnering in the*
　　U.S. and Haiti. Bloomfield, CT: Kumarian Press.
Koll, Karla Ann. 2003. Struggling for solidarity: Changing mission relationships between
　　the Presbyterian Church (USA) and Christian organizations in Central America dur-
　　ing the 1980s. Ph.D. diss., Princeton Theological Seminary.
Michenfelder, Joseph. 1969. *Gringo volunteers.* Maryknoll, NY: Maryknoll Publications.
Sherman, Amy K. 1997. *The soul of development: Biblical Christianity and economic*
　　transformation in Guatemala. New York and Oxford: Oxford University Press.
Van Marter, Jerry. 2007. Taking life on: PC(USA) missionary gave up comfortable pulpit
　　for mission service in Guatemala. http://www.pcusa.org/pcnews/2007/07657.htm.
　　(last accessed February 22, 2008).

Chapter 7
How Is Your Life Since Then?
Gender, Doctrine, and Development in Bolivia
Jill DeTemple, Erin Eidenshink, and Katrina Josephson

Scholars and practitioners have traditionally imagined development, in its basic form, as an effort to better the material circumstances of a population. Faith-based development, however, is equally, if not more, concerned with spiritual matters. When a Bolivian child is enrolled in Agape,[1] an international Protestant Christian development organization, for example, he or she is given a vividly colored "Life Finalization Plan" chart on which to keep track of fulfillment of yearly goals set by the organization. These goals include medical checkups, attendance at the organization's after-school programs, and finished homework. No chart is complete, however, without a sticker next to the box that marks a development indicator of special importance to Agape, the child's conversion to evangelical Christianity.[2] In Agape's development model, accepting Christ as a personal savior is a vital step toward good hygiene, academic progress and physical health. This chapter explores this interplay of material and social goals in Agape, and argues that by eliding spiritual and physical development agendas through "Bible-based" programs, curriculum, and media such as the sticker chart, the organization uses development as a tool that conflates evangelization, westernization, and material progress in the context of development programming.

Specifically, we focus in this chapter on gender. Though there are several works that explore the dynamic of gender in development (e.g., Mehra 1997, Jaquette and Summerfield 2006), and a small but increasing number of studies that examine the role of religion in development work (Bornstein 2005, Occhipinti 2005, Hefferan 2007), the intersection of faith, development, and gender remains largely unexplored. Clearly, however, both religious and secular development organizations reflect, and seek to influence, the construction of gender in the societies in which they work.

Indeed, gender is one area in which religious and development histories overlap. The women's movement of the late 1960s and early 1970s spurred debates in both religious and development circles about the role of women as mothers, social and religious leaders, and economic actors in society. At the same time that women gained the right to ordination in some liberal Protestant and Jewish congregations, the United Nations and other development entities implemented Women in Development [WID] programs, seeking to integrate women into development processes from which they had previously been excluded (Hirschmann 2006). The invention of the birth control pill and international family planning policies in the 1960s and 1970s also brought women's roles—and women's bodies—into the combined and often combustible sphere of development policies and religious ideologies.

Agape, as an evangelical development organization, has both witnessed and participated in the religious and development manifestations of this debate. Examining how Agape staff members model and teach about gender, then, is indicative of the ways in which the organization balances its function as a development agency concerned with material progress, and as a religious organization concerned with conveying social and spiritual ideals. Gender, as a socially constructed and malleable facet of human identity and social organization, is also a useful lens through which to explore the ways in which Agape addresses culture as an asset of, and impediment to, its spiritual and material goals.

Agape in Context: Cochabamba

Research for this chapter was conducted in the summer of 2007 in Cochabamba, a departmental capital of approximately 600,000 inhabitants. A highland city approximately eight hours from La Paz by bus, Cochabamba is home to several government and non-governmental development organizations, many of them faith-based. For several of these organizations, Cochabamba serves as a hub for services targeted at rural populations outside the city. Agape is no exception, and though it has offices in Cochabamba, many of its clientele live in small, less developed communities well removed from the paved streets, Internet cafes, and service-sector economy the capital offers.

Agape's particular positioning as a faith-based development organization active in Bolivian cities and in its countryside is the result of its history as a post-World War II mission targeting children, and of the rise of Protestant Christianity in Bolivia. Formed after the end of the war, Agape implements and maintains programs throughout the developing world. Project sites are formed in partnership with local evangelical churches, many of them Pentecostal. Each church is responsible for hiring Agape site staff and for overseeing day-to-day project administration.

The existence of such local evangelical churches, in both rural and urban settings, is the result of an increase in the number of Protestants in Bolivia, an expansion which mirrors a general trend in Latin America.[3] Officially Catholic in the colonial and immediate postcolonial eras, Bolivia opened its borders to

Protestant missions in the late 19th century under a liberal government, which sought to cut legal ties to Rome. The Brethren Assemblies, Canadian Baptists, Methodists, Andean Evangelical Mission, and the Seventh-day Adventists established permanent missions in Bolivia beginning in 1895, with another wave of Protestant interest coming after World War II. Much of this early Protestant activity manifested in strategies aimed at gaining individual converts, something early missionaries cited as difficult in Bolivia's communal society (Wagner 1970, 44). Indeed, such a western, individual approach to both conversion and development carries on through the present day. Agape focuses its mission on individuals, particularly individual children, though they are individuals in the distinctly communal milieu of Andean culture.

Specifically, Agape is an organization focused on child development, and it employs a child-sponsorship model to fund its project sites around the world. Participants are matched with donor sponsors and contact them several times a year through letters. Each site employs a site director, programs director, sponsorship director, and finance director, giving a uniform structural framework to each project.

Agape program participants, mostly indigenous children ages 3-20, attend a half-day program three days a week, designed to supplement attendance at state schools, which also run on half-day schedules. Depending on the size of the church's facilities and finances, some centers operate six days a week in order to accommodate a greater number of children. The program provides a snack, lunch, and occasionally clothing. Meal schedules are prepared by an Agape nutritionist. Program curriculum is developed in-country by Agape employees and outside education specialists.

Agape's spiritual goals are most directly embodied in its education curriculum, which organization personnel uniformly describe as "Bible-based." Indeed, lesson plans utilize a variety of Christian scriptures, often to teach the importance of individual responsibility for a myriad of tasks, ranging from spiritual issues to cleaning one's room. Lesson plans emphasize that God is everywhere, and that scripture may be used to discern God's will in every daily task, be it large or small. Job 8:21 ("He will yet fill your mouth with laughter, and your lips with shouts of joy" [NRSV]), for example, is used to teach oral hygiene, one component of Agape's larger goal of creating "responsible, Christian adults." Indeed, staff members frequently mention the Bible as the basis for all teaching. Alejandra Vásconez,[4] an administrative assistant at the country level, remarked that, "Everything that we teach the children, everything is based on biblical principles. Everything, everything, everything." She was adamant that Agape's program had its basis in the Bible, though, notably, she never addressed the possibility of variations in biblical interpretation.

For Agape staffers, then, it seems clear that development, at least in relation to the curriculum they design for the young participants in Agape after-school programs, is a religious endeavor. Material progress, in the form of better nutrition and increased earning potential through higher education, is melded to the spiritual and social realms through the use of biblical authority. In Alejandra's words,

> Our purpose is the development of the child, this is our mission, our vi-
> sion: to succeed in developing the child, so that more than knowledge, the
> child develops physically, is healthy, that the child knows God, biblical
> truths, etc; and also that the child develops socially and emotionally; that
> the child can take part in society, make friends, have a peaceful family
> life. This is our objective so that he or she can be adult, responsible, so
> that he or she can be Christian. That is, he or she can support him- or
> herself.

Alejandra's choice of language makes it evident that Agape envisions development as both spiritual and material, intertwined and largely inseparable. Agape's mission is to develop children cognitively and physically, but more importantly, spiritually, with a final goal of financial independence.

What the Word Says: Negotiating a "Biblically Based" Development

While an idyllic listing of blended material and spiritual goals is relatively easy to articulate, staff members often contest the primacy of each mode of development within the organization and its activities. Agape staff in program sites and teaching roles most frequently defined development in terms of material change: infrastructure, basic services (light, water), schools, and increased access to medical care. Staff at the administrative level, however, overwhelmingly described development as a process of raising social and religious consciousness. One administrator at the country office, for example, defined development as "higher levels of personal relationships," clarifying that God calls people to feed and clothe the needy in the community. "God created us with potential and everyone has their talents and gifts," he continued. "Development is reaching this point."

Indeed, Agape's overall mission and programming appear to relate more closely to such a relational understanding of development. Agape does not focus on infrastructure, but rather on individuals, whose development administrative officials consider central to the long-term improvement of the communities in which they work, and of Bolivia more generally.[5]

How, then, do Agape's religious goal of individual salvation and its more generalized development goals of increased social consciousness and material progress relate? As with many faith-based NGOs, Agape employs a "holistic" approach to development that assumes effective development will address the inseparable physical, spiritual, and psychological well-being of development clientele (Bornstein 2005; DeTemple 2006). No one can be "developed" in this model, no one may reach his or her potential as a human being, if he or she is not physically, mentally, and spiritually healthy.

Agape puts this holistic approach into action by employing religious imagery and activities in every corporate function, and by frequently invoking the Bible as the basis for the agency's inception and continued work. Staff members offer prayers before meals, decorate classrooms with Bible verses and stories, and share in daily devotionals. These overarching and pervasive spiritual themes give uniformity to Agape's programming, and also encourage individuals to see Jesus Christ as the catalyst for all other actions, both within and outside of organizational activities. This consciously "Christ-centered" mode of operation gives the staff freedom to use spiritual explanations for material goals and progressions, and allows a successful negotiation between development as a social and material ideal.

Such a conflation of material and spiritual goals also allows a reproduction of evangelical exceptionalism vis-à-vis Bolivian, and specifically Catholic, culture. Following an evangelical theological tenet to be "in the world but not of it," Agape staff emphasize that a "Christian" life is fundamentally different from that of non-Evangelicals. In discussing appropriate gender roles in the home, for example, one teacher at an Agape after-school program indicated that "in Catholic families, not in all, but the majority, the husband rules because he works, period." While she supports an ideal that places men in leadership roles in the home, she explicitly distanced what she considers to be an evangelical understanding of biblical lines of authority from what she saw as a secularized or nominally Catholic *machista* social structure where men have power simply because they work outside of domestic spaces.

Agape programming and staff encourage this kind of exceptionalism, both in rhetoric that focuses on developing "Christian adults" who can correctly implement biblical teachings in daily life, and in emphasis on conversion as a vital step toward a genuinely fulfilling, prosperous, and moral life. Children receive a sticker on their life plan charts for a public acceptance of salvation, mp3 players are awarded to children for the best Christian testimony, and students applying for scholarships must describe how they are different as a result of a personal conversion experience in the church, answering the application question, "how is your life since then?" Accepting Christ as a personal savior, something Agape and other evangelical entities identify as a spiritual necessity that distinguishes them from Catholics and other "false sects," is perceived and lauded as a radical transformation that positively affects both religious and social realities. How such exceptionalism plays out in the arena of gender in the course of Agape's development enterprise is our focus in the remainder of this chapter.

The Partial Reformation of Machismo:
Equality, Gender and Biblical Authority

In her seminal 1995 work on Colombian evangelicals, *The Reformation of Machismo*, Elizabeth Brusco states that "In a prescriptive sense, the modernization and development of a country depend on its citizens acquiring habits and attitudes that are consistent with capitalist economic behavior" (Brusco 1995, 142). She then proceeds to argue that for many women, converting men to a shared evangelical lifestyle is economically and socially advantageous for family life. This "reformation of machismo," as she frames it, allows evangelical men to opt out of machista societal norms that encourage the maintenance of several women, as well as persistent and expensive indulgence in alcohol and tobacco. The reformed man is a domesticated man, able to invest in hearth and home.

In its consistent blending of capitalist and spiritual ideals in singular events such as testimony competitions, and in broader media employed in daily classroom use, Agape appears to be similar to many of the evangelical churches Brusco studied, especially in its presentation of idealized gender roles. Indeed, Agape rhetoric and didactic materials are rife with references that equate evangelicalism with enhanced gender equality, as well as harmonious domestic relationships and generalized prosperity.

Specifically, Agape is consistent in communicating an ideal of gender equality, both in the rhetoric staff members employ and through the medium of its curriculum. In interviews targeted at discerning attitudes about gender roles, staff members commonly commented that God had created males and females as equals, and all of the lesson plans we reviewed also emphasized this point. This equality, however, tended to be qualified. Staff frequently added that men and women were created with equal worth, but for different purposes, having subsequently different roles.

A female pastor of a Pentecostal church with which Agape partners, for example, described the male role as, "The man, when he is married, a father, is priest [*sacerdote*], the head of the family, is the one who can spiritually—is the one who assumes the priesthood of the family and who ministers the word of God to the family." When we asked what exactly being the head of the household means, she answered, "To be the head of the household means that he represents it, as Christ represents the church." "As for woman," she continued, "as the Bible says, she should oblige the blessing of God in this sense. She assumes the role of being subject to her spouse, of being in submission to her spouse, but in the sense of the church being subject to Christ." She also quoted Proverbs 31, which describes a capable and industrious wife as "more precious than jewels" as an example for how a woman was to oversee her household and become a "tremendous wife." When asked for a specific idea of how roles were to be split between the genders, she concluded, "I base myself on biblical teachings, so I believe that the man is the head and the woman is the help and the housewife [*doña*]. That's it in summary: head and help and housewife."

Images in Agape classrooms support such normative roles and reify notions of their scriptural basis. One particular poster in a classroom for seven- and eight-year-olds was titled "our sexuality" with a caption that read, "God created men and women with well-defined gender roles."[6] On one side of the poster a fair-skinned boy sits in an airplane-wallpapered room, soccer ball in hand, smiling above the caption, "masculine sex." On the opposite side of the poster, "feminine sex" is represented by a young girl in a pink room complete with a castle, tea set, fuzzy pink slippers, and a Barbie doll. Boys are to be boys, and girls are to be girls, with gender-specific, and, by implication, biblically mandated, interests and activities.

Figure 1 - Agape poster demonstrating "well defined" gender roles

Such scenes signal two important aspects of gender ideology and modeling within the Agape context. First, gender is domesticated. While staffers referenced external employment and activities, especially in relation to appropriate male conduct, most of the teaching and casual talk about gender located specific roles for men and women within the context of the home. Girls and boys are pictured in bedrooms, and men's and women's roles as "head and help and housewives" are squarely in the context of family relations. The "responsible

Christian adults" that Agape seeks to develop are invariably mothers and fathers, husbands and wives.

Certainly, this is not unique to Agape. Gutmann (1996), Burdick (1993; 1998), and Brusco (1995) document the ways that Catholic and Protestant doctrines and teachings uphold the home as a female domain in Latin America. Indeed, when Brusco discusses the "reformation of machismo" in Colombia, she argues that a conversion to evangelical Christianity allows a domestication of men, admitting them fully into the household, and therefore into normatively female spaces. Gutmann's work, while less concerned with religion, also cites Catholic images of female domesticity as an impediment to engaged fatherhood (Gutmann 1996, 64). For evangelicals, then, including Agape staff members, the home is a space apart from greater society where ideal, religiously based, and more egalitarian gender roles may be implemented and maintained. Development, in this regard, starts at home.

And, indeed, many Agape employees consistently contrasted an ideal evangelical home with those in greater Bolivian society when speaking about development work focused on gender. Most of the on-site support staff offered that in general Bolivian society, the notion of women's roles is one that conditions females, from a young age, to accept certain traditional roles with defined responsibilities. Usually this tradition relegates young girls to cooking, cleaning, and caring for brothers and sisters. Staff also indicated that boys generally take on little, if any, responsibility in the home, and spend their time playing soccer or doing schoolwork, something they attributed to a machista ethic that allows men to escape what staffers see as a God-given domestic responsibility.

Agape curriculum, didactic materials, and staff members continually emphasized the role of men as the "head" [cabeza] of Christian households, though there were, notably, a wide variety of interpretations as to what this role entails. Employees differed broadly in their description of the roles that men and women were to take on in the house with regard to spiritual leadership, material provision, and responsibility for household tasks. The female pastor defined the head of the household as "the one who represents the family, though decisions are made by the two of them, husband and wife." The husband, she went on to clarify, is like Christ, representing the church. "He is the one who defends the church, the lawyer." A teacher at the same site was markedly less egalitarian in her view, noting that "the man brings the idea and then talks to the wife about it." As a woman, she was adamant that she could not dictate household policy.

While Agape staff and curriculum support a generalized ideal of men as the "head" of households, then, they do so in ways that attempt to distinguish biblically supported patriarchy from what they perceive as secular, and detrimental, machista norms in Bolivian society. One teacher emphasized greater responsibility taken on by boys in evangelical homes in recalling an activity focused on nutrition and cooking. In this activity, the girls went to cook, and rather than playing soccer outside, the boys moved tables and then sat down to watch. The teacher explained what he saw as a positive change in the children's behavior in terms of biblically correct gender roles, where men take greater interest in and responsibility for the home. Part of that participation includes a paternal stance towards wives, so that "Christian" husbands take on roles as protectors. In this vein, another male staff member likened women to flowers that need to be tended and cared for. He remarked that

> They say that the woman is the delicate one . . . that the woman is delicate and sometimes one has to protect her. As the Bible says, the woman is more delicate, and one should protect her as a rose . . . it says that the man is the head and must make a decision for the good of the household. And if you have a beautiful rose, you need to be grateful.[7]

Agape staff members thus cast male authority as biblically mandated male protection for delicate and therefore needful women. This authority, however, is to be wielded with a certain air of thankfulness. The evangelical interpretation of gender roles is different from machista views of male authority because women are treated with "respect" and "gratitude."

By emphasizing gender in domestic spaces, then, Agape reinterprets culturally predominant gender roles, moving men more squarely into domestic spaces under the banner of scriptural authority. Men retain power in households, but it is to be a kindler, gentler power based on fidelity and responsibility, a power that they are to use with gratitude. The gender norms of Bolivian culture are converted, leaving the essence of patriarchal authority in place, but separating that patriarchy from what Agape describes as a secular, machista base.

While there is an overt rhetoric of difference between evangelical and cultural gender roles within households, Agape classrooms often mimicked stereotypical machista interactions between genders. Although many of the sites we visited included boys and girls equally in classroom instruction and activities, a proportionally significant number of teaching sessions exhibited markedly uneven participation between boys and girls. In one classroom, boys wandered in and out while playing soccer as girls worked on an Agape lesson plan that detailed eating disorders, causes, and treatments. In the same classroom, the boys' return was marked by a paper-burning incident, to which the teacher responded by calling the perpetrator "mischievous." This particular scene is indicative of a certain modeling of gender roles that does not support women's authority in the classroom or, by extension, in the home. Delicate flowers are not likely to wield authority, after all, nor are they likely to thrive in the competitive atmosphere of public life. While an evangelical reformation of machismo may bring men into the home, it does not necessarily bring women fully into the workplace, political office, or marketplace. A full reformation of machismo has yet to be completed.

In the Image and Likeness of God: Gender, Christianity and Prosperity in the Western Context

One reason for this lack of completion, and a second major aspect of gender ideology and modeling in Agape practices, is Agape's elision of "Christian" families with Western social and material norms, an elision that takes place in the specific context of development, and with the specific authority of scripture. The images of the boy and girl used to teach "well defined" gender roles, for example, model a household setting in which each child not only has a plethora of personal toys, but a private room in which to put them. This certainly does not reflect the reality of most Bolivian children, who share rooms, and most likely beds, with siblings, and often with their parents, especially in rural settings.

Indeed, most of the assumptions about family life that underlie Agape programming and ideologies both encourage and presume an ideal of Western nuclear families able to participate actively in a consumer economy. In the vast majority of classroom didactic materials and in curricular guides, families are depicted as consisting of a father, a mother, and two children, most often a boy and a girl. Despite the fact that these lesson plans and posters are created in Bolivia, by Bolivian staff, typical Bolivian homes with multiple generations of family, fictive kin, and, quite often in these days of out-migration, absent fathers, are notably lacking from the literature. "Christian" families are small, nuclear families, with husbands acting as helpful heads; wives happy to be submissive, industrious mothers and homemakers; and children, "boys" and "girls" in English as well as Spanish in the poster, who spend their days playing with manufactured toys.

Once again, such images are linked in Agape classrooms to development cast in terms of material improvement, and to an overt agenda of Christianization. Agape staff employ scriptural passages to encourage children to sit in Western-style chairs, use desks, eat with silverware and don the Western clothing the projects provide, often with the explicit suggestion to "improve" themselves so that they might become more successful in mainstream Bolivian society. Traditional Andean dress, customs and language become impediments to the individual development and self-improvement the programs emphasize.

Moreover, they become impediments to becoming the "responsible Christian adults" that Agape seeks to develop. In everything from didactic materials representing Adam and Eve in the aesthetic of Western comic book heroes, to ideological emphases on prosperous nuclear households with a father as the authority figure, Agape conflates Christianity with material success and "civilized" ways of living, often in stark contrast to local, Andean realities. Material goods become markers of developmental and even spiritual success, leading to a particularly Westernized ideal of development that comes to carry the authority of scripture.[8]

Figure 2 - Agape textbook depicting Adam and Eve with the caption, "authority"

"Christian" families in Agape literature, for example, are notably Western-ized in their dress, speech and occupations. Though the majority of the children Agape serves in the Cochabamba region are indigenous, and have parents who wear traditional Andean dress, the after-school programs distribute T-shirts, jeans, and sweatshirts to the children. Staff members also wear Western dress, with the exception of site cooks, who are most often indigenous women in tradi-tional garb, and who work away from the public eye. Though many of the chil-dren speak Quechua at home, Spanish is the language of instruction at the after-school programs. As one staff member put it, "Learning Spanish is a way of improving themselves."

To become "developed" in the Agape context, then, is not only to become a responsible Christian, it is to become, at least nominally, Westernized, speaking Spanish and trading indigenous clothing for Mestizo or even North American wear. Once again, such development has significant implications for the ways in which gender is constructed and reproduced in the overtly religious context of the organization. As Marisol de la Cadena has noted, indigenous women in the Andes are imagined to be more naturally "traditional," retaining indigenous dress and domestic roles that set them apart from "mainstream" economic and social functions in which men more easily participate (de la Cadena 1995). By emphasizing the role of women as Christians in the home, even in materials that represent "developed" families as prosperous and active in the economy, Agape curriculum furthers a notion that "Christian development" is primarily for men, who then share the rewards of economic mobility with their household.

In this regard, then, Agape's programming troubles the possibility of a genuinely indigenous development, even as it works to maintain gender roles that could be construed as "traditional" in a predominately machista, Bolivian society. Girls are encouraged to find happiness and prosperity primarily in their future roles as mothers and wives, even should they work outside of the home; boys are to represent their families in productive public careers while being "responsible" to wives and children. They are to do so as Evangelicals in Western clothing, notably different from mainstream, Catholic Bolivians with whom they live. They are to do so as men and women created in the image and likeness of a distinctly Western, and upwardly mobile, God.[9]

Religion and development come together in countless ways when faith-based NGOs design and implement projects in the countries in which they work. By examining how one faith-based NGO concerned with children models and teaches about gender, however, we can better see some of the ways in which religious doctrine, social ideologies and material goals intertwine. By linking ideas of material progress with "Bible-based" doctrines, Agape both encourages evangelical separation from Bolivian society and reifies many gender-based roles for men and women within that society. It also, consciously or unconsciously, elides "Christian" homes with those based on a Western model, effectively giving patriarchy and Western modes of consumption the imprimatur of biblical authority.

Notes

Research for this project was conducted with a grant from the Richter Foundation and the Honors Program at Southern Methodist University. The authors are grateful to both programs for their support.

1. A pseudonym.

2. "Evangelical" is a notoriously slippery term, especially in the Latin American context. For the purposes of this chapter, "evangelical" refers to Protestant Christians who place an emphasis on personal conversion experiences that lead to a "personal relationship" with Jesus Christ. In the wider Bolivian context, *evangélicos* are simply non-Catholic Christians, including Seventh-day Adventists and "mainline" Protestants such as Methodists. Mormons and Jehovah's Witnesses are often included in this category by Catholics, but are excluded by many self-identified *evangélicos*.

3. According to the 2001 census conducted by the Bolivian National Statistical Institute, 78 percent of the population is Roman Catholic, and Protestant denominations account for 16 to 19 percent of the population, with more Protestants (roughly 20 percent of the population) in rural areas. As recently as 1985, the population was as much as 95 percent Roman Catholic.

4. A pseudonym.

5. David Stoll, for example, contrasts an evangelical emphasis on individual change to that of mainline Protestants and the Catholic Church. "In contrast to liberal Protestants and much of the Catholic Church," he writes, "prominent [evangelical] figures ...advised Latin Americans to concentrate on improving themselves rather than working for structural change." (Stoll 1990:19). See also Ethan Sharp's chapter in this volume, in which he discusses ways in which conservative Protestant approaches to drug abuse reflect neoliberal concerns with individual responsibility and reform.

6. "Dios creó hombres y mujeres con una conducta sexual bien definida." While the literal translation of "conducta sexual" is "sexual conduct," we have chosen "gender roles" to better render the more limited meaning of the phrase in the context of the poster.

7. The staff member's implication that this is a literal biblical mandate springs from unclear origins. The only reference to roses in the Bible comes from the Song of Solomon, in the context of the "rose of Sharon," an allegory with no obvious referent. His allusion to a biblically-based chain of authority in the household is also debated within Christian circles. While conservative Christians will cite Timothy 2:12-14 ["I permit no woman to teach or to have authority over a man; she is to keep silent. For Adam was formed first, then Eve; and Adam was not deceived, but the woman was deceived and became a transgressor"] as the text establishing men as "spiritual heads" of households and religious bodies, liberal and moderate Christians do not generally find a preordained line of household authority in biblical texts.

8. Such an emphasis on nuclear families is not limited to evangelical ideology. See Nilanjana Chatterjee and Nancy Riley (2001) for a discussion of the ways in which the Indian state equated modernity, prosperity and development with two-child families.

9. See Hogue's chapter in this volume for an analysis of the relationship between the values of faith-based aid organizations and the structures and norms of local social systems.

Works Cited

Bornstein, Erica. 2005. *The spirit of development: Protestant NGOs, morality, and economics in Zimbabwe.* Stanford, CA: Stanford University Press.

Brusco, Elizabeth E. 1995. *The reformation of machismo: Evangelical conversion and gender in Colombia.* Austin: University of Texas Press.

Burdick, John. 1993. *Looking for God in Brazil: The progressive Catholic Church in urban Brazil's religious arena.* Berkeley: University of California Press.

———. 1998. *Blessed Anastácia: Women, race and popular Christianity in Brazil.* New York: Routledge.

Chatterjee, Nilajeena, and Nancy Riley. 2001. Planning an Indian modernity: The gendered politics of fertility control. *Signs.* 26(3):811-845.

De la Cadena, Marisol. 1995. Women are more Indian: Ethnicity and gender in a community in Cuzco, in *Ethnicity, markets and migration in the Andes: At the crossroads of history and anthropology,* ed. by Brooke Larson, Olivia Harris, and Enrique Tandeter, 329-48. Durham, NC: Duke University Press.

DeTemple, Jill. 2006. "Haiti appeared at my church": Faith-based organizations, transnational activism, and tourism in sustainable development. *Urban Anthropology and Studies of Cultural Systems and World Economic Development* 35:155-181.

Gutmann, Matthew C. 1996. *The meanings of macho: Being a man in Mexico City.* Berkeley: University of California Press.

Hefferan, Tara. 2007. *Twinning faith and development: Catholic parish partnering in the U.S. and Haiti.* Bloomfield, CT: Kumarian Press.

Hirschmann, David. 2006. From "home economics" to "microfinance": Gender rhetoric and bureaucratic resistance, in *Women and gender equity in development theory and practice,* ed. Jane S. Jaquette and Gale Summerfield, 71-86. Durham: Duke University Press.

Jaquette, Jane S., and Gale Summerfield, eds. 2006. *Women and gender equity in development theory and practice.* Durham: Duke University Press.

Mehra, Rekha. 1997. Women, empowerment and economic development. In *The role of NGOs: Charity and empowerment (Annals of the American Academy of Political and Social Science),* ed. Alan W. Heston, Neil A. Weiner, and Jude L. Fernando, 136-42. Thousand Oaks, CA: Sage Publications.

Occhipinti, Laurie A. 2005. *Acting on faith: Religious development organizations in northwestern Argentina.* Lanham, MD: Lexington Books.

Stoll, David. 1990. *Is Latin America turning Protestant? The politics of Evangelical growth.* Berkeley: University of California Press.

Wagner, C. Peter. 1970. *The Protestant movement in Bolivia.* South Pasadena: William Carey Library.

Chapter 8
"God Wants Us to Have a Life that Is Sustainable": Faith-Based Development and Economic Change in Andean Peasant Communities
Emily Hogue

An FBO's Place in Andean Peasant Communities: What Neoliberalism Leaves Behind

Campesinos and *campesinas*[1] from the communities surrounding Combapata, Peru flow little by little into the meeting room of the most formidable building in the district. The tile roof, concrete floors, and flush toilets make this two-story cement building a considerable structure in an area where adobe walls, dirt floors, and thatched roofs prevail. The meeting's attendees are the political and social leaders of their communities; presidents, vice presidents, committee leaders all come to participate in this meeting, which they hope will bring about change and progress for their community in the coming year. They come in their dirt-covered clothes, having worked their fields and walked the long dusty road to the meeting. They carry a few necessities for the day's journey in brightly colored *llikllas*[2] on their backs. Their commitment to this meeting and concern over its outcomes are evident in their willingness to miss a day's work in the fields and make the long hike—as long as fourteen hours round-trip for some—to the meeting.

The building is the office of the local Area Development Project (ADP) for World Vision International (WVI), which describes itself on its home page as a "Christian relief and development organization dedicated to helping children and their communities worldwide reach their full potential by tackling the causes of poverty" through child sponsorship. WVI[3] is a transnational faith-based organization (FBO), committed to bringing integrated sustainable development in the primary areas of health, education, social justice, Christian values,[4] and economic development (WVI Cusco 2006). The transnational nature of the organization and its strategy for global redistribution through child sponsorship are premised in the "dawning awareness that the global problems we confront . . . require transnational solutions," as noted also by Tim Fogarty (this volume). WVI is one of the largest FBOs operating in the world today, working in one hundred countries and serving more than 2.2 million children (Stafford 2005). In the department of Cusco, Peru, WVI has ten operating ADPs, which provide assistance to tens of thousands of families.

This paper examines WVI's intervention in Andean indigenous communities in the Cusco area. Drawing on twelve months of fieldwork in the area, which included participant observation, document analysis, and surveys and semistructured interviews with beneficiaries, WVI staff, and targeted communities, this paper explores the relationship between WVI ideologies of desirable economic and social behavior and shifts in religious and economic values, ideologies, and practices[5] among WVI recipients and targeted communities. Situating this research in Anthony Giddens's concept of "structuration,"[6] I argue that shifts in local values, ideologies, and practices are directly tied to WVI's work in the area, and that the more linked that households and communities are with WVI, the greater those shifts are. Essentially, social structures such as ideologies and values exist among members of a group, orienting their practices and actions; those practices, in turn, bring about the enduring maintenance or the transmutation of structures. Through this interplay between structure and practice, WVI introduces new ideologies and values to reorient practices, as only practical changes rooted in structural change will result in sustainability.

Returning to the WVI scene opening this chapter: the day's meeting is a "participatory budget meeting." Members from participating communities are coming together to decide how in the coming year the ADP will allocate the funds destined for community development projects. This particular ADP, named ADP Salcca after the river that runs through the district, serves eighteen communities from three different political districts,[7] thirteen of which belong to the district of Combapata, where the ADP office is located. To support the interests of its members, each of the eighteen communities sends representatives to the budget meeting.

The development projects promised by WVI are considerable, exceeding those promised by the districts' local governments or other state-run programs, both in number and probable impact. For example, WVI has helped build and plans to fund the building of several more new schools in areas of the district where the government has never built and has no plans to build. The budget of WVI also greatly exceeds that of the local government and other state programs operating in the area. However, the differences in impact between the FBO and the local governments are not just material or financial, as WVI also offers the communities far more in terms of capacity building, technical guidance, and social support. While the local government historically would have claimed responsibility for designing and delivering these social and economic services, the government's limited budget—primarily the result of neoliberal structural adjustments—currently prevents it from doing so. Thus, many Combapata community members feel that the government has "abandoned" them.

The Peruvian political economy in the last two decades has been shaped primarily by neoliberal structural adjustment programs (NSAP), which have greatly impacted the economic and social life of the Peruvian peoples, as well as the Peruvian development sector. In the Peruvian context, NSAPs are defined as "a compilation of liberal political measures whose objective is to reform the institutional production that controls production, allocation, distribution, and consumption, redefining the economic roles of the market and the State, the rules of the (economic) game and the organizations at the micro-economic level to develop a competitive and open capitalist economy" (Gonzales de Olarte 2000, 23). Neoliberal reform came to Peru in the early 1990s, when the Fujimori administration enacted strict NSAPs in an attempt to curb the serious economic decline and hyperinflation brought about through the heterodox economic reforms of Garcia's administrations in the 1980s. Fujimori's neoliberal reforms, commonly known as "Fujishock," mimicked the neoliberal reforms touted by the Washington Consensus and carried out by other Latin American nations. However, Fujimori's reforms were decidedly more radical than those of most other Latin American nations (Arce 2005; Dancourt 1999; Gonzales de Olarte 1998). Among others, these policy reforms have included: 1) tax reform; 2) the privatization of social security pensions; 3) social sector reforms targeting poverty alleviation; and 4) the decentralization of health care.

While neoliberal reforms appear to have brought about economic improvements for Peru as a whole—e.g., GDP has increased significantly—in actuality, reforms have reinforced a center-periphery relationship between the capital and the rest of the nation. For example, deregulated imports have made the value of local agricultural products plummet, leaving rural agrarians with little economic recourse but to migrate or to orient agricultural production to more lucrative markets, both options greatly affecting sociocultural patterns among Peruvians. This has debilitated the economic capacities of peripheral areas, such as the area where the present study takes place.

Although neoliberal reforms in Peru included poverty alleviation policies to counter the effects of market deregulation, those policies have done little to assuage the pains of neoliberalism-induced poverty (Arce 2005; Gonzales de Olarte 2000). In general, poverty alleviation programs have had limited impact. The National Compensation and Development Fund (FONCODES) created in the early 1990s, which has focused on building basic infrastructure for health and education programs (Gonzales de Olarte 2000), largely has funded short-term projects carried out through local base-level organizations (Arce 2005; Portocarrero et al. 2002). Yet the FONCODES program—which is centralized through the national government—tends to procure materials (Gonzales de Olarte 2000) and technical assistance from the core areas, thereby reproducing the core-periphery division, providing little economic inclusion or boost to the periphery areas. Moreover, the base-level organizations created to work with FONCODES only exist for the duration of the short-term projects for which they are funded (Arce 2005; Portocarrero et al. 2002). Generally, the inability of social aid programs in Peru to counter the onset of structural adjustment has meant greater poverty, near starvation, and extreme malnutrition for numerous poor (Gonzales de Olarte 1998; Starn, Degregori, and Kirk 1995).

Given these realities, neoliberal platforms generally invite private organizations to cover the social and economic needs of national populations (Pfeiffer 2004), executing the "privatization of development" discussed in the introduction to this volume. Indeed, the number and scope of NGOs operating in Peru has grown decidedly since reforms began in 1990, though the Peruvian state's reaction to and interaction with those NGOs varies along a spectrum ranging from mutual support to hostility (Portocarrero et al. 2002). Yet, the majority of NGOs are seen working together with local governments and state-run programs like FONCODES to carry out development projects (Avila 2000).

Congruent with the neoliberal context, WVI has entered the scene to fill the void of social programs and to soothe the pains of the State's "abandoned" citizens. Where once the Combapatinos[8] looked to national and local government programs for assistance, their faith and hope in those programs has waned considerably. WVI and other local NGOs are now considered the main source of change, development, and aid among surveyed Combapatinos. While feeling that their government has "forgotten" them, many local citizens see WVI as "the only one who listens" to their needs.

WVI's Intervention: A Call for Change

The ADP meeting scene that opens this chapter reveals WVI's strength and prominence in the local communities' development processes. At the same time, as the meeting unfolds, it becomes clear that determining the budget is not the only thing on the minds of WVI staff. This community gathering, like all other events, encounters, and meetings of WVI, has an additional purpose: to shape the values, ideologies, and practices of program participants. Unlike organizations that work to provide only material improvements, WVI also focuses intently on moral and spiritual improvements. In this way, the organization's approach aims for "holistic" development—involving the "inseparable physical, spiritual, and psychological well-being" of participants—that DeTemple, Eidenshink, and Josephson describe (this volume). The FBO operates with a strategy to bring about what it considers "Sustainable Transformational Development."[9]

This concept is rooted in the notion that sustainable development occurs primarily through changes to mentalities, values, ideologies, and, hence, practices which arise out of objective spiritual realities and the commandments of Jesus. Importantly, the change WVI is hoping to promote is not about conversion or adopting a new religion, but entails a spiritual transformation in which people develop a stronger relationship with God (Jesus) and, thus, adopt beliefs and practices which are pleasing to him and beneficial for them. As one WVI senior staff member in Peru said, "the projection of development that World Vision asserts, stemming from a knowledge of Jesus, [is that] only Jesus can transform people and that people transformed by Jesus can attain social transformation."[10] In this way, WVI acts as an appendage of Jesus to bring about social transformation that is advantageous for these communities economically, socially, and spiritually. This orientation solidly places WVI into the category of "faith-saturated" FBOs, discussed in the introduction to this book.

A staff member starts the meeting with a video featuring images of undernourished children, adults on crutches, and people wearing rags. A Christian song plays in the background, as text proclaiming the love of Christ and God's eternal search to regain his lost children overlays the final scenes of poverty. During a period of reflection that follows, WVI staff discuss God's love for those present and His desire that His people not suffer in poverty and sickness. A second video then is screened, focusing on Christian hope and faith. Afterward, with most community representatives now present, a WVI staff member asks an attendee to begin the meeting with a prayer. The prayer is in the local language of Quechua, but it is decidedly Christian in pleading for the help and mercy of God for those present. After the prayer, the WVI staff holds a devotional, or time of Biblical reflection, with the *comuneros*.[11]

The theme of the day's devotional is the wise and industrious use of resources, which God finds pleasing. Prefacing his comments with a reading of Matthew 25:14-30,[12] the WVI staffer assures the *comuneros* that God will multiply resources to His children who use them correctly. Those who squander or hide their resources and talents not only will not have theirs multiplied, they will instead lose them. "God wants our resources to be well administered, so that we can have life and life in abundance," he persuades them. He then suggests that the traditional, and still practiced, productive activities of the *comuneros* do not provide sustainability, since seasonal crops of low economic value, such as potatoes and corn, do not provide a steady financial base for local families. Because these agricultural practices do not provide economic equilibrium, WVI believes they hinder the economic progress of local communities. The staff member follows this by saying that "God wants us to have a life that is sustainable." In this context, development and change are not "good" simply because the UN, USAID, or private NGOs say so, but rather because God says so. To those who heed the WVI staff member's words, it seems obvious that God calls for change and that he is using WVI as his earthly voice.

This discussion forms a foundation for the rest of the day's work: the budget. The *comuneros* are asked to acknowledge what they have, that is, what

God has given them; and then to consider what will be the most efficient way to use these gifts in the coming year. For WVI, this meeting is not just about material and economic decisions. It is also about promoting the "Christian Values" WVI views as key to development: solidarity, transparency, punctuality, good health practices, equality, honesty, responsibility, politeness, cleanliness, love, faithfulness, and gratefulness (WVI Cusco 2007). In the orientation of its projects, initiatives, meetings and goals, WVI focuses not only on righting global economic inequities by redistributing resources at the global level through child sponsorship, but also on "tackling the causes of poverty," which are said to include supposedly inefficacious local social values, ideologies, and norms.

WVI and Change in the Salcca Valley

World Vision International began working in the district of Combapata, Peru in 1996 through a small-scale project that would become ADP Salcca. The mid-1990s were a time of renewal for most communities in southern Peru. President Alberto Fujimori's administration had rid the nation of leftist terrorist groups like *Sendero Luminoso*,[13] and the national economy was quickly on the upswing after devastating poverty and five-digit inflation had ravaged the country. WVI chose to work in Combapata and the Salcca Valley because of its relatively stable social situation and existing connections between WVI and the local Peruvian Evangelical Church.[14] As a Christian organization, WVI views the Church as one of its "principal allies," according to WVI senior staff in Cusco. The Church's strong and ever-growing foothold in the district created a promising environment for WVI's work in the area.

The vision of WVI in Peru is "life in all its abundance for all children" (WVI Cusco 2007). WVI's program concentrates on children, with the goal of improving their living conditions though projects addressing its five main development areas of health, education, social justice, Christian values, and economic development. Because WVI believes that the child "cannot be seen outside of the context of the family"[15] or the community, WVI works not only with children, but also with parents, local households, community leaders, and community political structures. While WVI's efforts to improve living conditions are based, in part, on bringing capital and material improvements to the area, the crux of its work is focused on transforming the values, mentalities, and practices of the people it aids. It does this through its strategy of Sustainable Transformational Development. Accordingly, much of WVI's effort is based in capacity-building workshops, spiritual devotions,[16] and courses on values. Always addressing the five developmental areas of health, education, social justice, Christian values, and economic development, WVI uses instruction and the teaching of Christian values as a force to change people's thoughts and actions.

Households in the eighteen communities where WVI Salcca works are dedicated primarily to small-scale agricultural and livestock production. Approximately 91 percent of the surveyed residents in the Salcca area are small-scale agriculturalists and livestock producers, the vast majority of whom produce first for consumption and second for sale to markets. The production of these farmers is fairly low due to factors of climate, soils, and available technologies. The great majority of the farmers uses a yoke of oxen and pick axes to plant and work their crops. More mechanized technologies are scarce; for example, only two tractors are available for the 1,856 families[17] living in the area.

Historically, the residents of the lower altitudes[18] of the Salcca area have focused their agricultural production on crops of potatoes, corn, and fava beans (*habas*); residents at medium altitudes produce potatoes and *habas*; and soils and climates at higher altitude zones allow farmers to grow only varieties of small potatoes. In terms of livestock, lower altitude residents raise cattle, sheep, chickens, and guinea pigs (*cuyes*). Communities in the medium and higher altitude levels raise primarily sheep, llamas, and alpacas, since these species are physically better suited than other farm animals for high altitudes. The production of these crops and livestock has remained fairly consistent over the last several hundred years. While use of chemical fertilizers and pesticides was popular in lower altitude communities for several years, most households in the study sample say they have ceased using them because they make the crops unhealthy and poor tasting. Other than the short-lived use of fertilizers, community members contend that practices have remained much the same in the area, except for the shifts that WVI is implementing. Still, these shifts are sizeable.

Interviewees commented on the ways WVI programs have changed market orientations and agricultural production among their communities. Owing largely to the influence of WVI programs, cattle production is now the key source of cash income for most families in the lower altitudes of the Salcca area. WVI improved cattle production by helping residents to build cow sheds for more hygienic and efficient cattle fattening, encouraging the purchase of more valued breeds of cattle, and providing seed for better feed sources, like alfalfa and clover. In the medium and higher altitudes, cattle production is much more problematic. For this reason, WVI has focused primarily on vegetable production in medium altitudes and alpaca production in high altitudes.

The vegetable production initiatives of WVI have reoriented nutritional and agricultural practices and ideologies while also creating a source of cash income for families previously producing primarily for subsistence. Through educational and capacity-building workshops, WVI has encouraged what it considers to be better eating patterns that promote health, nutrition, and education. Through WVI educational sessions, families have come to revalue autochthonous foods such as quinoa and tarwi beans, which are much higher in protein and vitamins than more recent staples such as the white rice that the Spanish brought with them. Because vegetable produce (carrots, cabbage, beets, spinach, onions, and garlic) yields a higher profit and is more in demand than the traditional crops of corn and potatoes, reorienting households to swap traditional crops for more "desirable" vegetables generates a higher cash income for families. From WVI's perspective, in order for families to afford the costs associated with other key areas of development—like education, where money is necessary to pay tuition and buy books and uniforms—they need to transition away from subsistence farming toward activities that offer cash incomes.

Within the areas of economic development, health, and nutrition, WVI's capacity-building efforts and activities have seriously altered the way many households eat, produce, subsist, and think about subsistence. WVI has used educational and capacity-building workshops to foster ideologies that orient households towards economic practices that will allow for a "transformed" lifestyle, often by explicitly invoking a vision where children can "live the life of plenty that God has for them." In essence, WVI initiatives have encouraged many *comuneros* to accept that their children deserve a better type of life, for which a cash income is often necessary. WVI advocates new production practices as the most efficient and lucrative way to get that cash income.

WVI and Structural Change in the Community of Orosccocha

So, how does WVI's promotion of certain values and ideologies impact the social structure (values, ideologies, and norms) of community members where it works? My research findings suggest that there is a relationship between WVI and changes to structure and practices in the five areas of development, as I discuss below, and that the magnitude of those changes is contingent upon variables concerning: 1) the intensity of the participant's relationship with WVI (attendance to WVI events, participation in WVI projects, etc.) and 2) the religious orientations of the participant. An analysis of ideological and practical changes in the area of economic development reveals how WVI is participating in processes of structuration in the communities.

In this section, I present the community of Orosccocha as a useful illustration of the effects WVI's intervention has had on some households, and of how those effects are associated with the two variables described above. I chose Orosccocha as one of five sampled communities in the area because of a strong relationship it had developed with WVI, very evident changes that I could see taking place, and high levels of evangelization going on in the community in the years since WVI had entered. Orosccocha was very welcoming and committed to WVI's efforts, and, thus, the FBO had channeled its work into Orosccocha and other equally responsive communities a bit more than it had in other, less-responsive communities. Orosccocha is one of just five communities that I sampled throughout the area, but I feel that some of the stories and experiences which came out of the community were particularly illuminating in terms of the economic changes that WVI's faith-based work is initiating.

Numerous households in Orosccocha report having experienced structural changes to their own values, ideologies, and norms as a result of interactions with WVI. These shifts center around WVI ideologies of family integrity, the importance of children's well-being, the prudent use of economic resources, and the use of new technologies. The theological framing of those ideologies suggests a transcendent reason for change, as seen in the remark of one interviewee from Orosccocha who said, "God doesn't want to see people living like that" (i.e., how they lived before). WVI suggests its teachings and stances are ordained by God and that they enable a way of life God wants for his children. In this manner participants are encouraged, on a spiritual level, to adopt these changes with the motivation of living the way God views as correct, pleasing God, and incurring his rewards. Those structural changes were reported as key to initiating changes in the life practices of households and establishing an ideological foundation and motivation for practical shifts. It is also important to recognize that while interviewees claim that structural changes are the cause of practical changes, changes to technologies and infrastructure have occurred simultaneously with those structural changes. For example, installed sprinkler systems have facilitated year-round production, shifting agricultural calendars dramatically from the one-harvest tradition.

WVI's mission focuses on the well-being of children in the communities, with the result that much of the FBO's effort and projects are aimed at fostering a strong family unit to create a healthy living environment for the sponsored child. Because of this ideological position, WVI staff members stress practices that will keep families intact and interacting in presumably "positive" ways. For example, in explaining how his family's interaction, as well as earning and spending practices, had changed because of WVI, one interviewee commented that WVI taught him that his children were valuable and that their futures were important. He explained that he and his wife had reoriented the family's earning and spending so that their children's school matriculation and supplies were top priority in their spending budgets. Several other interviewees discussed similar changes to family interaction and spending, as WVI redirected priorities toward their children. Notably, the interviewees most often expressing changes to family interaction were WVI "promoters" or team leaders who regularly attend WVI trainings and then act as conduits to take knowledge from the training back to their communities. These promoters have the most interaction with the organization, and, therefore, are most likely to be affected by its ideological platforms regarding family values.

Altered family values, along with the newly installed sprinkling irrigation systems, have greatly encouraged year-round cultivation. As a result, seasonal migration has decreased, as families focus on providing a stable family life and environment for their children. Previously, heads of household or the entire family would migrate to work as day laborers on plantations located in the jungle and coastal areas during the months their lands were not producing. Now, families see that migrating has negative impacts on the family as it reduces their time together, takes children away from one or more of their parents at times, causes children to miss school, and does not create economic stability. Several men claimed that they now remain in the household throughout the year to uphold their role as father-figure, guide, and provider; however, they discussed that role in terms of responsibility, not dominance. Their comments echo the Evangelical concept of "biblically mandated male protection" in the household also described by DeTemple, Eidenshink, and Josephson (this volume). Female interviewees commented that migration created unhealthy habits in the family, as tensions from economic instability, members' absences, and moves between spaces caused fighting and a breakdown in household relationships.

In addition to reduced seasonal migration, WVI's instructional programs and the installation of sprinklers have prompted and enabled entire communities to change from only potato and *haba* production to growing a variety of vegetables, reorienting economic production. Some 70 percent of randomly surveyed households[19] in Orosccocha reported that they utilize the sprinkling system and now cultivate vegetables that do not grow without irrigation. Of those growing the new crops, 71.4 percent dedicate some portion of the new production to local markets for sale. The planting and agricultural practices of households also change with the new crops, as these are generally less labor intensive than potato crops, resulting in the potential decline of practices that previously entailed mutual aid between households. In addition, the sprinkling system has to be used in rotation as water pressure is too low to supply more than one or two households simultaneously. Thus, households have had to shift typical daily and weekly work schedules to accommodate the sprinkler schedule. Yet, they described these changes in schedules as relatively insignificant compared to the benefits received from the new technology.

The new crops and commodities signify cash income for participating households, as they now have some higher value product to sell in markets. Both men and women engage in the commercialization of their products and taking them to market; however, men primarily remain in charge of production strategies for commercialization. Those households that engage in commercialization reported cash incomes between two to nine times higher than households that did not use the sprinkling systems and grow the new crops. The new production strategies introduced by WVI mean greater diversity in crops and an increase in crop yields.

As one Orosccocha *comunero* says of these changes in his community, "we all wanted to do better, to not be like before. Before, we didn't know, right? Now we figure our accounts, see if things are producing well or if they aren't . . . We all want to improve. We don't want to stay in poverty. We want to get ahead." He states that the new crops bring an "advantage" to them, so that they can "better [them]selves, for [their] children." The man continues, remarking, "[before WVI's intervention], we were lost, really lost. When World Vision began to come, they trained us, no? In all areas, in agriculture, cattle production, raising *cuyes*. [. . .] They began having talks with us. For that, we thank World Vision, that they have taught us so much, in everything."

The new income generated from these shifts is generally directed in two directions: back into the household, and toward the educational needs of household children. Most households are using greater cash incomes for improvements to their homes, such as building outhouses, and for reinvestment back into production strategies. Again, those most deeply involved with WVI through trainings and participation in WVI projects experienced the greatest shifts in production practices and consumption orientations. One interviewee who is also a WVI "promoter" had continually put his income back into projects for raising guinea pigs and growing vegetables. Savings and investment are two capitalistic principles that WVI also promotes, and the investment of income into the home and production are part of WVI's strategy for sustainable development. The use of income for educational needs also demonstrates the new emphasis on children as well as the reorientation toward investing, this time in a future made possible through education. In terms of education, WVI claims there have been real changes in the region, as communities are choosing to orient communal funds offered by WVI for building schools; also, more children are attending educational activities, more parents are attending workshops regarding their children's education, and more teachers in the communities have been trained on various educational methods.

All male interviewees from the community of Orosccocha[20] say that their interaction with WVI has helped them to value their families and time with their families. Numerous male interviewees from throughout the area said that WVI's intervention has affected how they interact with their wives and how they view women's roles within the family and community. Claiming that WVI had encouraged them to value their wives' opinions and knowledge on household issues, male participants commented that reevaluations of gender roles had led to a reduction in arguments and violence within the home. On a community level, *comuneros* continually described how violence had dissipated inside and outside of homes because of the influence of WVI values. Interviewed women were not as talkative about these issues and did not discuss major changes to gender roles within their household. Their disinclination to talk in detail about the issue may be due to cultural norms which traditionally prevent women from speaking on such family matters. Despite shifts toward greater equality within the household, women still remain much less at ease speaking in public to people they do not know well, as was evident throughout my research. However, many women discussed how WVI has created programs that highlight women's productive contributions, such as the marketing of artisan work traditionally created by women.

In this way, WVI's stressing of greater appreciation and respect for spouses as well as more equal gender roles within the household confirms the assertion by DeTemple et al. (this volume) that in Evangelical Protestant beliefs, "the home is a space apart from greater society where ideal, religiously based, and more egalitarian gender roles may be implemented and maintained." Yet, while many Evangelical Protestant movements juxtapose social relationships among their adherents to the rigorously traditional and *machista* roles maintained within Catholicism, my research revealed that WVI usually contextualized such issues within the Bible, not within any certain religion or denomination. Because it works with such a large percentage of the population (the majority of which is not Evangelical Protestant), WVI in Cusco tries to not differentiate between participants based on their religious orientation.[21] In fact, over half of the staff employed by WVI in the Cusco area is Catholic. Creating rifts between Catholics and Evangelicals would undoubtedly prove disastrous for the organization's program.

WVI has concentrated its efforts in Orosccocha more than other communities, citing greater responses in participation from Orosccocha households as the reason. Perhaps the religious orientation of the community partially explains the greater enthusiasm for WVI projects in Orosccocha. Currently, 70 percent of Orosccocha households are Evangelical Protestant Christians and 30 percent are Catholic. Importantly, over half of the surveyed Evangelicals say their conversion occurred in the last ten years, the time when WVI was working in the area. While Evangelicals may be more responsive to and accepting of WVI's work in the area, WVI may also perceive that it is more desirable to work with Evangelicals. Assuredly, there is a relationship between Evangelical religious orientations and WVI's involvement in the area; Evangelical households much more frequently stated that they felt their communities had experienced positive changes, correlating those changes to WVI's intervention. Participants from Orosccocha cite much greater changes in the five areas of development than the four other studied communities.

Conclusion

Giddens (1984, 25) contends that "[a]nalyzing the structuration of social systems means studying the modes in which such systems, grounded in the knowledgeable activities of situated actors who draw upon rules and resources in the diversity of action contexts, are produced and reproduced in interaction." I have focused here on one particular "mode" in which social systems in Combapata are produced and reproduced: through interaction with WVI.

Empirical evidence from this study suggests that WVI's intervention in the studied Andean indigenous communities is initiating changes in economic and social practices through the proliferation of religiously based ideologies and values. Through biblical teachings, devotionals, educational trainings, and workshops, WVI is promoting certain beliefs that it feels will strengthen people's relationships with God and encourage them to act in ways that provide a healthier and happier life. These beliefs are biblically based, Christian-centered ideological platforms that address how people should live and the type of life God wants for people.

In the areas where WVI is working, many *comuneros* are heeding the beliefs set forth by these platforms, and their acceptance is causing real social and economic change within some households as they reorient behaviors to live a life that is pleasing to God and themselves. In social terms, the beliefs promoted by WVI are causing changes such as the reevaluation and redirecting of family relationships and gender roles as well as the prioritization of family integrity and children's needs. These social changes are foundational for the type of healthy and sustainable community WVI is endorsing, but they require even more profound shifts in economic practices—including primarily production and consumption—to create real social transformation and true development. The primary economic changes among households in the studied communities involve an increase in the commercialization of household production and integration into markets, an intensification in year-round agricultural production and a turning away from seasonal migratory work, and a reorientation of consumption practices toward investments and children's needs.

This research also reveals that changes to structure and practices in the studied communities are conditional on 1) the intensity of the participant's relationship with WVI and 2) the religious orientation of the participant. Individuals who attend WVI capacity-building sessions or take some leadership role within WVI-sponsored community initiatives are more likely to be influenced by WVI's ideological positions, and more likely to adopt them. In the same vein, households that have already felt some influence of an evangelical Christian church or movement are more likely to positively receive WVI and its platforms for change. Hence, changes to ideologies and practices are not evenly distributed among communities or within a community. The degree to which changes are occurring varies greatly between households and individuals, but data convey that notable changes are occurring and bringing about social and economic transformation throughout the area.

As research findings in this chapter indicate, indigenous communities in the Cusco area are experiencing economic changes, and those economic changes are specifically related to social changes in religiosity and values. Nevertheless, many questions remain unanswered regarding the cultural implications of WVI's development strategy as well as its impacts on people's identities and worldviews. Future research is still needed to explore further the relationship between WVI (and other FBOs) and the stated religious orientations of the household, conversions to evangelical Christian religions, and changes in the ideologies and practices of people in the communities where WVI works. As the work of WVI and other faith-based development organizations continues and impacts an ever-growing number of communities and populations, it will be the job of social scientists to seek out answers to the many questions that are created in this space where faith and development intersect.

Notes

1. Spanish term meaning peasant, male and female.

2. Quechua term identifying the cloth frequently used to carry a bundle on the back.

3. World Vision International has been the subject of much anthropological research in recent years. Studies by Andrade (1990), Bornstein (2001; 2002; 2005), Cruz (1999), Guamán Gualli (2005), and Tripp (1999) have examined the FBO in terms of how it incorporates faith in its organizational structure, how it integrates concepts of faith and development, and the role it plays in evangelization. This study is distinctive from previous research because it focuses on communities' reactions to WVI and the changes within communities that result from WVI's intervention. In this research, the focus is on community members receiving WVI assistance (the population sample), as opposed to the FBO and its staff.

4. See below for a definition of WVI's Christian Values.

5. For this paper, "values" are defined as principles about what is good or right that orient behavior among individuals and social groups; "ideologies" are complex sets of beliefs that guide individuals and social groups; and "norms" are unwritten social rules that orient behavior.

6. Anthony Giddens's concept of structuration posits that 1) action necessitates structure (rules and resources) as a prerequisite condition for its production and that 2) structure, conversely, is maintained or transformed through the social system, defined as "reproduced relations between actors of collectives, organized as regular social practices" (1984, 25).

7. A district in Peru is roughly equivalent to a township in U.S. counties. The district of Combapata, where this research primarily is based, covers 182.55 square kilometers and has a population of 7,335 community members (Combapata Municipal Government 2000).

8. A citizen of Combapata.

9. In Spanish, *Desarrollo Transformador Sostenible.*

10. WVI staff member's direct quote: "La proyección del desarrollo que postula Visión Mundial, desde el conocimiento de Jesús, es aceptar que solo Jesús puede transformar al hombre, y el hombre transformado por Jesús se puede transformarse socialmente."

11. Spanish term meaning community members.

12. Matthew 25:14-30 covers the Parable of the Talents.

13. *Sendero Luminoso*, or the Shining Path, was a Maoist terrorist group that fought for revolution against the Peruvian government throughout most of the 1980s and early 1990s.

14. *Iglesia Evangelical Peruana.*

15. Personal interview with WVI senior staff.

16. A term meaning a time of Biblical study, reflection, and prayer.

17. See Malqui et al. 2007.

18. The Salcca area, like most Andean highland zones, is separated into three altitude zones based on meters above sea level (or masl): low [2,500–3,500 masl], medium [3,500–3,999 masl], high [4,000 masl and above] (Combapata Municipal Government 2000). The distinction between these zones is based primarily on the flora and fauna that exist or can survive at that altitude (See John Murra's [1981, 1985] work on the idea of vertical ecology).

19. Sampling for surveys included both households that participated with WVI and households that did not. All sampled households in Orosccocha reported that they participate with WVI.

20. Orosccocha is a small community of 52 households, and the sample size (n=10) reflects 19 percent of the population. Approximately 20 percent of households were sampled in each of the five studied communities, in which male and female participants were equally represented among those surveyed.

21. While some WVI staff members are Evangelical Protestants and do occasionally express disdain for Catholic practices and beliefs in personal conversations, I never observed a staff member speaking badly of Catholicism to participants or other non-Evangelical staff members.

Works Cited

Andrade, Susana. 1990. *Visión mundial: Entre el cielo y la tierra. Religión y desarrollo en la sierra ecuatoriana*. Quito: Abya-Yala CEPLAES.

Arce, Moisés. 2005. *Market reform in society: Post-crisis politics and economic change in authoritarian Peru*. University Park, PA: Pennsylvania State University Press.

Avila, Javier. 2000. Los dilemas del desarrollo: Antropología y promoción en el Perú. In *No hay país más diverso: Compendio de antropología peruana*, ed. Carlos Iván Degregori, 413-42. Lima: Red para el Desarrollo de las Ciencias Sociales en el Perú.

Bornstein, Erica. 2001. Child sponsorship, evangelism and belonging in the work of World Vision Zimbabwe. *American Ethnologist*. 28(3):595-622.

———. 2002. Developing faith: Theologies of economic development in Zimbabwe. *Journal of Religion in Africa*. 32(1):4-31.

———. 2005. *The spirit of development: Protestant NGOs, morality, and economics in Zimbabwe*. Stanford, CA: Stanford University Press.

Combapata Municipal Government. 2000. *Plan urbano de ordenamiento del centro de Combapata*. Cusco, Peru: Combapata Municipal Government.

Cruz, Marcelo. 1999. Competing strategies for modernization in the Ecuadorean Andes. *Current Anthropology*. 40(3):377–83.

Dancourt, Oscar. 1999. Neoliberal reforms and macroeconomic policy in Peru. *CEPAL Review* 67:51-73.

Giddens, Anthony. 1984. *The constitution of society*. Berkeley: University of California Press.

Gonzales de Olarte, Efraín. 1998. *El neoliberalismo a la peruana: economía política del ajuste estructural, 1990-1997*. Lima: Instituto de Estudios Peruanos.

———. 2000. *Neocentralismo y neoliberalismo en el Perú*. Lima, Peru: Instituto de Estudios Peruanos.

Guamán Gualli, Julián. 2005. Visión mundial en el ámbito del desarrollo local. In *Experiencias en gestión y desarrollo local*, ed. Mario Unda, 85-199. Quito: Centro de investigaciones CIUDAD, Universidad Andina Simón Bolívar.

Malqui, Cesar, Ronald Torres Bringas, Guadalupe Hinojosa, Hernán Vásquez Arellán, Tanya Reynaga Liguria, and Rosario Maribel Vásquez Flores. 2007. *Evaluación intermedia del programa de desarollo del area Salcca: Informe final de evaluación*. Cusco, Peru: World Vision Peru Office of Monitoring and Evaluation.

Murra, John. 1981. Socio-political and demographic aspects of multi-altitude land use in the Andes. In *L'homme et son environnement á haute altitude*, ed. CNRS, 129-35. Paris: Séminaire CNRS NSF.

———. 1985. "El archipiélago vertical" revisited. In *Andean ecology and civilization: An interdisciplinary perspective on ecological complementarity*, ed. S. Masuda, I. Shimada, and C. Morris, 3-14. Tokyo: Tokyo University Press.

Pfeiffer, James. 2004. Civil society, NGOs, and the Holy Spirit in Mozambique. *Human Organization* 63(3):359-72.

Portocarrero, Felipe S., Cynthia Sanborn, Hanny Cueva, and Armando Millán. 2002. *Más allá del individualismo: el tercer sector en el Perú*. Lima, Peru: Universidad del Pacífico.

Starn, Orin, Carlos Iván Degregori, and Robin Kirk, eds. 1995. *The Peru reader: History, culture, and politics*. Durham, NC: Duke University Press.

Stafford, Tim. 2005. The Colossus of care: World Vision has become an international force—and a partner with the poor. *Christianity Today* 49(3).

Tripp, Linda. 1999. Gender and development from a Christian perspective: Experience from World Vision. *Gender and Development.* 7(1):523-43.

World Vision International. Home page. http://www.worldvision.org (last accessed December 2, 2008).

WVI Cusco. 2006. *Nuestra inversion en la niñez.* Cusco, Peru: WVI Cusco.

———. 2007. WVI Cusco. *Aprendiendo a vivir mejor.* Cusco, Peru: WVI Cusco.

Chapter 9
A Chilean Faith-based NGO's Social Service Mission in the Context of Neoliberal Reform

Javier Pereira, Ronald J. Angel, and Jacqueline L. Angel

Introduction

During the 1970s and 1980s the nations of Latin America adopted wide ranging market-based neoliberal reforms in response to serious economic and debt crises as well as directives from multilateral agencies including the World Bank and the International Development Bank. Although each nation introduced its own structural reforms, in general these involved the privatization of important economic functions, the decentralization of planning and management, and government retreat from the direct delivery of social services. Although these reforms had their intended effect of stimulating aggregate growth, structural adjustments that included drastically reduced public spending had a serious impact on the well-being of the poorest segments of the population. In nations with high levels of income inequality and poorly developed and articulated social service and health care systems, the result was an increase in poverty and growing inequities in access to basic social services, including health care (Lloyd-Sherlock 2000). Although the neoliberal reforms were introduced in all sectors of the economy, in this discussion we focus on the impact of structural readjustment policies on access to social services for the poor and the response by civil society to the retreat by the state from the direct responsibility for the delivery of such services. In order to focus the discussion we consider one faith-based non-governmental organization in Chile and deal primarily with its elder care functions as an example of the organization's response to a new set of social needs that accompany the rapid aging of the population.

Chile was at the forefront of market based reforms in the delivery of social services, and its experience with basic structural adjustments provides insights into the intersecting roles of the state, the market, and the non-governmental sector in addressing basic human needs. In the context of authoritarian military governments and the state's retreat from direct social service delivery, non-governmental organizations of necessity assumed greater importance. Many new organizations came into being, and older organizations found themselves confronting new challenges. In different countries the Catholic Church responded to both social service and human rights challenges differently. In Argentina the Church hierarchy often allied itself with the dictatorship (Verbitsky 2006). In Chile, on the other hand, the Catholic Church assumed the role of defender of human rights and largely opposed the most blatant abuses of the military government.

In what follows we present a description of perhaps the most important Catholic NGO in Chile, *Hogar de Cristo*, review its history and structure, and assess its role in providing social services to the poor. Given the extent of need among all age groups, Hogar de Cristo's original mission to minister to poor street dwellers expanded to include the care of other needy groups. As the social and political situation has changed, Hogar de Cristo's role has evolved and extended into such domains as the care of destitute and dependent elderly individuals. Hogar de Cristo's success has clearly been facilitated by the fact that Chile is a staunchly Catholic nation in which the Catholic Church is a powerful social institution. In many ways this makes Hogar de Cristo unique, and its successes may be hard to duplicate elsewhere. Nonetheless, identifying the major sources of this organization's effectiveness is theoretically useful, and an examination of its operation can potentially provide practical lessons concerning the role of faith-based initiatives in the alleviation of human suffering generally. In what follows we investigate the institutional, political, and social factors that account for Hogar de Cristo's success.

The Evolution of Neoliberalism in Practice: A New Role for Faith-Based NGOs

For purposes of discussion we divide the period from the original neoliberal reforms of the 1970s to the present into three somewhat arbitrary periods. The first phase consists of the original radical privatization and decentralization initiatives that profoundly changed the social contract in Chile and undermined the state's traditional paternalistic role in social services. In the 1980s, reformers called for the radical introduction of a neoliberal orthodoxy and the retreat of the state from productive and social services. During this period the responsibility for social service delivery was shifted from governmental agencies to NGOs and other civil society entities. This shift in responsibility for social service delivery included an increase in the level of funding directed to private organizations, as well as an increase in the number of contracts granted to NGOs. The objective of these reforms was greater economic efficiency.

The second phase consists of a period during the 1980s and 1990s characterized by a response to the serious social dislocations that the retreat of the state and the heavy reliance on the market introduced, especially for the most vulnerable citizens. There was a strong focus on managerial reforms in an attempt to achieve greater efficiency in public management. It was during this period that the concept of citizen participation in management and policy decisions was introduced into the discourse on reform. Such participation was intended to increase equity in access to services and provide a mechanism for assuring improvements in the quality of public services and greater transparency in their administration. In health care the new impetus toward client and community participation was reflected in the growth in the number of patient committees and a rhetoric that called for community input into the management of public hospitals and clinics. The objective was to increase system responsiveness to citizens' needs and to introduce greater client orientation into the system as a whole. Yet in reality continuing decentralization and economic and administrative rationalization meant that civil society and patient participation in governance and real citizen input in the key phases of planning and administration was limited. The role of NGOs in social services, including health care, increased and became more institutionalized. Through this period civil society organizations continued in their role of providers of services rather than serving as policy advocates or guarantors of citizen and patient rights (González Bombal, Garay, and Potenza 2003; Bebbington and Farrington 1993; Nelson 1995; Vivian 1994). In general, the second-wave reforms with their focus on increased equity and citizen participation showed mixed results, but they clearly signaled the emergence of a new state/civil society relationship that rejected an excessive reliance on either the state or the market. It was clear that although the neoliberal market-based orthodoxy that defined the first wave of reforms might be modified, the more open and competitive models of social service delivery were here to stay.

The third phase, which continues today, represents a period in which the state's role, as well as civil society's role, is being redefined. It represents an attempt to introduce corrective measures to deal with the effects of the withdrawal of the state from direct responsibility for social welfare that was part of the first wave. This third wave involves an ongoing process of reaffirmation, and in many important ways a recentralization, of regulatory and monitoring functions of the state. While decentralization and municipalization continue to be the objectives in service delivery, the clear necessity of national and regional coordination makes the need for a significant state role clear. The third wave seeks to further redefine the role of the community in the planning and oversight of social service delivery, as well as to extend the benign supervisory and coordinating role of the state.

Decentralization and the devolution of responsibilities and administrative roles to more local levels of governance informed the core logic of the first wave of neoliberal reforms. Today we are witnesses to a process of the "recentralization" of oversight and coordination functions. If the state's role ceases to be that of a direct service provider, its new role consists of greater system rationalization and oversight (Barrientos 2000). Such recentralization, though, is informed by a clear understanding of the state's limitations in its capacity for coordination and control. In the new regime, civil society organizations continue to play a central role and, theoretically, provide effective mechanisms for enhancing transparency and the sort of rationalization that maximizes system outputs while assuring the greatest level of equity. The new phase of reforms recognizes the role of civil society organizations and NGOs as "embedded" within those of the state (De la Maza 2000; Evans 1996). This new public/private partnership philosophy acknowledges the artificial distinction between state and society upon which most traditional health care systems are based and conceives of the relationship as highly interconnected.

The tasks that remain for the third wave include the further consolidation of democracy and the assurance of citizen participation, local control, and greater equity in the assurance of social rights. The challenge in this new phase of reform, as it was during the second, is to foster basic social rights, while assuring that the system as a whole remains modern, flexible, and competitive (Fernández and Ochsenius 2006). Few would advocate returning to the past, and the reality of a relatively high degree of privatization and rationalization in the direct provision of services represents the new norm. Any new reform in the delivery of health care must take this new reality into account. In this new economic and political environment, civil society organizations, including NGOs, have a new and important role, one that is different from the adversarial posture that many assumed during the dictatorship. Today, NGOs face the traditional dilemma of balancing the roles of service provider and advocate for the powerless. As service providers NGOs run the risk of depoliticization and becoming agents of the state rather than advocates for basic social change.

Along with the evolution of social policies related to social service delivery, today a new discourse has emerged in the discussion of the role of civil society in Latin America generally. Growing concern with the failure of previous reforms to address the problems of serious inequities in access to and quality of social services has resulted in an increased interest in the concept of "active citizenship" and the empowerment of consumers and users of services to allow them to participate in the decision-making processes concerning the distribution and nature of services. Many parties, including the multilateral agencies that originally championed neoliberal reforms, have recognized the need to increase citizen and community involvement in the planning and administration of health care services in order to assure the legitimacy and sustainability of reform efforts (Chiara and di Virgilio 2005; Tussie, Mendiburu, and Vázques 1997). In the health care sector, for example, this new focus has resulted in a series of reforms intended to increase civil society and citizen input into management and policy decisions. As of yet, the ways in which this objective can be effectively achieved are not clear, but the changing discourse in which problems of equity are directly addressed is promising.

Social Security for the Elderly

Like most other Latin American nations, Chile has traditionally looked to the family as the primary source of care for the old and infirm (Soldo and Freedman 1994). In developed nations, the needs of these individuals are largely addressed through the market, at least for the middle class. In Chile market-based solutions for the care of the poor and infirm are rare. Institutional long-term care for those in need is simply too expensive for the majority of families or for the nation as a whole. In 2002, for example, fewer than two percent of elderly Chileans resided in nursing homes (Marín, Guzmán, and Araya 2004). Of course, for the poor market solutions are irrelevant. For these individuals the absence of a formal state-sponsored safety net means that someone else must provide support or they must do without. This population is the most seriously affected by the lack of formal support services, and it was the segment of the overall population most harmed by neoliberal reforms. In order to focus our discussion of Hogar de Cristo's role, we pay particular attention to its role in the care of destitute and infirm elderly persons.

From our perspective, Hogar de Cristo is a civil society organization despite the clear power of the Church in Chile. As we noted earlier, during the initial neoliberal reform period civil society organizations were largely confined to the role of subcontractors to public agencies. For the most part, their role was limited to the provision of services in exchange for funding, and their role in the design of any new system of distribution was limited. One result was growing criticism of the exclusion of NGOs and other civil society organizations from the policy debate, design, and implementation processes. The continuing discussion of participation is partially a response to the restricted service delivery roles that many NGOs accepted. Even with greater focus on the political aspects of service delivery, though, NGOs remain major service delivery organizations and in Chile their applied roles are, if anything, expanding.

Data

Our assessment of Hogar de Cristo's elder care functions is based on published and unpublished sources (Lowick-Russell, Parga, and Carmona 2004) and in-depth interviews with directors and secretarial staff. The first author conducted seven interviews with Hogar de Cristo personnel, including high-level officers of the organization. This data collection effort was part of a larger project focused on the role of NGOs in the provision of health services in the Southern

Cone. The project's fieldwork also included in-depth interviews with members and directors of health related NGOs (twelve), governmental health service providers including municipal and ministerial services (nine), public health administrators and officials (seven), users and clients of health services (eighteen), academic informants and consultants (eleven), and one representative of the most important Chilean NGO association (Acción). Interviews were preceded or followed by direct observations at four different facilities in Santiago, including the central headquarters of Hogar de Cristo in Estación Central. Lastly, two former employees of the organization now living in the city of Austin, Texas also served as valuable sources of information for checking data and providing additional insights.

Hogar de Cristo's Role in Elder Care

Hogar de Cristo was founded in 1944 by Father Alberto Hurtado, a Jesuit priest who felt compelled to respond to the large number of homeless people in Santiago. By 1951 the organization had already provided shelter to 700,000 people and distributed 1,800,000 meals (Erlick 2002). Initially, the elderly did not represent a core focus but have come to represent a large fraction of the clientele served. In addition to its mission of ministering to the needs of the poor, Hogar de Cristo's activities include advocacy and public relations aimed at raising the public's awareness of the problem of poverty in Chile. Since its beginning Hogar de Cristo has become professionalized and has adopted managerial, administrative, and fund-raising strategies that have allowed it to increase private donations and avoid dependency on the state or on the Catholic Church. In 2002, nearly 32,000 people received services daily (AmeriSpan 2004). In Santiago alone, 2,654 clients aged sixty and over receive services on a daily basis. National survey data indicate that Hogar de Cristo is the most trusted organization in the country (CERC 1996). Although religion remains an intrinsic part of the organization's life, employees, volunteers, and those who receive help can be of any religion.

From the perspective of institutional theory, we may see Hogar de Cristo's full range of services as an adaptive response to a changing elder care environment, where purposive institutional design, resource control and management, and the avoidance of dependency are key elements of its effectiveness (Scott 1995; Meyer and Scott 1992). Viewed as incomplete social systems, NGOs in general and Hogar de Cristo in particular are challenged to "manage dependency" as they seek the resources to reproduce institutional structures and maintain legitimacy at the same time that they retain autonomy in order to accomplish their care mission in a changing environment. The successful resolution of the tension between resource generation and the need to maintain autonomy requires some degree of professionalization in terms of organizational structure, management, and the supervision and skills of the care providers. High levels of specialization and expertise, training of staff and volunteers to provide high-quality services, and the advancement of a professional institutional environment emerge as salient institutional features that may allow for effectiveness and service scaling-up. The successful NGO, then, must combine the often conflicting needs of organizational professionalization and bureaucratization and the desire to remain close to the community and clients on which its unique approach is based.

Among those deemed to be in greatest need are elderly couples and individuals with low levels of autonomy who are living alone, elder persons who are providing care to a disabled family member, and older persons living in families that lack the economic resources to provide for the older person's needs (Hogar de Cristo 2004). This formal targeting of services is based on the recognition that the elderly do not comprise a homogeneous population. For certain individuals, especially those who were unable to save or accumulate assets during their working years, old age brings with it the serious risk of poverty and illness. Those with the fewest social and economic resources are the individuals that are often not well served by poorly coordinated government programs. Within the population in need each individual's situation represents a combination of unique factors that require personalized intervention strategies. In order to address complex needs, individuals with a wide range of professional skills and knowledge of the community participate in the elder care programs.

The increasing share of the elderly among the organization's target population and the growing challenge it faces in providing assistance to families in the community who care for elderly individuals require new adaptations. Hogar de Cristo offers a continuum of care that addresses the full range of needs. The four options that make up the continuum include: (1) in-home assistance; (2) day care centers; (3) self-managed residential homes; and (4) protected residential homes. On a daily basis the organization serves 2,654 older individuals through these programs in Santiago. Several factors are considered when determining an elderly person's eligibility for admission to residential programs. These include age (one must be sixty years old or over); income (one's family income must be lower than the poverty threshold, which was 40,000 Chilean pesos in 2005, or approximately 68 U.S. dollars per month); available housing quality and safety (one must be homeless or living in substandard housing or the victim of mistreatment/violence); and health (suffering from alcohol abuse, and/or afflicted with a disease or health problem) (Lowick-Russell, Parga, and Carmona 2004).

The types of services the organization provides to community residents include transportation to health care facilities, help with medications, legal and financial assistance, and help with food, household items, clothing, and other daily necessities. Another intervention model is embodied in social support programs that are focused on the prevention of isolation. These programs are based in day care centers that provide educational services, recreational activities, occupational therapy, family intervention, nutritional and health information, transportation to and from the centers, assistance with hygiene and hairdressing, laundry services, household repair, temporary care, and other services as needed. These services overlap and complement those of the independent living initiatives.

The most ambitious and extensive interventions are part of the organization's housing and assistance programs, which include institutionalization in the most serious cases. Hogar de Cristo is perhaps unique in actually providing long-term care in its own facilities. These programs are geared toward those elderly individuals who are too impaired, or who do not have the family resources, to live in the community. These residential services, which are offered on a temporary or longer-term basis depending on need, are provided in housing units where the residents receive the full range of services offered by the other programs. In Santiago a total of 1,260 people receive services in these residential facilities (Hogar de Cristo 2004).

Hogar de Cristo's success has led to an increasing demand for its elder care services. To help fill the gap, the NGO has supported the work of service delivery entities by signing *convenios* (contractual agreements) with third-party organizations through which they supervise, monitor, and fund elder care services. These subcontracts include such ancillary service providers as foundations, parishes, other NGOs, and religious congregations. These third parties administer aspects of the service delivery programs, and in certain cases they also contribute funding and infrastructure. For the most part, though, Hogar de Cristo funds the subcontractors and provides supervision, consultation, and assistance with the targeting through its centralized screening procedures for determining who receives services. Such subcontracted services represent a large share of the total number of individuals served. In 2003, for example, while 831 individuals were housed in Hogar de Cristo's own long-term care homes, 378 were in subcontracted home situations. Of the 606 individuals receiving day care services, 335 were served by subcontractors.

Reflecting its high level of professionalization, Hogar de Cristo employs best practice management techniques and innovative fund-raising strategies. The fact that the organization receives relatively little of its funding from the state makes it an exception to other NGOs in the region. Indeed many NGOs have become little more than state agencies, a fact that has resulted in much criticism (Gideon 1998). Although Hogar de Cristo is a faith-based organization, it does not receive direct funding from the Catholic Church (Nonprofit Enterprise and Self-sustainability Team 2000) although it does receive funds from national and international Catholic fund-raising sources. Most of Hogar de Cristo's financial support comes from private donations rather than public funds or private grants (Nonprofit Enterprise and Self-sustainability Team 2000). Hogar de Cristo offers membership and the organization has strong membership support, which is a major factor that allows it to remain financially independent. An important source of revenue is a funeral home founded in 1954. The project was begun in response to the fact that many Chileans could not afford to pay the burial expenses and other costs associated with the death of a loved one. The funeral home has contracts with *Parque del Recuerdo* (Memory Park) cemetery, *Prever* (a funeral service company), and *Cinerario Hogar de Cristo* (a crematory). One of the most effective fund-raising mechanisms is the selling of *Coronas de Caridad* (Crowns of Charity), which are memorial cards that convey expressions of love for a departed loved one and serve as replacements for traditional funeral wreaths. These cards have become a national symbol throughout Chile and are a valued vehicle for expressing affection while supporting the work of the organization.

Hogar de Cristo's fund-raising capacity is so highly developed that it has, in practice, become a foundation and it serves as a source of funding for other organizations, NGOs, and grassroots projects. In recent years international donor agencies have reduced their contributions to intermediary NGOs in Latin America. In this environment Hogar de Cristo's capacity for self-sufficiency in fund-raising has persisted and makes it stand out within the NGO domain. Hogar de Cristo employs a very detailed system of accountability. Every unit keeps detailed records of all services provided, persons served, and money spent. This information is transmitted to a central accounting department which compiles the data. The detailed system of accountability enables the organization to calculate the daily cost of the different services provided to recipients, including the elderly. The informational system is very important for planning, identifying inefficiency and waste, and identifying effective and ineffective programs. Since the organization raises the majority of its funds from the general public, public accountability is more of an issue than governmental accountability. The public favorably views the organization because of its reputation and commitment to service (Nonprofit Enterprise and Self-sustainability Team 2000).

Conclusion

This case study offers several insights into the potential role of faith-based civil society organizations in providing social services to vulnerable individuals and communities in contexts in which state-sponsored services are unavailable or inadequate. As the Chilean population ages and the long-term care needs of the elderly increase, the role of NGOs in their care will evolve. The question we end with is whether Hogar de Cristo offers a useful paradigm for other nations to follow or whether this organization and its context are so unique as to offer few generalizable findings. The attempt to understand the sources of the success of organizations like Hogar de Cristo is important for several reasons. Perhaps the most important of these is the fact that the state is not well suited to directly provide assistance to all elderly individuals who might need it. The state is best suited to deal with issues related to defense, the regulation of commerce, international relations, and the provision of high-cost technical health care. Much of what older dependent individuals need is low-cost, nontechnical, and best provided by family members or volunteers who are in close contact with the person.

The aging of the populations of Latin America will only increase the old age dependency burden for families and states. Under the leadership of President Ricardo Lagos, and now Michelle Bachelet, the Chilean government has made health care reform a major priority. In theory, the newly implemented health reform plan (Plan AUGE) grants free universal basic health coverage in public clinics and hospitals to all Chileans over the age of sixty suffering from a select set of illnesses. Yet the elderly have many other needs that the formal system cannot address, and, as a result of the privatization of health care, a two-tiered system of care has emerged in which the elderly are disadvantaged. In Chile today the public health system, FONASA, provides care to the poor, a population that includes many elderly, while a minority of younger and wealthier individuals is privately insured (Rojas 1998). The public and private systems differ not only in terms of the age and income of their beneficiaries, but in terms of health service utilization patterns and the quality of care provided as well. The shift of elderly individuals to the public system represents a potentially serious increased burden for the public system and lower quality care for recipients.

It is clear from our analysis that even though Hogar de Cristo has enjoyed great success, the state clearly defines the operational environment in which it carries out its functions. The state's influence and the means in which it structures the regulatory, market, and organizational environment in which civil society organizations operate is manifested through several mechanisms. These include the state's policies of the privatization of service delivery, the decentralization of services and a greater emphasis on municipal administration, and democratization. While these create greater opportunities for civil society in framing and addressing social problems, they also alter civil society organizations' relationships not only to the state, but to other organizations as well.

As we noted in the introduction, the evolution of civil society in Chile has changed the relationship of the non-governmental sector to the state. During the 1970s, in the context of the highly politicized Pinochet regime, Hogar de Cristo adopted a position of political neutrality as a strategy to effectively engage in service delivery and to counteract some of the negative effects of the government's neoliberal economic and social service reforms. With the upsurge of participatory politics in the postdictatorship era (Paley 2002), the organization cautiously adopted a more contentious language characteristic of the rights rhetoric that pervaded Chilean social programs of the 1990s. While remaining loyal to its politics of neutrality, the organization progressively adopted a public stance that drew greater attention to the rights and aspirations of socially excluded elder groups.

Despite this shift, though, the organization's relation to the state is clearly one of greater practical cooperation. In 2004, for example, the national health system, FONASA, and Hogar de Cristo entered into an agreement designed to expand the social safety network and health coverage to older individuals in poor households. Recipients of the national antipoverty program "Chile Solidario" or eligible patients sixty years of age or older may be transferred after discharge from public services to a Hogar de Cristo facility. As part of this agreement, within five days of an individual's discharge from the public facility Hogar de Cristo assumes responsibility for the provision of integral medical treatment to those with any of a select set of the most common illnesses. In this way Hogar de Cristo clearly augments the limited service capacity of the public system and furthers the privatization initiative that has formed the core of Chilean social policy since the Pinochet administration. In addition to complementing the caregiving functions of FONASA Hogar de Cristo engages in community outreach to inform the population about the new benefits of Chilean health reform (Plan AUGE). In conjunction with the medical school at the Universidad Santiago de Chile Hogar de Cristo is participating in a national campaign to inform poor communities about eligibility criteria and the group of pathologies that are covered by Plan AUGE. The new Chilean President, Michelle Bachelet, has stated elder care priorities that are clear extensions of the system in which Hogar de Cristo plays a major role.

Despite the state's role in defining the organizational environment in which Hogar de Cristo operates and the increasing cooperation with the government in providing services to the elderly we must reemphasize the uniqueness of Hogar de Cristo in the extent to which it has been able to avoid economic dependency on the state. Many NGOs function largely as state agencies in carrying out mandates funded by governmental agencies (Arellano-Lopez and Petras 1995). It may well be the case that Hogar de Cristo will move further in this direction in the future. Its independence from the state does not come without costs, though; perhaps most notably in the fact that even given its size Hogar de Cristo does not have the resources to adequately address the full range of needs of poor elderly Chileans. Even as it has expanded its services in the area of elder care, the limitations of Hogar de Cristo's reach make the inherent limitations of such a nonstate approach obvious. Most high-tech and complicated medical services remain in the domain of public hospitals. In health and social services our study suggests that NGOS are best suited to labor-intensive rather than high-cost technology-intensive functions.

Hogar de Cristo is also unique in the extent to which it has been able to avoid the difficulties that emerge with the need to compete with other organizations for scarce resources, including funding. As we noted, Hogar de Cristo's relationship with other NGOs and similar organizations is one of sponsorship or contractor. The position of the Catholic Church in Chile represents a major source of social and cultural power, and Hogar de Cristo's institutional survival is assured by the unique conditions that grant it a great amount of popular support, a large contributing membership, and a favorable and valuable public image. Whether aspects of this organizational success could be adopted by or transferred to other nongovernmental organizations remains to be seen.

Acknowledgments

We gratefully acknowledge support for this project from the Policy Research Institute, International Program, the RGK Center for Philanthropy and Community Service, LBJ School of Public Affairs, and the Population Research Center, University of Texas, Austin.

Works Cited

AmeriSpan. 2004. Private shelter for elderly adults. http://www.amerispan.com/volunteer_intern/VolunteerProgramDetail.asp?Volunteer_Program_ID=288 (last accessed March 3, 2005).

Arellano-Lopez, Sonia, and James Petras. 1994. Non governmental organizations and poverty alleviation in Bolivia. *Development and Change* 25(3):555-68.

Barrientos, Armando. 2000. Getting better after neoliberalism: Shifts and challenges of health policy in Chile. In *Healthcare reform and poverty in Latin America*, ed. P. Lloyd-Sherlock, 94-111. London: University of London, Institute of Latin American Studies.

Bebbington, A., and J. Farrington. 1993. Governments, NGOs and agricultural development: Perspectives on changing inter-organizational relationships. *Journal of Development Studies* 29:199-219.

Centro de Estudios de la Realidad Contemporánea (CERC). 1996. National Survey of Trusted Organizations. La confianza en las instituciones. *Diario El Mercurio* (Santiago), p. 31, November 24.

Chiara, Magdalena, and Mercedes di Virgilio. 2005. *Gestión social y municipios: De los escritorios del Banco Mundial a los barrios del Gran Buenos Aires*. Buenos Aires: Prometeo Libros-UNGS.

De la Maza, Gonzalo. 2000. Sociedad civil y construcción de capital social en America Latina: Hacia donde va la investigación? In *4th International Conference of the International Society for Third Sector Research*. Dublin: ISTR.

Erlick, June Carolyn 2002. Chile's Hogar de Cristo. Tradition and modernity. *Revista* Spring 2002:23-24.

Evans, Peter. 1996. Government action, social capital and development: Reviewing the evidence on synergy. *World Development* 24:1119-32.

Fernández, Margarita, and Carlos Ochsenius. 2006. *Innovaciones, arreglos institucionales y participación ciudadana: Contribuciones a la reforma de salud*. Santiago: Universidad de los Lagos.

Gideon, Jasmine. 1998. The politics of social service provision through NGOs: A study of Latin America. *Bulletin of Latin American Research* 17:303-321.

González Bombal, Inés; Candelaria Garay, and Fernanda Potenza. 2003. *Organizaciones de la sociedad civil y políticas sociales en la Argentina de los noventa*. Buenos Aires: Universidad San Andres/CEDES.

Hogar de Cristo. 2004. *Adulto mayor*. http://www.hogardecristo.com/hacemos/a_mayor.htm (last accessed March 3, 2005).

———. 2005. *Aspiraciones y expectativas de los adultos mayores: Una consulta participativa*. Santiago: Universidad del Desarrollo—Hogar de Cristo.

Lloyd-Sherlock, Peter. 2000. *Healthcare reform and poverty in Latin America*. London: Institute of Latin American Studies, University of London.

Lowick-Russell, J., M. I. Parga, and G. Carmona. 2004. Una experiencia a compartir. El trabajo del Hogar de Cristo con los adultos mayores. Santiago: Fundación de Beneficencia Hogar de Cristo.

Marín, L., Pedro Paulo, José Miguel Guzmán M., and Alejandra Araya G. 2004. Adultos mayores institucionalizados en Chile: ¿Cómo saber cuántos son? *Revista médica de Chile*, 132(7):832-38.

Meyer, J. W., and W. Richard Scott. 1992. *Organizational environments: Ritual and rationality.* London: Sage.

Nelson, Paul. 1995. *The World Bank and nongovernmental organizations: The limits of apolitical development.* New York: St. Martin's Press.

Nonprofit Enterprise and Self-sustainability Team. 2000. *Hogar de Cristo, Mobilizing local resources.* http://www.nesst.org/documents/HogardeCristoinglespage1FINAL.pdf (last accessed March 3, 2005).

Paley, Julia. 2002. Toward an anthropology of democracy. *Annual Review of Anthropology* 31:1469-96.

Rojas, Patricio. 1998. Sistema de salud de Chile. *Cuadernos Médico-Sociales* 39:46-53.

Scott, W. R. 1995. *Institutions and organizations.* Thousand Oaks, CA: Sage.

Soldo, B. J., and V. A Freedman. 1994. Care of the elderly: Division of labor among the family, market, and state. In *Demography of Aging*, ed. Linda G. Martin and Samuel H. Preston, 195-216. Washington, DC: National Academy Press.

Tussie, Diana, Marcos Mendiburu, and Patricia Vázques. 1997. Los nuevos mandatos de los bancos multilaterales de desarrollo: Su aplicación al caso de Argentina. In *El BID, el Banco Mundial y la sociedad civil sus nuevas modalidades de financiamiento internacional*, ed. Diana Tussie, 63-98. Buenos Aires: FLACSO / Oficina de Publicaciones del CBC-UBA.

Verbitsky, Horacio. 2006. *Doble juego: La Argentina católica y militar.* Buenos Aires: Editorial Sudamericana.

Vivian, J. 1994. NGOs and sustainable development in Zimbabwe: No magic bullets. *Development and Change* 25:167-93.

Chapter 10
Faith-Related Education NGOs in Latin America: The case of Fe y Alegría in Peru
Paul A. Peters

Faith-related NGOs have a long history of providing social services in development contexts. The diverse collection of social service, advocacy, research, and evangelical groups that comprise faith-related NGOs are often promoted as an effective and efficient means to reach target populations and respond to rapidly changing needs. Religious and faith-related agencies are involved in such diverse areas as poverty alleviation, provision of education services, low-income housing, and health care provision. Commonly stated benefits of these agencies stem from their innate ability to interact with civil society, their emphasis on efficiency, their promotion of individual responsibility, and the encouragement for clients to become personally invested in their own well-being (Smith and Sosin 2001). The benefits of faith-based agencies often follow those promoted by neoliberal policies whereby NGOs are seen as a new form of social agent that can represent specific societal interests and respond more efficiently to the needs of populations. However, critical enquiry of neoliberal reforms, particularly in Latin America, questions the move to social service provision by NGOs from more traditional organizational activities (Arce 2006; Bebbington 2004; Cowen and Shenton 1995; Olson 2006).

Inherent in much of the discussion surrounding faith-related agencies is the assumption that these organizations operate differently than non-faith-related agencies in the way that they administer services, cooperate with the state and market, and interact with civil society. Some authors suggest that the perceived benefits of these agencies are causally linked to their connection with religion, such that it is religion *itself* that provides the benefit to individuals and society (DiIulio 2002). With an increasing proportion of social services being provided by civil society agencies, many of which are faith related, it is important to understand what aspects of faith and the agency's relation to faith provide for any increased effectiveness and, more importantly, whether it is religion in and of itself that provides these apparent benefits.

Theories of social capital are often cited to explain the positive effects of religious affiliation, whereby the sacred commitment to God and social closure within the community are important sources of social capital. Starting from the assumption whereby faith-related agencies are assumed to have benefits *above and beyond* their secular counterparts, this article questions whether it is the affiliation of these agencies *in and of itself* that provides the benefit, or if this can be obtained via other social mechanisms. The implications of this discussion extend to both sides of the argument: those that desire to see faith agencies play an increased role in providing state and market services, and those that question the motives and abilities of such agencies. The results of this paper suggest that it is not religious affiliation in and of itself that provides for the perceived effectiveness and efficiency of these agencies. Rather, the flexible organizational structures of NGOs in general, coupled with the legitimacy and authority afforded by faith relationships, allow these organizations to operate more freely and to promote positive organizational myths that support their actions.

This article deconstructs the organizational myths of faith-related education NGOs in Latin America. Using the organization Fe y Alegría as a starting point, the features of faith-related agencies are examined in relation to the role of social service agencies within neoliberal contexts. Theoretical and empirical evidence from educational sociology suggest that this religiously based organization would, as a provider of basic educational services, provide additional benefit to the school and community. Additionally, neoliberal policies promote such organizations as an alternative to the (assumed) highly regulated and inefficient public system, where the economic costs are borne outside the public sector with social benefits realized by often disadvantaged communities. The purpose of this chapter is to examine the assumptions that faith-related NGOs are somehow "better" than others and are "different" from other types of public service provision. This examination is from a largely theoretical perspective and provides a basis for understanding faith-related agencies in neoliberal development contexts.

Organizational Structure and Legitimacy

To begin with, this chapter discusses the manner by which organizational legitimacy is created by these organizations within a given community. Relating legitimacy to the aims of neoliberalism, the approach taken here is to examine formal organizational structures that promote the liberalization of markets for goods, services, and factors of production. An area where this has been prevalent is in the provision of basic education, especially in impoverished areas. National governments in Latin America have placed a greater emphasis on education as a means of national socioeconomic development programs. While some of the increases have been for public education programs, large components have been directed to fostering private education provision, including that by NGOs. How these agencies operate as mechanisms to increase social capital and the manner by which legitimacy is formed by organizational structures is not completely understood.

Neoinstitutionalist theory approaches the analysis of organizations by emphasizing the ways in which organizational environments shape structure and processes (DiMaggio 1998). Meyer and Rowan define formal organizations as "systems of coordinated and controlled activities that arise when work is embedded in complex networks of technical relations and boundary-spanning exchanges" (1977, 340). Their definition is based on a modern, institutionalized context in which "professions, policies, and programs are created along with the products and services that they are understood to produce rationally" (1977, 340). Organizations that employ methods embedded within the prevailing bureaucratic norms of society stand to increase their legitimacy and their prospects of survival, irrespective of the efficiency of their acquired practices and procedures. Institutional products, services, techniques, policies, and programs serve as myths which organizations may adopt ceremonially, often in conflict with organizational efficiency (Meyer and Rowan 1977). Thus, it is not the institutional elements themselves that support organizational legitimacy, but rather it is the interaction between myth and ceremony within the broader societal and bureaucratic environment. It is this final point from which the purported benefits of religious agencies can be dissected, whereby affiliated agencies can build upon the existing myth and ceremony of religion to construct legitimacy with target communities.

Meyer and Rowan additionally note that "institutional rules may have effects on organizational structures and their implementation in actual technical work which are very different from the effects generated by the networks of social behavior and relationships which compose and surround a given organization" (Meyer and Rowan 1977, 341). This is a useful point in that it stresses that organizations themselves are embedded within societal and bureaucratic structures and that these relationships have as much effect on organizational effectiveness as institutional rules and regulation. NGOs in general, and religiously related NGOs in particular, are heavily influenced by broader civil society and bureaucratic norms. This point is mirrored in educational literature, especially within environments such as Latin America where "context matters" (Peters and Hall 2004). However, unlike in public education systems where schools are clearly defined bureaucratic arrangements, NGO structures are diverse and the analysis of structure and agency is predicated by how these organizations are defined.

NGO Legitimacy

Legitimacy is a multifaceted concept that encompasses the regulatory (conformity with rules and laws), cognitive (conformity to societal norms), normative (congruence between organizational and societal values), and pragmatic (self-interest of an organization's clients) domains (Scott 1995; Suchman 1995). Legitimacy can be defined as "a generalized perception or assumption that the actions of an entity are desirable, proper, or appropriate within some socially constructed system of norms, values, beliefs, and definitions" (Suchman 1995, 575). This definition, as implied in the description of myth and ceremony above, emphasizes that the social construction of an organization's legitimizing environment varies by cultural, political, and economic contexts.

Lister (2003) further disaggregates the concept of legitimacy according to different organizational domains and target audiences. Different actors will focus on different characteristics or behaviors of an organization to develop perceptions of legitimacy. For example, in interaction with local actors, agencies will use language reflective of cultural traditions while in the interaction between funding agencies, language will reflect current international development norms. Importantly, Lister recognizes that the "approaches, interests, and perceptions of the stakeholders, not the agency, determine which characteristics create legitimacy" (Lister 2003, 179). In particular, agencies use myths and symbols to enhance their legitimacy with concerned actors and to justify internal agency goals. Legitimacy is dynamic, increasing and decreasing over time as broader views of development change. Organizational myths are constructed based on relationships with external actors as much as internal desires for efficiency. Thus, these agencies are able to flexibly adapt to both the attitudes of local actors and the desires of external funding agencies, creating legitimacy on multiple levels simultaneously.

For faith-related NGOs, as for faith itself, the construction and perpetuation of legitimacy is inherently linked to the perception of faith itself within the broader social environment (Weber 1946). Thus, the legitimacy of an NGO can be analyzed through its relation to the external environment, its multifaceted nature, and the use of symbols to enhance its legitimacy. It is through this last point that faith-related NGOs can be seen as advantaged, where the unique symbology created through identification with faith itself provides for an advantage for creating legitimacy within the broader societal context (Lister 2003). As with educational institutions, the exact nature of NGO faith relations is diverse, with the characteristics of these relationships influencing how organizations operate and are perceived.

Implications for Religious NGOs in Latin America

This section furthers the discussion of faith-related NGOs by examining a specific example of a faith-related NGO in Latin America. This example is pertinent to the other chapters in this volume as it highlights benefits and drawbacks from alignment with faith and exposes the ability of religion to provide legitimacy while at the same time stressing the importance of strong organizational frameworks. The NGO Fe y Alegría was started in 1955 in Venezuela, growing from ongoing missionary work in the slums of Caracas where education was seen not only as a means to improve the well-being of individuals but also to spread Christian values. Despite this explicit recognition of missionary work and religious conversion, the principal goal of Fe y Alegría is to provide a quality education to disadvantaged and marginalized children, with social development goals placed ahead of religious teachings. The founder of Fe y Alegría, Father Jose Maria Velaz, stated that "an uneducated person is a dominated person, a vulnerable person, and an oppressed person. In contrast, an educated person is a free person, a transformed person and an individual that controls their own destiny" (Fe y Alegría 2004). Education was thus perceived to be the major transformative force in society and, when combined with Christian service, could impart major change in individual lives and communities. It is this and other powerful statements that guide the programs and activities of Fe y Alegría and reinforce the construction of myth and ceremony as guided by the doctrine of the Catholic Church.

Mission and Values

Central to the construction of institutional structures are dominant mission and value statements that oversee program activities and services. The slogan of Fe y Alegría is a "Movement for Integral Popular Education and Social Development"—translated from the Spanish "*Movimiento de Educación Popular Integral y Promoción Social.*" The organization has chosen this slogan deliberately and defines how it meets each element of the slogan individually:

Movement – it unites people in the process of growth, self-criticism, and the search for answers to the challenges presented by human needs.
Education – it promotes the development of individuals who are cognizant of their own potential and the reality around them, who are free, committed, and who seek to be protagonists towards improving their own well-being.
Popular – it sees education as part of a political and pedagogical process for social transformation rooted in local communities.
Social Development – it makes a commitment to facing injustices and the needs of individuals in an effort to create a society that is just, fraternal, democratic, and participative (Fe y Alegría 2004).

While many of these terms lose some strength when translated into English and appear to be little more than rhetoric, the importance placed on social development is evident as is the link to Christian values. The stated mission of Fe y Alegría is further elaborated with clarification on how important aspects of its mission are to be interpreted by the broader organization. First, the term *popular education* is defined as a historical and social process whereby individuals and communities are supported in efforts to realize their own potential and become central actors in their own development path. It is felt that the desire for education should be initiated within communities themselves and reflect their own cultural and social expressions, so as to encourage participants to become active agents in the development of their own history. As a social process, education is strongly influenced by the unique conditions of the local community and seeks to provide individuals a voice of their own and in relation to other social groups.

Second, central to their mission is the term *educación integral*. This term, while having only a partial translation into English, can be roughly translated as "holistic education." The organization views this process as encompassing ordinary people in all the elements of their daily life (relationship to themselves, to nature, to God; their basic needs of food, clothing, shelter, and health; and their stage of personal growth). It attempts to view people from within their own historical context, with their own cultural, social, economic, political, and religious values—but with openness towards other cultures and worldviews. While there is a commitment to varied pedagogical processes and openness to institutional flexibility, all work is carried out in accordance with the Gospel and Christian values. This is reinforced by a commitment to an *evangelizing pedagogy* as a central element of their mission, whereby a relationship with God can bring liberation to individuals and allow integration into a broader community. These commitments mirror the sources of social capital as proposed by Coleman, whereby "the precept derived from religious doctrine that every individual is important in the eyes of God" can guide and inspire the pedagogical practices of educators (Coleman 1990, 321).

Organization of Fe y Alegría

From its inception, Fe y Alegría has been based on the premise that schools are to be built by and within the community, generally with the financial and labor contributions of parents. These initial roots are continued in the current organization, where communities not only initiate the request for a school, but also contribute to its construction and maintenance. Fe y Alegría has attempted to place ownership in the hands of the community and parents rather than the federal Ministry of Education, although they often work with both national-level ministries and regional offices to coordinate program planning and funding.

Local schools affiliated with Fe y Alegría have strong ties to the community, with parents and civic leaders encouraged to be intimately involved in daily activities. Schools are coordinated from a central district office where evaluation and program development is centered. Uniquely, each school is officially a public school, charging no fees to students. Teacher salaries are most often paid for by the government, although teacher housing and expenses are often paid by Fe y Alegría. Teachers in Fe y Alegría schools are generally selected by the organization itself, and additional training is provided above that required by national ministries (World Bank 2004). The national and regional offices of Fe y Alegría are committed to covering building costs, equipment, and innovative education programs (Podsiadlo 1998). Fe y Alegría works closely with all national ministries of education in developing the curriculum and materials for students in their schools, with many of the materials developed by Fe y Alegría, such as indigenous language textbooks, available to all other public schools throughout the country.

Overall coordination of programs is provided through the central office in Venezuela, although national offices enjoy a high degree of autonomy. The statement of guiding principles to which all schools in the system adhere is the International Mission Statement of Fe y Alegría elaborated above. Each national office develops its own mission statement, and each school within a federation has its own, locally developed mission statement. McMeekin characterizes this as a "network of networks," allowing a contextual flexibility for individual schools and regions (McMeekin 2003).

Many studies have found that Fe y Alegría schools perform better than their public counterparts (see below, Table 10.1), and they are described as a "more efficient type of public school" (Swope and Latorre 2000, 159). There are several reasons for these positive benefits. First, affiliation with the Catholic Church provides a common grounding in a region that has strong historical ties to the Catholic faith. Second, pedagogical inputs are important and schools are encouraged to develop their own teaching models and philosophies of education

Country	Gross Repetition Rates		Gross Dropout Rates	
	Fe y Alegría	*Public Schools*	*Fe y Alegría*	*Public Schools*
Peru	25.43	32.48	9.86	25.72
Bolivia	20.35	72.88	9.00	26.80
Venezuela	22.03	40.24	16.18	38.65
Nicaragua	24.07	39.11	13.75	10.00
Ecuador	7.21	12.80	29.20	38.60
Guatemala	20.49	19.04	22.30	38.20
Colombia	21.33	19.21	10.50	8.00
El Salvador	29.03	20.20	39.70	40.40
Paraguay	27.44	33.88	8.37	5.00

Table 10.1: Fe y Alegria compared to other public schools, 2000 (McMeekin 2003, 9).

in conjunction with parents and the community. Third, the nature of the schools' network provides for an overall vision, a common set of objectives, and the management tools to effectively implement educational practices. McMeekin observes that "such an institutional environment makes it easier for members of school communities to enter into the kinds of informal transactions that contribute to effective teaching and studying and good performance" (McMeekin 2003, 10).

McMeekin suggests that the successes of Fe y Alegría are centered on four primary factors (McMeekin 2003). First, they are focused on creating a school community. Local populations invite Fe y Alegría to establish a school, providing a starting point for close relationships with parents and community leaders. Fe y Alegría selects its own school directors and teachers whenever possible. Teacher turnover is very low, and they are encouraged to actively participate in school-building and community development projects (McMeekin 2003). The result is a strong personal commitment on the part of most teachers.

Second, there is strong involvement on the part of parents and the external community. Key aspects of this are "student retention strategies" that involve parents and the community. Activities and workshops stress the importance of parents supporting schoolwork in the home and being actively involved in the education of their own children. This is often achieved through the commitment of a key actor within Fe y Alegría who provides a leadership role within the organization and the community. This relationship between regional actors and the community is clearly important to the ability of Fe y Alegría to operate effectively. In cases where this actor has either left the organization or has lost credibility within the broader community, the organization as a whole clearly suffers.

Third, there is flexibility in the development of formal rules within educational institutions. Fe y Alegría does not require the establishment of uniform formal rules across all schools in the network. Rather, it encourages rules to be developed by the communities themselves in coordination with teachers and directors. Most of the schools in the Fe y Alegría network are found to be quite orderly, and informal rules and enforcement mechanisms such as teacher-director and teacher-peer relationships provide a high degree of conformity within and between schools (McMeekin 2003).

Finally, there is an environment of cooperation and trust fostered between the different organizational levels. Teachers generally remain in positions for extended periods of time, and relationships between directors and teachers tend to be positive. Parents are encouraged to motivate and support their children to stay in school and study. Educational programs reflect the desires of parents and community groups, and content such as agricultural techniques, indigenous language instruction, and teaching of traditional histories is often developed within each network and school (Swope and Latorre 2000).

Agency and Relation with Civil Society

The unique pedagogical organization of the Fe y Alegría schools network has a clear positive impact on schooling outcomes and overall program success (McMeekin 2003; Reimers 1993). The nature of these public-private partnerships has inspired national governments to examine education service delivery and other NGOs to develop similar programs. However, it is still unclear how much of the success of Fe y Alegría is due to its organizational structure, relationships to the state and market, or the tie to faith. While most schools within the Fe y Alegría network perform above average, they are also supported by additional and stronger local administrative planning networks than their public counterparts. Local school officials and regional administrators generally have direct ties to the community itself and thus more involvement in community needs and desires. These additional factors themselves may account for a large part of the success of Fe y Alegría, although given the explicit role of religion within the organization as a whole it is clear that faith has a large impact on community programs.

In describing how Fe y Alegría is able to be successful, Father Gabriel Codina notes that "the most important thing, without question, is the sense of 'mission,' the charisma of Fe y Alegría itself and its choice and spirit of service to the poor. This provides a 'value added' that is a particular characteristic of Fe y Alegría in all of Latin America" (Codina 1994, 344). It is this aspect that is most unique, that the inclusion of faith within the organizational structure unifies individuals and strengthens the bonds between local and national actors through a common value system or institutional myth. However, this is not necessarily from faith in and of itself. Building from this, the organizational structures of faith-related agencies can be further deconstructed with regard to their construction of myth and ceremony as key elements in the creation of legitimacy in the community.

Deconstruction of Faith-Related Agencies

As expressed in the introduction to this volume, NGOs in general and faith related agencies in particular do not fit neatly into common definitions of institutional or organizational structures. These organizational types are often characterized by flexible structures that respond to changing funding sources, client needs, program shifts, and state interventions. As such, it is difficult to place individual agencies into a single category, or even to classify NGOs themselves (Salamon and Anheier 2004). Using Meyer and Rowan's six propositions on organizational structure, the nature of how religiously based social service agencies operate between civil society, the state, and market can be deconstructed. In some cases faith-related NGOs conform to these propositions, while in other cases there are clear differences, suggesting that these organizations require different modes of institutional analysis.

Proposition 1: As rationalized institutional rules arise in given domains of work activity, formal organizations form and expand by incorporating these rules as structural elements (Meyer and Rowan 1977, 345).

This proposition suggests two central ideas. First, that as institutionalized myths begin to shape new domains of activity, formalized organizations begin to appear. Second, as new rational institutional myths appear within current domains of activity, existing organizations expand their structures so as to become more similar to these myths (Meyer and Rowan 1977). The activity of NGOs often takes place within existing institutional environments such as education or health, where formal organizations already exist and operate with a given set of rules. NGO activity within these domains may exert forces of change on customary formal structures such that existing organizations will adjust to become isomorphic to these myths. In these respects, many NGOs can be seen as prominent actors constructing new institutional myths within existing domains of activity by challenging conventional operational structures.

Proposition 2: The more modernized the society, the more extended the rationalized institutional structure in given domains and the greater the number of domains containing rationalized institutions (Meyer and Rowan 1977, 345).

This proposition implies, first, that formal organizations themselves are more likely to develop and networks of relation to become increasingly complex in more modernized societies. Second, formal organizations in more modernized societies are likely to have more developed institutional structures, which are seen as rational means to attain desirable ends (Meyer and Rowan 1977). Meyer and Rowan further suggest that "once institutionalized, rationality becomes a myth with explosive organizing potential . . ." (Meyer and Rowan 1977, 346). As organizations adapt to changing institutional environments, they begin to incorporate externally legitimated structures rather than focusing on internal efficiency. This adherence to externally created myths demonstrates that an organization is acting on collective societal values.

This proposition clearly diverges from the realities of Latin American governance and bureaucracy (or the similar experiences in other world regions), which are not generally considered highly modernized, and from the structures apparent in many NGOs. Formal bureaucratic structures in Latin America are generally weak and subject to rapid changes from economic or political change. This weak environment allows NGOs to emerge within traditionally structured fields of activity and to shape structures to accomplish their goals. Those NGOs that work closely with the state are often able to mold national policies based on their own organizational goals. Additionally, as NGOs create new institutional myths and as these become increasingly rational means of operation, this rationality itself can become the organizing potential for further activity within the specific domain of activity.

This influence within existing structural domains is not, however, limited to Latin America in particular or developing regions in general. NGOs within the United States are often recognized as having considerable power to influence broader structural domains and legislative environments. The flexible definitions of NGO activity and breadth of fields within which NGOs operate allow these organizations to move between legislative arenas and to both provide services on the one hand and to act as agents of change on the other. This flexibility has led to calls from popular media and certain governmental agencies for stronger regulation and stricter definitions of NGOs.

Proposition 3: Organizations that incorporate societally legitimated rationalized elements in their formal structures maximize their legitimacy and increase their resources and survival capabilities.

This proposition clearly rings true in the case of faith-related NGOs in Latin America, where the societally accepted norms of the Church strengthen the legitimacy and authority of related organizations within the community. Thus, actions of these faith-related organizations are legitimated not necessarily by the outcomes of their programs and services, but by the perceived infallibility of their word. This legitimation is furthered by the historic involvement of the Church in Latin America and its strong institutional structure as compared to the state. Thus, the formal rules and doctrines of the Church may often be accepted more readily than those of the state itself, further allowing these organizations to operate with relative impunity. Weber echoes this by stating that:

> These types [religious associations] are constructed by searching for the basis of *legitimacy* . . . the legitimacy of the power-holder to give commands rests upon rules that are rationally established by enactment, by agreement, or by imposition. The legitimation for establishing these rules rests, in turn, upon a rationally enacted or interpreted "constitution." Orders are given in the name of the impersonal norm, rather than in the name of a personal authority; and even the giving of a command constitutes obedience toward a norm rather than an arbitrary freedom, favor, or privilege (Weber 1946, 295).

Thus, when operating in unstable economic and political environments, faith-related NGOs are able to provide a rational basis for action within the community and maintain fundamental myths even when faced with external pressures for change. This differs from Weber's interpretation, where religious power is strongly likened to political power. In the case of Latin America, political power is fragmented, weak, and often seen as illegitimate by large sectors of the population. Thus, the methods of control and domination by political structures are often based on coercion or domination (social, economic, or military in nature). In contrast, religious structures in Latin America, for the most part, maintain a certain level of infallibility, with power supported by the bestowal of sacred values.

Proposition 4: Because attempts to control and coordinate activities in institutionalized organizations lead to conflicts and loss of legitimacy, elements of structure are decoupled from activities and from each other.

As was elaborated in the definition of NGOs earlier in the paper, one of the distinguishing features of NGOs is their ability and desire to maintain flexible organizational structures. The formal structures of NGOs are often promoted more in name than in reality, where actual program activities within communities may not be entirely reflective of those activities described in formal literature and funding requests. This decoupling of activity and appearance allows NGOs to vary their activities in response to practical day-to-day considerations rather than from internal or externally imposed formal arrangements. A key element of this decoupling is the acceptance of agency participants that the organization is acting in "good faith." Clearly, for faith-related organizations, where legitimacy is directly derived from this premise, these types of groups have a clear advantage.

Proposition 5: The more an organization's structure is derived from institutionalized myths, the more it maintains elaborate displays of confidence, satisfaction, and good faith, internally and externally.

For most NGOs, and for faith-related NGOs in particular, organizational structure is often based on elaborate mission statements and goals, most of which reflect shared societal ideals such as individual well-being, education for all, or basic health and sanitation. For faith-related NGOs, organizational structure is generally reinforced by the historically derived myths of the Church, thus furthering the legitimacy of the organization beyond its immediate domains of activity. This has been noted earlier in this discussion, but in terms of NGOs, a relation with faith allows not only a flexible structure, but also the inherent strength of myths supported by the Church.

Proposition 6: Institutionalized organizations seek to minimize inspection and evaluation by both internal managers and external constituents (Meyer and Rowan 1977, 359).

The evaluation of NGO activity has begun to receive increased attention in recent years by academic researchers, donor agencies, and NGOs themselves. Appearances are that many NGOs are hesitant to adhere to strict evaluation criteria, particularly those based on quantitative measures and external evaluation. Rather, many organizations desire to create legitimacy through the creation of inclusive networks between international donors, the state, market, and civil society. Faith-related NGOs have an additional advantage in this respect, where the acceptance of their "doing-good" is further bolstered by institutionally created myths supported by religious doctrines of charity.

Discussion

This paper has outlined an organizational perspective on how faith-related NGOs operate within broader institutional environments in comparison to other NGOs. Faith-related NGOs, rather than being substantially different from NGOs in general in terms of their ability to respond to the needs of the community, exhibit distinct organizational advantages in terms of the construction of institutional myths and ceremony. From an examination of the six propositions proposed by Meyer and Rowan, it is apparent that the appearance of advantage within institutional domains of activity does not necessarily come from religion itself, but rather from the legitimacy obtained by the NGOs' relation with faith. Using an organizational approach, this article shows that the construction of myth and ceremony by faith-related organizations provides the perceived advantage and legitimacy among local communities and funding agencies.

First, NGOs construct new myths within existing domains of activity, thus adapting traditional activities to reflect their organizational missions and goals. Second, weak states and markets in many developing regions allow NGOs to emerge within traditionally structured fields and to alter these domains to fit their agendas. Third, the historic legitimacy of the Church allows faith-related NGOs to operate with a certain level of impunity, bolstered by historic legitimacy and infallibility in the eyes of the local population and the state. Fourth, NGO activity is inherently decoupled from base organizational structures, with legitimacy maintained primarily by the construction of institutional myths. Fifth, religious organizations have an advantage of socially constructed legitimacy that is reinforced by the strength of historical institutional structures. In Latin America, where the Church has been a driving force in development from the time of the Conquest, these structures have the additional advantage of maintaining legitimacy beyond the state. Finally, organizational structures of NGOs are based on elaborate missions and goals using culturally adapted norms, framed within the language of local populations.

Thus, it is these distinct characteristics which provide faith-related NGOs with a perceived advantage over other NGOs and institutions involved within related domains of activity. Despite this, the specific differences between faith-related and completely secular NGOs may be unclear on the surface and the mission and ideology of successful organizations may not differ greatly, irrespective of religious affiliation. Religious affiliation may just provide an advantage in terms of defining organizational roles, ideological commitments, broader perceptions by related agents, and traditional domains of activity. In this respect, it may be possible for *any* NGO to create institutional legitimacy based on the construction of myth and ceremony, and, likewise, to lose that legitimacy when the presented myths and ceremonies are challenged.

These findings run counter to what some sociological theory suggests. It appears that in the case presented here and from the analysis undertaken of faith-related organizations in general, the relation to faith provides a "shortcut" to creating legitimacy. While this shortcut is often promoted as being explicitly faith-related, it is not necessarily so. This argument is particularly relevant within the field of education, where faith-related schools have long been studied as examples of places where faith can provide a genuine benefit to students and communities. It has been suggested in some cases that it is faith in and of itself that provides this benefit. However, based on an examination of the placement of faith-related NGOs within commonly defined institutional domains, this suggestion becomes doubtful. While faith may indeed provide benefit to individuals, how closely it is related to organizational outcomes and effectiveness is questionable.

The research presented in this paper suggests that the current emphasis on faith-related agencies in the provision of key social services may be better served by strengthening the institutional structures of all organizations operating within those fields, whether related to faith or not. Regulation of the NGO sector in general may not serve to accomplish this by itself. Rather, the legitimacy of NGOs needs to be strengthened through broader accountability between appearance and action, in addition to clarity on how program activities may influence existing institutional domains and regulatory structures.

These definitions should not necessarily infringe on the various aspects that make NGOs unique actors within societal domains, as this may negate what makes many NGOs effective alternatives to the market or state in providing essential services or challenging existing norms (Joseph 2000). While this suggestion is concrete in nature, the discussion in this article is necessarily theoretical as there appears to be a gap in the understanding of how faith and religion interact with organizational structures and the effectiveness of institutional practices. To further elaborate on this argument, the myths and ceremonies of various institutions need to be dissected in terms of their ideological statements, perceived impacts, and actual practices. However, from the initial findings of this paper, the role of religion and faith on organizational effectiveness may not be as strong as is often promoted.

Works Cited

Arce, Moisés. 2006. The societal consequences of market reform in Peru. *Latin American Politics and Society* 48(1):27-54.

Bebbington, Anthony. 2004. NGOs and uneven development: Geographies of development intervention. *Progress in Human Geography* 28(6):725-45.

Codina, G. 1994. La experiencia de Fe y Alegría. In *Cooperación internacional y desarollo de la educación*, ed. M. Gajardo, 321-46. Santiago: Agencia de Cooperación Internacional de Chile.

Coleman, James S. 1990. *Foundations of social theory.* Cambridge, MA: Harvard University Press.

Cowen, Michael, and Robert Shenton. 1995. The invention of development. In *The power of development*, ed. Jonathan Crush, 27-43. London: Routledge.

Dilulio Jr., John J. 2002. The three faith factors. *The Public Interest* Fall 2002.

DiMaggio, Paul J. 1998. The relevance of organization theory to the study of religion. In *Sacred companies: Organizational aspects of religion and religious aspects of organizations*, ed. N. J. Demerath III, P. D. Hall, T. Schmitt and R. H. Williams, 7-23. New York: Oxford University Press.

Fe y Alegría. 2004 Program outline. Fe y Alegría 2004 Available from http://www.feyalegria.org (last accessed December 2, 2008).

Joseph, Jaime A. 2000. NGOs: Fragmented dreams. *Development in Practice* 10(3/4): 390-401.

Lister, Sarah. 2003. NGO legitimacy: Technical issue or social construct? *Critique of Anthropology* 23(2):175-91.

McMeekin, Robert W. 2003. Networks of schools. *Education Policy Analysis Archives* 11(16).

Meyer, John W., and Brian Rowan. 1977. Institutionalized organizations: Formal structure as myth and ceremony. *The American Journal of Sociology* 83(2):340-63.

Olson, Elizabeth. 2006. Development, transnational religion, and the power of ideas in the High Provinces of Cusco, Peru. *Environment and Planning A* 38(5):885-902.

Peters, Paul A., and G. Brent Hall. 2004. Evaluation of education quality and neighbourhood well-being: A case study of Independencia, Peru. *International Journal of Educational Development* 24(1):85-102.

Podsiadlo, John J. 1998. Schools for the poor in Venezuela. *America* 178(18):8-13.

Reimers, Fernando. 1993. Education and the consolidation of democracy in Latin America: Innovations to provide quality basic education with equity. In *Advocacy Series Education & Development 4*. Washington, DC: US Agency for International Development (USAID).

Salamon, Lester M., and Helmut K. Anheier. 2004. The challenge of definition: Thirteen realities in search of a concept. In *Defining the nonprofit sector: A cross-national approach*, ed. L. M. Salamon and H. K. Anheier, 11-28. New York: Manchester University Press.

Scott, W.R. 1995. *Institutions and organizations.* Thousand Oaks, CA: Sage.

Smith, Steven Rathgeb, and Michael R. Sosin. 2001. The varieties of faith-related agencies. *Public Administration Review* 61(6):651-70.

Suchman, M. 1995. Managing legitimacy: Strategic and institutional approaches. *Academy of Management Review* 20:571-610.

Swope, John, and Marcela Latorre. 2000. *Fe y Alegría schools in Latin America: Educational communities where the pavement ends*. Santiago: Centro de Investigación y Desarollo de la Educación.

Weber, Max. 1946. *From Max Weber: Essays in sociology*. Trans. and ed. H. H. Gerth and C. W. Mills. New York: Oxford University Press. Orig. pub. 1922.

World Bank. 2004. Latin America: Fe y Alegría - A Jesuit education movement supported by AVINA. Paper presented at Scaling Up Poverty Reduction: A Global Learning Process, Shanghai Poverty Conference, Shanghai.

Chapter 11
Soka Gakkai in Brazil: Buddhism, Recruitment, or Marketing?
Suzana Ramos Coutinho Bornholdt

Introduction

This paper discusses the possibilities regarding the articulation between a specific religious group—Soka Gakkai International—and its engagement with social causes. It is based on a case study done in the southern part of Brazil on Soka Gakkai International [of] Brazil (henceforth BSGI, literally "International Society for the Creation of Value"), a lay Buddhist organization of Nichiren Shoshu that was founded in Japan in 1930 and is now considered one of the most successful Japanese religious movements (Clarke 2000, 326).

Based on anthropological fieldwork, this essay provides an ethnographically informed approach to understanding how Soka Gakkai creates innovative strategies of interpretation and accommodation in a specific religious field by presenting itself in Brazil primarily as an NGO and not as a religious group. The contradictory way in which BSGI uses the image and practice of an NGO responds to its own need: the recruitment and maintenance of membership. This chapter intends to show the ambiguities of a group that tries to address some of the necessities of a country plagued by immense social inequalities but, at the same time, uses this process as a marketing strategy and a plan of action to recruit new members.

Buddhism and Soka Gakkai in Brazil

Soka Gakkai International (henceforth SGI), the largest lay Buddhist organization in Japan, began in 1937 as a lay association of Nichiren Shoshu, one of several denominations tracing its origins to Nichiren (1222-1282). Although Nichiren Buddhism dates from the thirteenth century, Soka Gakkai is a contemporary religious group. Tsunesaburo Makiguchi (1871-1944), a Japanese educator, founded the organization in 1930 as part of a movement to reform Japan's educational system. After the Second World War a disciple of Makiguchi, Josei Toda, reconstituted Soka Gakkai and became its second president. Toda began an intense effort to spread Nishiren Daishonin's teachings to the lay population, but it was through the current president, Daisaku Ikeda (1928-), that the movement has continued to expand. Ikeda succeeded Toda in 1960 as third president of Soka Gakkai, and since then he has been traveling abroad to bring encouragement to members dispersed in small numbers all over the world.

The first SGI district established outside Japan was inaugurated in the city of São Paulo, Brazil, on October 20, 1960. At that time, the association had fewer than 150 members, all of them of Japanese ancestry. However, in recent decades, the Brazilian Soka Gakkai branch has evolved into a Buddhist group with centers in almost every region of Brazil. According to official information collected from the BSGI headquarters in São Paulo in May 2006, there are currently 160,000 Brazilian members, 90 percent of whom are of non-Japanese origin. In Brazil, the history of Buddhism is mainly related to Asian, and particularly Japanese, immigration. Buddhism came to Brazil with the Japanese immigration which began in 1908. Clarke (2001, 197) points out that it was not until the 1960s that different Japanese new religious movements began to make an impact beyond the boundaries of Japanese immigrant communities. Moreover, it was only in the 1980s, with the immigration of Chinese and Tibetan groups, that the number of different Buddhist groups increased and Buddhism became widespread in Brazilian society.

Buddhism is represented in Brazil by a large number of groups (Shoji 2004), and Soka Gakkai has competed and struggled to maintain its place in the religious market, not only against other Buddhist groups, but also the Protestant, Catholic, Spiritist, and Afro-Brazilian religions. Although Gakkai cannot be considered a numerically significant religion in Brazil, this group has drawn attention to itself for different reasons. Soka Gakkai has grown very rapidly in the last decades, even in states whose specific sociohistorical contexts do not include significant Japanese immigration. With this in mind, it is relevant to analyze the current situation of Soka Gakkai and to try to understand the politics it has developed and applied in order to attract new members and to establish itself in the Brazilian religious market.

Gakkai, the World, and Brazil

Since its beginning—and especially under Ikeda's leadership—Soka Gakkai has struggled to relate its image to the ideal of an international organization committed to social causes. In 1963, the movement was legally recognized in the United States as a nonprofit organization. Soka Gakkai International was set up in 1975, and Ikeda became its president. SGI was registered as a non-governmental organization with the United Nations High Commission for Refugees and the Department of Public Information in 1981. Additionally, in 1983, it was registered with the UN's Economic and Social Council. Dobbelaere (1998, 8) notes that Ikeda regularly meets with world leaders, politicians, scientists, and artists to discuss solutions to world problems and related issues.

Soka Gakkai uses different strategies in different countries, and its work to spread and legitimize itself presents different characteristics, depending on the degree of emphasis given to specific aspects of its activities. In France, for example, SGI established the Victor Hugo Museum in 1991. In the United States, the Soka University inaugurated its branch in Los Angeles in 1987, and founded the Boston Research Centre for the 21st Century in 1993. In Brazil, as in other branches around the world, Soka Gakkai tries to create the image of an institution engaged in activities to promote peace, culture, and education based on Buddhism, clearly following the tendencies of national politics.

The rapid growth of the Brazilian branch of Soka Gakkai drew Daisaku Ikeda's attention; as a result, he visited Brazil in 1960 and again in 1966 (*Terceira Civilização* 2005). Although preparations were made for a third visit in 1974, the military dictatorship of the 1960s and 1970s had placed nationwide restrictions on religious groups and movements that attracted public involvement or large crowds. As a result of these policies, Ikeda was denied a visa to enter the country in 1974. This apparent setback provided the impetus for Soka Gakkai to re-evaluate how BSGI's image was being presented within Brazil. Until this time, all efforts had been concentrated on the Japanese community and the immigrants established in the country. After this incident, Soka Gakkai started to invest in optimizing its image in the broader community, and promoting its ideals widely within different spheres of Brazilian society as a whole.

Political liberalization and a declining world economy contributed to Brazil's economic and social problems in the early 1980s. Brazil's own economic crisis (e.g., an annual inflation rate of 239 percent in 1983) led to the mobilization of class organizations and unions, and between 1978 and 1980, widespread strikes took place in the industrial sector in major cities. As a response to this social reality, BSGI created the Education Department in the early 1980s. In addition, in connection with the Rio 92 worldwide conference on the rainforest and other environmental issues, Soka Gakkai founded the Amazon Ecological Research Centre (AERC) in the city of Manaus, a project that is part of the Education Department. Both projects, the AERC and the Education Department, may be considered the most important marketing strategies of SGI within Brazil and in the world at large (Pereira 2001). While promoting BSGI on the world stage, these programs also promote the institution to potential new members within the country. These programs will be discussed below.

Social Action: A Brief Historical Overview
and Its Success in Brazil

The concept of "nonprofit" has gained more and more visibility in Brazil. The presence of and questions about nonprofit status have led to numerous discussions about political empowerment, redefining of the role of the state, democracy, pluralism, and ethnic and cultural identity; and have been increasingly invoked as they point to important possibilities for redrawing boundaries between the public and private spheres. These debates reflect not only different lines of thought in contemporary political and sociological discourse (Landim 1997) but also the diversity within and among so-called nonprofit organizations. In order to understand the reasons that led Soka Gakkai to choose a specific external image, it is necessary to know the history of these organizations and how they received such legitimacy among the Brazilians.

The history of voluntary associations in Brazil is linked to the colonial origins of the Brazilian state. The system of clientelism (based on the rules of patriarchal dependency) did not provide fertile ground for the development of autonomous voluntary associations such as those that emerged in the North American colonies (Landim 1997). Rather, considering that one of the pillars of Portuguese colonization was the close relationship between the colonial government and the Roman Catholic Church, the office of the papacy played an important role in organizing civil society. In a relationship that lasted for four centuries, until the proclamation of the Republic in 1889, Catholicism was the official religion of the state. To be Catholic was indispensable for the exercise of citizenship. The Church functioned as the civil registry, founded schools, provided social and medical assistance, and played a crucial role in conflict resolution (Landim 1997; Ribeiro de Oliveria 1985). In practice, all social work was carried out by the Church under the mandate of the state.

After the proclamation of the Republic, separation between church and state was institutionalized in the 1891 constitution. The constitution prohibited the government from providing financial assistance to religious groups and as a result the Catholic Church, aiming to maintain hegemony, started to establish new links with the population and institutions in order to increase resources. The 19th century also saw the beginning of a Protestant presence in Brazil, primarily as a consequence of the 1810 trade treaty with Britain and the massive European immigration to Brazil's south.

By the end of the nineteenth century, secular and religious voluntary associations had gained considerable prominence in Brazil. At that time, as a consequence of a massive immigration of agricultural and industrial workers from Europe and Japan (primarily to Brazil's South and Southeast), mutual aid support societies multiplied, helping members and their families financially in cases of illness, unemployment, disability, or death. Despite the domination of public life by the state, the private nonprofit sector was active. The government policy at the time was a selective support of organizations linked to either the apparatus of production or organized religion, while excluding the majority of the popular associative movements. Although a great number of civil associations sprang up during the 1930s (both left- and right-wing), most of them were repressed by the authoritarian regime installed in 1937. After the end of the dictatorship (1937-45), there was intense activity on the part of civil society, which gave a leading role to nonprofit organizations (Landim 1997, 330).

During the democratic period of the 1950s, church-based organizations were again active in community development and leadership training projects. At the same time, the lay movement linked to Catholic Action was forming progressive, left-wing groups within the Roman Catholic Church (Landim 1993). During these years, left-wing organizations of different kinds and affiliations had ample room to grow, both in number and in influence.

Fear of the rule of the "left" caused the military to seize power in 1964, in reaction to the social revolution and the power structure created in the 1930s. A new authoritarian era began under the military government, leading the country into a sphere of control of international capital. The policies of the military government limited the participation and the engagement of different groups committed to social causes. The only organization left relatively intact was the Catholic Church, which, although it had supported the military coup of 1964, began three years later to suffer not only political persecution but also the detention and torture of religious activists.

After the end of the military dictatorship, two simultaneous processes brought profound changes to Brazilian organizations working with and on behalf of the poor. The first was secularization and subsequent loss of influence of the Church: some existing NGOs no longer emphasized their religious roots, and new social initiatives established NGOs without any religious connotations. The second process was the strengthening of popular initiatives into well-structured autonomous popular organizations, or the "emancipation" of Brazilian popular movements. Breaking away from dependency on a church, they began to structure their own organizations at a local and subsequently national level.

These different institutions for and of the poor had an important role in the political redemocratization that took place between 1979 and 1988. The end of military repression made it possible for many organizations to act. This also explains why many Brazilian NGOs were established in the 1980s, in the wake of a nationwide secularization process (Poelhekke 1996).

Scholars attempting to describe nonprofit organizations in Brazil have encountered several difficulties. Landim (1997, 332) points out several of these: firstly, the term "nonprofit sector" has not yet gained currency in sociological and economic Brazilian literature; secondly, research of the topic is rare compared to what has been done in other countries. Beyond its legal definition, the term "nonprofit sector" denotes primarily membership organizations, representing a broad variety of forms and activities; in Brazil, the term suggests organized civil society in contrast to the State. Landim groups existing terms into five descriptive categories which are not mutually exclusive: a) civil societies or nonprofit organizations; b) associations; c) philanthropic or charitable organizations;

d) non-governmental organizations (NGOs); and e) foundations. Although the classification of BSGI as an NGO according to this model may be inaccurate, for analytical purposes I will focus the discussion in this direction by considering BSGI as an NGO.

"NGO" is not a legal term, and although it has subtle political connotations, it is not linked to any particular political ideology. Rarely used in Brazil until the mid-1980s, the adoption of NGO as a category of self-identification for these new organizations indicates a process of the creation and recent recognition of a common identity (Landim 1988, 62). In the Brazilian context, non-governmental work means strengthening the capacity of the poor to gain access to governmental services to which they are entitled by law, but which, in practice, are not only insufficient, inadequate, or nonexistent, but could also be done *by* the poor, *with* the poor, and *on behalf of* the poor. The roots of this trend are in the "Centers of Popular Education" or "Centers for Consulting and Support to the Popular Movements." "They were born and flourished at the height of the dictatorship, with their 'backs to the State' and 'under the shadow of the Church'" (Landim 1997, 399). They grouped together activists with a middle-class background, both religious and nonreligious, intellectuals seeking alternatives to academia, and ex-militants from traditional leftist groups.

The more these organizations became secularized, the more they embarked on a process of institutionalization and professionalization, as a result of which many became NGOs. The widely diverse collection of priority issues chosen by recent social movements (women, blacks, the environment, AIDS, street children, etc.) demonstrates NGOs' organizational commitment to civil society, social movements, and social transformation. The reasons for which BSGI chose to classify itself as an NGO will be discussed in the following section.

BSGI: Brazilian Context and Social Action

Following the national trend, the beginning of the 1990s was a starting point for a different mode of conduct led by BSGI. It was clear during my interviews that part of the legitimization process of Soka Gakkai in Brazil consisted of an effort to be accepted and recognized. What can be seen today is a well-projected and deliberate strategy to conquer public spaces and to emphasize the participation of members.

My ethnographic field research, done mainly in the state of Rio Grande do Sul and also at the national branch in São Paulo and Manaus, allowed me to get closer to the members of Soka Gakkai in Brazil. I lived in Porto Alegre for eleven months (from October 2005 to September 2006), and during that time I conducted interviews, read the most important materials produced by BSGI, visited members at their homes, traveled around the country to get to know key people and places—especially Rio de Janeiro, São Paulo, and Manaus—and attended the local meetings in Porto Alegre and its surroundings (i.e., Greater

Porto Alegre and its countryside). That experience allowed me to know the two "faces" Soka Gakkai presents in Brazil.

The time spent in Rio Grande do Sul was decisive in getting to know the religious face of BSGI better. But it was during the visits to the national branch in São Paulo and Manaus that I began to understand how they elaborate a more secular image in Brazil. In that sense, it is possible to affirm that Soka Gakkai carefully creates a dual discourse. Externally, the emphasis is not on religious practice, but on activities identified with the secular world, emphasizing BSGI's effectiveness as an NGO and aiming to create a positive public image. Internally, the organization remains interested in the doctrine and practice of members. While the religious discourse belongs to the members' ambit, the secular face of BSGI as an NGO is more prominent externally. This dual perspective is also noted by Pereira (2001), who researched the group at the end of the 1990s in the Brazilian Federal District. My intention in this chapter is to focus on the social activity and engagement of Soka Gakkai in Brazil, which is developed mainly in the state of São Paulo and the state of Amazonas.

In 1992 Brazil—the country that includes the greater part of the Amazonian rainforest—played host to the Rio 92 worldwide conferences on environmental issues. That same year, BSGI founded the Amazon Ecological Research Centre (AERC) in Manaus, in the state of Amazonas, representing the Environmental Education sector of the BSGI Education Department. Primarily, though, the Education Department has invested in two main projects: the Makiguchi Project in Action and the Literacy Nucleus. Brazil is one of the few countries in which the Tsunesaburo Makiguchi pedagogy is applied on a large scale. The Education Department developed a forty-hour literacy program for teenagers and adults, the Makiguchi Project in Action (a volunteer effort to revitalize education in public schools using Makiguchi's value-creating educational theories), and the Research Department for the science of education. Both projects, the AERC and the Education Department, may be considered the most important marketing strategies of SGI in Brazil today. One of its marketing strategies is that while it promotes BSGI on the world stage, it also promotes the institution to potential new members within Brazil.

The Education Department is subdivided into three groups: a) the Makiguchi Project in Action, b) the Literacy Department for Youth and Adults, and c) the Support Group or "Science of Education Research and Development Department." In the following paragraphs I will offer some information about BSGI's social activities in different areas within Brazil. For the sake of length, the activities of the group in the country are briefly described, presenting to the reader the main pursuits achieved by social engagement, and how they insert themselves into the specific fields. It is worth mentioning that, although this paper does not present many case studies and the description of the cases is not developed from a critical perspective, the analysis is based on my anthropological fieldwork conclusions, where I offer a critical perspective and discuss the ambiguities and conflicts which result from BSGI's social action in the country. When put in context, the description of their activities is very useful for understanding how they are used more as a strategy of insertion than a relevant social action.

Education Department

Makiguchi Project in Action

The Makiguchi Project in Action is based on the principles of *Soka Kyoiku-gaku Taikei* (The System of Value-Creating Pedagogy), a work published in 1930 by Tsunesaburo Makiguchi, the founding president of Soka Gakkai. Participants in the Makiguchi Project in Action are educators who have volunteered their time without financial remuneration. More than five hundred volunteers have participated in the BSGI Education Department over the years.

In 1996, Brazil's Federal Law Number 9394, the "Law of Guidelines and Foundation of National Education," put in place numerous components relevant to the desired quality of education. In the National Curriculum Parameters by which this law would be implemented, the Ministry of Education encouraged school initiatives in the formulation of educational projects. In a country where the responsibility for implementation of educational directives rests primarily with schoolteachers, the BSGI Education Department found a great opportunity to present to the teachers innovative approaches both to obtain support and to achieve the desired results in schools. Based on this demand, the BSGI Education Department decided to apply Tsunesaburo Makiguchi's theory in the Brazilian educational setting. The Portuguese translation of Makiguchi's book "The System of Value-Creating Pedagogy," published in Brazil in April 1994, was a remarkable moment for the people involved in the BSGI Education Department. It was in September of the same year that the Makiguchi Project in Action was initiated at Caetano de Campos (a public elementary and junior high school) as the "Spring Program," and was offered to second-year students at the elementary level.

In 1995, the BSGI subdivision "Science of Education Research" devised a plan for the Makiguchi Education Project which would tailor the project to the unique educational circumstances and needs in Brazil. The science of education research group joined the Education Department, and their participation soared to approximately 1500 students in forty-one classes. By May of 2000, the Makiguchi Project in Action was being offered in the classrooms of fifty-five municipal and state public schools in the state of São Paulo and one school in Curitiba, in the state of Paraná.

Literacy Nucleus

Although the nation has achieved greater economic and industrial development in the last twenty years, Brazil still faces a high level of illiteracy. Specialists believe that social exclusion is one of the primary results of illiteracy (Foweraker 2001), which is found more frequently within the elderly segment of the population and in poor and/or urban areas. Another aspect that must be considered in terms of this analysis is that more than one-third of the Brazilian adult population is considered functionally illiterate—unable to use reading and writing in daily activities.

After five years of experimentation, from 1983 to 1987, the Literacy Department for Youth and Adults was created within the BSGI Education Department. The program consists of forty-hour courses for each fundamental level primary grade, for a total of 160 hours. Initially, the objective was to teach reading and writing to adults who were considered functionally illiterate, aiming to support BSGI members with poor reading skills in their study of Nichiren Buddhism and the proclamations of President Ikeda (M.S., personal communication, June 2006). As the program expanded, BSGI started to offer courses equivalent to formal schooling.

Each forty-hour course is organized into weekly meetings, which usually take place on a Saturday morning and last for four hours. Students who complete all the lessons are eligible to obtain a fourth grade level public school certificate. Qualified staff—teachers, monitors, and assistants—are all volunteers and members of BSGI. According to my informants, between August 1987 and the first semester of 2000, 884 students completed their studies and were qualified to take the public examinations.

Support

In 1994, a group of psychologists within the Education Department began to participate in the Makiguchi Project in Action by offering lectures to parents and teachers in the Caetano de Campos School. In 1998, the group named itself the Psycho-Pedagogical Research and Development Nucleus and expanded its objectives and research to the teaching of learning. When the Education Department was formed, the nucleus became the Science of Education Research and Development Department. Its function is to support the activities of both the Makiguchi Project in Action and the Literacy Nucleus by providing research on the foundations of education, supplemental resources, suggestions, courses, lectures, and workshops; and, most importantly, to offer the BSGI Education Department a scientific face.

AERC (Amazon Ecological Research Centre)

The relevance and impact of the Amazon rainforest is one of the major arguments used by Soka Gakkai in Brazil for the conception and creation of the AERC. The United Nations Special Conference on the Environment, held in Rio de Janeiro in June of 1992, emphasized the need for humanity's harmonious coexistence with the natural world. One of its most important results was that it drew attention to the value of the Amazon rainforest.

In 1992, inspired by Ikeda's essay "A New Strategy for Environmental Protection"—which he wrote in response to the Earth Summit—BSGI officially initiated activities which subsequently became the AERC. The centre has 52.6

hectares of land in the middle reaches of the Amazon, on the outskirts of Manaus, and is located in a very exclusive tourist area where it is possible to observe the "meeting of the waters" (*encontro das águas*), where the Rio Negro and Rio Solimões join but do not mix due to differences in velocity, density, and temperature. The confluence of these two rivers results in the formation of the Amazon River, one of the largest rivers in the world. The exclusive location and modern facilities of the AERC indicate the high investment of Soka Gakkai in the project.

In November 1993 BSGI, the Soka University Ecological Centre, and the State of Amazonas Secretariat of Environment, Science, and Technology (SEMACT) signed an agreement to dedicate the centre to ecological research. The main aims of the project are: a) to create a seed bank and act as a forest seeds supplier; b) to be a model of reforestation and education environment; and c) to serve as a refuge for forest animals.

In June 1994, after the inauguration of the administrative local branch, the AERC started a reforestation program in its immediate area. This project succeeded in planting some 20,000 seedlings of thirty-four different tropical tree species for eventual transplantation onto the centre's land.

In 1996, based on the same project of tree planting and transplantation carried out in its own area, the AERC implemented a similar project in the city of Novo Aripuanã, a small and very poor city located around 300 km from Manaus. According to one of the leaders of the AERC, the process of tree planting can generate great economic value while benefiting the environment. The project to revitalize the rainforest not only focuses on conservation of the forest, but also serves as an experiment to "promote sustainable development that is economically viable and contributes to the betterment of the lives of the local people," as one of the local leaders described it (interview, June 27, 2006).

Beginning in 1997, the AERC came to be administered exclusively by BSGI and received autonomy from Soka Gakkai International to create its own structure and actions, working more closely with local communities. In 2001, AERC started construction of the building and installations for the laboratory Daisaku Ikeda. That same year they opened the place to visitors, and, through a partnership with the local government in the project "Environmental Itinerant School," they started to receive visitors from local schools.

Soka Gakkai Today: Ambiguities and Challenges in Brazil

It is essential to know the Brazilian social and political context in order to understand the actions of Soka Gakkai in the country. Decisive moments in national politics during the 1990s were used by the organization as propulsion for different ends. The result of the wide repercussions of Rio 92—not only in Brazil but internationally as well—and the moral strengthening of NGOs in Brazil played a decisive role in the political scenario of the 1990s. Soka Gakkai invests in different characteristics depending on the country where it is established. The specificity of BSGI relies on the fact that they started to elaborate a less religious and more secular image, investing in the relationship between Buddhism and NGOs. The organization started to define itself, as it is stated on its web page:

> The BSGI is the Brazilian representative of Soka Gakkai International (SGI), NGO with Buddhist base and affiliated to the United Nations and acting in the following areas: culture, peace, education, environment, nuclear disarmament and support to war refugees. (http://www.bsgi.br, last accessed September 20, 2007)

Whoever browses the site on the Internet is unable to associate the BSGI with a religious group; the emphasis is deliberately placed on its status as an NGO dedicated to peace, culture, and education.

It is worth mentioning that, like other religious groups, the chosen term for self-definition totally differs from their legal position. Soka Gakkai in Brazil is, in legal terms, a civil religious institution, but presents itself to the Brazilian community as an NGO with Buddhist principles or as a Buddhist association for laypeople. When asked about this ambiguous relation between NGO and religion, one of the leaders informed me:

> Actually, if we had to say openly, we would say that what is properly an NGO is the SGI, which is affiliated to the United Nations since 1975. So, SGI "gives a lift" to BSGI. It is a marketing strategy for us. BSGI develops work based on the same principles of SGI. That's why we say we are an NGO. But in legal aspects we are a religious entity (C.O.S., personal communication, May 2006).

Although Soka Gakkai promotes several social projects, the imbalance in proportion between the relatively small number of individuals benefiting from these projects and the huge investment of BSGI on the marketing and promotion of these activities became strikingly clear in my fieldwork. The reality of SGI's work on the ground was considerably different from the way they define themselves on their website as "an NGO with Buddhist principles," with extensive advertising of their "extremely relevant" social activity "spread nationwide." Notwithstanding its importance in the lives of many individuals and its reach in terms of absolute numbers, Soka Gakkai's educational project results are relatively minimal in a city such as São Paulo, the largest capital city in South America, with more than ten million inhabitants. Even more interestingly, during an interview in the institution's branch in São Paulo, I found out through my informants that the adult literacy project, known in certain circles worldwide as one of BSGI's most relevant projects, draws a majority of its participants from among Soka Gakkai members, with only a few nonmembers enrolled in its classes.

The history of the country clarifies, in many ways, why Soka Gakkai chose specific actions. During the period after the military dictatorship, i.e., the beginning of the 1980s, there was a clear policy not only to modify the organization's public image in Brazil, but also to extend the target public from Japanese immigrants to the national society at large (*Terceira Civilização* 2006). From the moment the institution opened its doors to Brazilian society, Soka Gakkai encountered a new reality which it had not previously faced. The beginning of the 1980s was marked by a period of political liberalization, and the worldwide economic decline contributed to one of the biggest economic crises in Brazil. These economic hardships exacerbated the problem of the rural exodus, and important cities such as São Paulo received a great proportion of these displaced masses. The organization's national expansion policy was successful in terms of attracting new members. A considerable proportion of these belonged to strata of the population that reflected the social problems faced by the country. The challenge then became not only the creation of a discourse attractive enough to convert new members, but the maintenance of these new members in the organization as well. One possible interpretation that explains the change of Soka Gakkai's strategy in Brazil is that it was necessary for the members to be able to read. Through reading, the new members would have access to the support material produced by Soka Gakkai as well as to the teachings of President Ikeda— seen by them as the "master of life." Constant stimulation and involvement in this structure of support would, it was believed, diminish the likelihood of withdrawal of recent converts (Y.K., personal communication, September 2006). It appears as though the educational project was created, first and foremost, as an internal necessity for the purpose of retaining new members.

The international political trend linked to the development of power alternatives to the state, and the way in which this new context brought hope for renewal within the country, meant that the image of a "third sector" appealed to Brazilian public opinion and carried with it significant credibility. This new tendency in Brazil, which had Rio 92 as its starting point, was used by Soka Gakkai as a great opportunity to expand its public activities. The new period within the country offered to the organization a unique opportunity for the elaboration of its public image and strategy of introduction into the Brazilian religious context. It was in this context that the AERC was created.

However, as with the educational projects, the gap between the gigantic investment of Soka Gakkai International in the promotion of AERC's activities and the actual benefits to the local population and environment came to me as a surprise. During my fieldwork in 2006, I had the opportunity to visit the modern facility of AERC. The building is relatively small, and the number of staff involved in day-to-day activities appeared to be so as well. The small scale of local activities—and here I am referring to the number of people that are effectively impacted by their projects—does not appear congruent with the massive promotion given to the project, as described previously. It is significant that, when designing and building the facilities for AERC, Soka Gakkai's architects in Japan designed the largest space of the building to be the projection room, devoted to the screening of institutional videos. This space, serving the external public, is larger than the meeting room where AERC's projects are discussed and, more importantly, significantly larger than the area reserved for the research labs. It is worth noting that Soka Gakkai's investment in the promotion of its research centre in the Amazon is so intense and its marketing strategy so effective as to have its discourse find its way into academic texts of researchers specialized in the institution (e.g. Seager 2006, 192).

BSGI's education and ecology projects must be considered as distinct projects with different purposes. The education project, established in São Paulo, was created partially but only secondarily to solve a specific social problem. The educational project aims to be not only the social response to the *kosen-rufu* prophecy—lasting peace through the spread of the teachings of Nichiren Buddhism—but also the response to a new institutional target: prospective members. When BSGI offers literacy classes, it includes in the same "package" lessons on how to read and correctly pronounce the mantra *Nam-myyoho-renge-kyo*, and how to interpret the messages of President Ikeda. And it is here that they begin to be involved in a new social network, partially responsible for strengthening their faith and maintaining cohesion within the group. Nevertheless, notwithstanding their differences and internal ambiguities, both come together in Soka Gakkai's effort to carve a space inside Brazilian society.

In short, both projects reveal the conflicts and ambiguities in the efforts of Soka Gakkai in Brazil. This ambiguity is reflected first in the discourse of the organization, which creates a dual sphere of action. Internally, Soka Gakkai in Brazil deals with the members—generally former Christians, with totally different religious backgrounds and with no experience in the new Buddhist religion—and with their religious experience. It is through the religious experience that Soka Gakkai develops strategies to maintain the members, using elements related to the Buddhist doctrine to involve the members in a specific network of relationship, engagement, and mutual support. The specific discourse used by the group internally, involving the religious aspect, totally differs from the external discourse. Externally, BSGI opts for a more secular face, avoiding any religious approach and trying to create a representation of a group committed to social causes. It is the external discourse that effectively produces a positive image for the Brazilian society and allows BSGI to find a favorable way to expand their ideas throughout the country.

If the first ambiguity of Soka Gakkai in Brazil is related to the dual discourse of the organization, the second is related to the action of the group. This posture of action, closely related to the commitment to social causes, is what effectively reveals Soka Gakkai's attempt to create a specific attractive appeal. Their endeavor in creating social projects can be considered ambiguous in the sense that, while engaging their efforts to reach a specific—and less privileged—stratum of the Brazilian population through their works, they also use this opportunity as an effective way to attract and maintain as many members as possible.

The ambiguity of both situations—discourse and action—lies in the fact that the social engagement of Soka Gakkai cannot be translated as an exclusive commitment to social causes, nor as a deliberate and dissimulative decision to enroll more members. It is necessary to face this specific reality beyond the uncritical analysis of faith-based non-governmental organizations, turning the attention to the importance of specific discourses, practices, and beliefs of the group when set against the national context. With the same perspective in mind, it is necessary to consider that the motivations of the group are not based merely upon practical reasons. Soka Gakkai daily faces the problems brought by its members such as illiteracy, debt, lack of support for health problems, and even starvation. The reality of Soka Gakkai's motivations is ambiguous and encompasses both rational strategy to attract more members, and their religious experience.

Works Cited

Clarke, Peter B. 2000. Buddhist humanism and Catholic culture in Brazil. In *Global citizens: The Soka Gakkai Buddhist movement in the world*, ed. David Machacek and Bryan Wilson, 326-48. New York: Oxford University Press.

———. 2001. Japanese new religious movements in Brazil: From ethnic to "universal" religion. In *New religious movements: Challenge and response*, ed. Jamie Cresswell and Bryan Wilson, 197-211. London: Routledge.

Dobbelaere, Karel. 1998. *Soka Gakkai: From lay movement to religion*. (Studies in Contemporary Religions). Torino: Editrice Elle Di Ci.

Foweraker, Joe. 2001. Grassroots movements and political activism in Latin America: A critical comparison of Chile and Brazil. *Journal of Latin American Studies* 33(4):839-65.

Landim, Leilah. 1988. A serviço do movimento popular. In *As organizações sem fins lucrativos no Brasil: Ocupações, despesas e recursos*, ed. Leilah Landim and Neide Beres. Rio de Janeiro: ISER/Johns Hopkins University.

———. 1993. A invenção das ONGs: Do service invisível à profissão impossível. Ph.D. diss., Universidade Federal do Rio de Janeiro, Brazil.

———. 1997. Brazil. In *Defining the nonprofit sector: A cross-national analysis*, ed. Lester M. Salamon and Helmut K. Anheier, 323-49. Manchester and New York: Manchester University Press.

Pereira, Ronan A. 2001. O budismo leigo da Soka Gakkai no Brasil: da revolução humana à utopia mundial. Ph.D. diss., Unicamp, Brazil.

Poelhekke, Fabio. 1996. *Brazil: NGO profile*. Ámsterdam: OM Oegstgeest.

Ribeiro de Oliveira, Pedro A. 1985. *Religião e dominação de classe*. Rio de Janeiro: Vozes.

Seager, Richard H. 2006. *Encountering the drama: Daisaku Ikeda, Soka Gakkai, and the globalization of Buddhist humanism*. Berkeley: University of California Press.

Shoji, Rafael. 2004. The nativization of East Asian Buddhism in Brazil. Ph.D. diss., University of Hannover.

Terceira Civilização. 2005. Especial. October.

———. 2006. Especial. October.

Chapter 12
Faith, Hope, Charity: Catholic Development Organizations in Argentina
Laurie Occhipinti

By this time, numerous critics have raised the possibility that "development," as it has been envisaged and enacted by a neoliberal agenda, causes more poverty than it remedies. The benefits of neoliberal development are, at best, uneven. Within this context, organizations that base their work on notions of social justice may offer an alternative model for development. A religious idiom of development reframes the terms of the debate, shifting the discourse from one which is narrowly focused on projects and outcomes to one which considers fundamental questions of how people live. The work of religious NGOs, at least in some cases, may represent a critical reformulation of development, the emergence of an alternative idiom within which to discuss poverty and wealth. Religious NGOs have the potential to envision "development" differently and the potential to carry out development projects within an alternative framework. Because they are based in religious institutions, they have social capital, moral standing, and financial and human resources to enact a development agenda that offers an alternative to the neoliberal development discourse.

As one of the most important sets of development institutions globally, nongovernmental organizations—NGOs—create and implement programs of economic development and social welfare. NGOs flourished under neoliberal policies of the 1990s, which promoted shifting many social services to the private sector. In an effort to begin to understand the ways in which religious organizations differ from their secular counterparts, I have conducted ethnographic fieldwork with two Catholic development agencies in Argentina. Such religious NGOs operate within a larger development discourse, but they also represent a distinct subset of development organizations. For these religious organizations, the motivation to engage in development work is not based on the neoliberal goals of economic maximization, improved living conditions, or growth. The driving force of these religious NGOs is social justice, interpreted broadly and inclusively. They are interested in improving the material conditions of the communities in which they work as a necessary step—but only a step—toward social justice. This paper explores the work of religious NGOs and the ways in which they are reformulating notions of development to fit it into a more moral framework. At times, they offer a popular, or perhaps populist, counter to neoliberalism and unchecked global capitalism, becoming a highly legitimizing voice of opposition. I argue here that the particular Catholic organizations of my case study actively envision the dominant capitalist society as the *cause* of poverty in the indigenous communities in which they work, and frame the indigenous local economies themselves as the solution. Bringing to bear the considerable moral and discursive resources of the Catholic Church, they pose a powerful critique of the neoliberal economy, and challenge not just the "poor" but all of us to live within a more just and moral economic framework.

Development and Discourse

Development projects affect a community on several distinct levels. Most obviously, development programs seek to change material conditions. On another level, development organizations may play a central role in changing understandings of the relations of production—the beliefs that people hold about "rightness" or justice in the distribution of resources. In this process, NGOs have an important role in negotiating between the "local" and the "global" visions of "development," in the definition of poverty, the strategies chosen, and the cultural (sub)text of local projects.

The notion of a discourse of development is one which has been explored by many anthropologists in the last fifteen years (see, for example, Escobar 1995; Shaw 1995; Pigg 1992; Little 1992; Ferguson 1994). According to this persuasive analysis, development agencies create a vision of the problems of poverty as fixable, subject to apolitical, technical, bureaucratic intervention. A discourse of development is shaped at many levels—internationally, by large development agencies, and locally, through the daily praxis of individuals and communities. The discourse functions to disguise the inherently political question of access to resources, diverting attention from what are in fact questions of poverty and power. The discourse of development operates to "shape . . . the nature of development practice, the interpretive community of development agents, and the facts they emphasize" (Porter 1995, 84). Recognizing and deconstructing this particular discourse is important not merely as an analytical exercise, but because it becomes a rationale by which resources are distributed, often in regions where resources are scarce.

The dominant, secular discourse of development emphasizes technical solutions to issues that are defined in highly limited and circumscribed ways. It tends to confine projects to specific ends and means. In the last five or ten years, there has been an increased shift towards universal, narrow development goals, embodied most directly in strategies such as the UN Millennium Development

Goals adopted in 2000 (UN 2007). This universalizing, technocratic aspect of development has been criticized extensively by anthropologists and others. Yet development, like any other discursive sphere, is not a monolithic, homogeneous entity but one which is multifaceted, with many voices and contestations (Grillo 1997).

Many Christian development organizations emphasize a "holistic" approach to development that goes beyond material needs and considerations. "Christian development discourse, unlike secular development, advocates humanness in its fullest 'potential,' explicitly striving to meet the needs of individuals spiritually and materially" (Bornstein 2001, 60). The Mennonite development agency, as one example, notes, "Physical survival needs must be met, but the ethical and aesthetic are also vital for strengthening human dignity and identity" (Yoder, Redekop, and Jantzi 2004, 296). Religious organizations may be less likely to shy away from addressing the deeply moral questions of power and inequality that are obscured by the larger discourse of development. The way in which "poverty" itself is defined by a development organization has clear ramifications for the kinds of programs it implements, its own methodology, and, just as importantly, the arenas of local life that it defines as outside the scope of its interests. Such definitions are not always fully articulated, but nevertheless inform the program's actions and philosophy. They are created in a process of dialogue with ideas of development gleaned from larger institutions and trends in global development, from an organization's own ideological background, in this case based on a liberal Christianity, and from conversations with local people, who are also involved in a separate but interrelated process of definition and discourse. As one might expect, the extent to which any organization has an explicit theory of development underlying its initiatives varies as much as the organizations themselves. Some may not even regard themselves as doing "development"; charitable giving has long been a part of Christian practice. Others have a highly complex economic and social agenda, with a highly self-conscious and reflexive philosophy and theology of their decision to engage in development work. In an era in which the forces of globalization are increasingly contested by local voices, religious organizations that base their work on notions of social justice may offer an alternative model for development.

Religious organizations themselves are highly cognizant of the differences between themselves and their secular counterparts. Deciding to engage in development work is often a step taken by religious organizations in order to effect change in the world based on a "reflection on the reasons for Christian involvement in development, the method of involvement, and the goal of involvement from a Christian and biblical perspective" (Samuel and Sugden 1982, 19). Such a holistic approach allows them to go beyond the narrow confines of specific projects. A religious idiom of development may permit religious organizations to be more creative in their approach to projects as well as to take on projects that are simply not part of the agenda for other institutions.

Supported by both government and private sector funding, NGOs have responded creatively in many cases to persistent issues of poverty, but, as critics have noted, NGOs, as private agencies, are unable to address the systematic *causes* of poverty. There is danger in the tendency to shift responsibility for social welfare from the government to the private sector. Even progressive NGOs committed to grassroots participation face a problem in creating development strategies that respond to local demands, as the very introduction of aid can create clientelism and cooptation. But the larger issue is that NGOs, in contrast to the state, have little power to change conditions that create poverty: unequal access to productive resources, regressive policies, highly inequitable systems of land and income distribution, and so on. Laura MacDonald notes that in Latin America, NGOs have been seen as the key to successful development by both critics and proponents of neoliberalism. She cautions that despite their popularity in development circles, "The apparent virtues of NGOs tend to obscure the real problems even the most well-meaning and effective NGOs encounter in attempting to promote development. The virtuous image creates unrealistic expectations about the possibility of quick fixes if only aid is directed to people at the grassroots. In most of Latin America, the decks are stacked against the poor, and NGO activity can do little in the short term to shuffle the deck" (1995, 32).

Communities and Organizations

> The faith of the poor, the religious dimension that allows them to maintain their traditions, their ancient customs of respect for the land, solidarity, [and] openness to others, knowledge which is often forgotten, are the riches that the poor offer to a society that is bleeding to death from having forgotten these values (OCLADE 1996, 1).

In 1997-98, I conducted field research with two religious NGOs in northern Argentina called OCLADE and Fundapaz. Both agencies have their origins in the Catholic Church, stemming from a progressive Catholic concern with poverty and social justice. Both work primarily with indigenous populations, which make up a small percentage of the Argentine population.[1] These small development organizations share a deep concern for social justice and inequality, and both are critical of the neoliberal policies which dominated the Argentine political economy in the late 1990s. They also both work within certain constraints, some stemming from the need to gain funding, and others from the limits of their own ability to effect change.

The two organizations work in very different cultural regions and ecological zones. In the province of Salta, where I conducted research, Fundapaz works with the Wichí, a lowland indigenous people, whose economy was based on hunting and gathering until the middle part of the twentieth century. Fundapaz promotes a variety of projects in the Wichí and the surrounding *criollo* (white) communities, according to local needs and preferences as well as to practical project considerations. The NGO has also had a long-term commitment to help local communities gain legal rights to the land that they occupy (Occhipinti

2005). In its promotion of social justice in the Wichí communities, Fundapaz faces formidable challenges. The material standard of living of the Wichí is much lower than elsewhere in the province or in the nation. Wichí communities generally have neither electricity nor a reliable supply of potable water. Public services such as health care and education are inadequate throughout the region. Household cash incomes range from virtually nothing to about $150 per month. The economy of these Wichí communities is based on a precarious combination of wage labor, subsistence agriculture, and foraging. The organization portrays its work as that of a "bridge" between poor rural populations and the dominant society—a bridge upon which ideas travel in both directions (Fundapaz 1989). As a private nonprofit organization, Fundapaz is not officially affiliated with the Catholic Church, but sees itself as having "Christian inspiration" and maintains close ties with the Church. Most of its funding comes from nonprofit European development agencies, many of which are religious in nature. Other funding comes from government sources and large international agencies such as the World Bank.

OCLADE is a nonprofit NGO established and run directly by the Catholic Church of the Prelature of Humahuaca. It runs programs throughout the Prelature, which encompasses most of the *puna* (*altiplano*) of northwest Argentina, as well as the valleys directly to the east. This area may well represent one of the poorest geographical regions in Argentina, with high indexes of illiteracy, infant and child malnutrition, and unemployment. Iruya, where I conducted research, is a scenic town in the high Andean valleys, a land of dramatic cliffs and swift rivers, and its people are generally referred to as Kolla.[2] The local economy is based primarily on subsistence agriculture, supplemented by meager sales of produce on the regional market and migrant labor to plantations in the lowlands. The average household has a cash income of perhaps $600 a year and holds less than half of a hectare of land. OCLADE's major programs focus on community organizing, economic development projects (mostly in subsistence agriculture), and various projects aimed at improving health and education for women and children. OCLADE has also acted as an important conduit of material resources into the community; projects have provided materials to construct systems for drinking water and for irrigation and to build health posts. There have also been several attempts to create productive associations and cooperatives for both agriculture and crafts. Funding comes directly from the Prelature, from various religious intermediary organizations, both Catholic and Protestant, from non-religious development organizations, and from several government programs.[3]

Like most small NGOs, both organizations have an array of projects underway at any one time, including child-feeding centers, agricultural training, infrastructure improvements such as building community centers and systems for delivering potable water, education, and health care. The diversity in their programming is intentional. Both organizations share a long-term commitment to the communities where they work. The goal is not to create one project, or to fulfill a single criterion, but to seek out projects that meet specific local needs. To a large extent, however, each NGO is limited because of its dependence on outside funding. Current trends in the nonprofit sector dictate that programs and spending are directed at short-term projects with narrowly focused goals aimed at the poorest sectors of society, resulting at times in ineffective programs which lack long-term strategies and links between different types of efforts. In "shopping around" for funding, the NGO is often limited to the kinds of projects and programs that are popular or current in mainstream development circles. This allows organizations to take advantage of the options that may be available and provides flexibility in the short term, in order to find new or existing sources of funding. However, it also leaves gaps in budgeting for long-term strategies and planning. For both Fundapaz and OCLADE, these long-term strategies and planning have included projects and issues which are not part of the mainstream development discourse, most notably land reform and issues of indigenous rights.

Despite the significant differences between both the organizations and their "client" populations (Occhipinti 2005), the two organizations share a common understanding of the larger project of development. As religious NGOs, OCLADE and Fundapaz draw heavily on the values and ideas of liberation theology and a progressive Catholicism. They frame pressing issues of local poverty in terms of the greater inequalities of global capitalism. Their solutions to problems of the communities in which they work employ the standard tools of development—microcredit, adult literacy, and the like—but do so within a discourse of morality and justice.

Development and the Theology of Liberation

Both Fundapaz and OCLADE have created a specifically religious idiom of development that emanates from their own Catholic, and specifically progressive Catholic, background. They draw impetus and inspiration from liberation theology, and this perspective shapes the work that they do and the role that they see themselves playing in the community. They share the perspective that human dignity, not wealth, is the end goal of development. Strategies to reduce poverty are merely a means to that end.

Liberation theology arose in the 1970s in Latin America as way to address the role of the Catholic Church in society. It offered a model of radical change and, ultimately, a vision of the participation of the entire population in political, religious, and economic life. Liberation theology did not express just theological questions, but a far-reaching critique of Western society, capitalism, and the marginalization of poor. Implicit (and occasionally explicit) in this moral economic philosophy is a critique of Western capitalism, characterized as having a long history of exploitation and oppression. In a practical sense, this critique is played out in the form of an emphasis on economic self-sufficiency and autonomy. As liberation theology was put into practice around Latin America, there was a strong emphasis on grassroots communities as the basis for all change, for social action. Liberation theologians were critical of what many termed *des-arrollismo* ("developmentalism"), used in a pejorative sense for reforms that failed to address issues of power (Berryman 1987, 34). Many argued that *des-arrollismo* emphasized "planned social change" without a consideration of people's real needs, creating a development model according to which "people have to overcome bothersome obstacles" like culture and religion (Van Kessel and Droogers 1988, 55). Liberation theology, by contrast, suggested a model of radical change, including land reform, nationalization of key industries, and educational reform, advocating the participation of the entire population in political, religious, and economic life (Benavides 1987, 128-29). In this vein, many new Catholic organizations were established and old ones revitalized by those influenced by liberation theology's message that the Church must exercise a "preferential option for the poor." Although liberation theology itself may have petered out as both a religious and a social movement, its influence is still felt not only in the Catholic Church where it originated but also in mainline Protestant churches (Yoder, Redekop and Jantzi 2004), evangelical organizations (Sider 1982, Bornstein 2003), and even in the Pentecostal movement (Kamsteeg 1998). The ideas of liberation theology remain influential and continue to resonate in northern Argentina in both the Catholic and mainline churches. The church, as one of the few stable local institutions, is seen as a powerful ally in the struggle of daily life. And, in fact, the church itself represents one of the few sources of material and ideological resources available.

NGOs such as Fundapaz and OCLADE were founded as a direct response to the idea that poverty must be understood as a theological problem and that Christians have a duty to work against unjust social conditions. As conceptualized by these NGOs, the end of development is not material prosperity, but a better quality of life for the individual, a notion which includes human rights and self-fulfillment. Poverty itself is understood as an impediment to self-fulfillment, and antipoverty programs take a center place for religious organizations just as in their secular counterparts.

The links between material and spiritual poverty are often actively theorized by religious NGOs (Bornstein 2003, 46). In a conservative Protestant organization studied by Erica Bornstein (2003), bringing development to the poor is understood as a Christian act. In this view, economic development has two purposes: to introduce Christian beliefs to individuals, and to restore their God-given potential (Bornstein 2003, 48). Molefe Tsele, a Lutheran minister and General Secretary of the South African Council of Churches, cites Gustavo Gutiérrez, a prominent Catholic theologian, to argue that development can be a "transformative and liberating process that goes beyond material and financial advancement to overcome other deficits including cultural, social, political and economical ones" (Tsele 2001, 204). Tsele goes on to argue that the church needs to demonstrate that it brings something substantative to development, beyond traditional charity efforts. He places this substantial contribution squarely in the spiritual realm, saying that it is "only by reintroducing faith-inspired motives in development . . . that the Church's development enterprise can become authentic" (2001, 209). The church has the potential to redefine the content and goals of development itself to focus on people, societies, and life. Development, Tsele says, is not like fixing cars (2001, 210). A religious idiom of development has emerged in conversation with liberation theology and with the dominant development discourse. Although the emphasis may vary from organization to organization, within and between faith traditions, it shares some themes that distinguish it from mainstream or secular frameworks for development. One of the most prominent of these themes is a critique of capitalism, and, more specifically, a general condemnation of the policies of neoliberalism.

In the work of Fundapaz and OCLADE, there is a clear critique of the structures of capitalism, and particularly of the neoliberal policies that shaped the Argentine economy throughout the 1990s. During this period, the federal government, under President Carlos Menem, was deeply involved in a program of neoliberal "reforms," which included the privatization of a wide array of industries and services, drastic cuts to social services, and shifting responsibilities from the federal to local and provincial governments. Although neoliberal reforms were largely successful in controlling inflation and creating stability in large financial institutions, they also resulted in high unemployment, a shrinking of the traditionally strong middle class, and increased (or at least increasingly visible) corruption. NGOs found themselves on the front lines of this shift in state policies. The director of Fundapaz commented that he felt that the NGO sector was effectively subsidizing the government by providing not only basic services but training and long-term community development. In effect, he noted, "We are seeing the privatization of aid." Another NGO administrator said, "Fundapaz can't act as the Ministry of Social Benefits! It is not the father of the people. We can't be—there are limits to our human and financial resources."

In this context, development projects that increase capitalist economic structures or that create strong ties to the market economy were frequently depicted as inappropriate or even impossible for the indigenous population. As one example, OCLADE has put much more emphasis on issues of health and education than on local economic development, despite local interest in improving market access. This emphasis is directly tied to OCLADE's religious motivations and its views of the community in which it works. In the late 1980s, for example, OCLADE did experiment with developing cooperatives, one for produce and one for crafts, but these quickly fell apart. The local co-op organizers had little training in either marketing or accounting procedures. In the case of the agricultural co-op, the co-op itself faced serious challenges from existing intermediaries, who both temporarily raised the prices they offered farmers and threatened to cut off producers who worked with the co-op. Rather than address these challenges directly, the NGO abandoned the attempt, and even used the failure of the cooperatives as a justification for avoiding similar projects. The resistance of OCLADE's leadership to projects aimed at improving market access for local producers is directly tied to its rejection of neoliberal capitalism. Increasing commercial production was not, at its base, compatible with ideals of cooperativism and collective action. It raised the specter of increasing local inequality and was seen as inimical to maintaining cultural traditions. The NGO tends to tends romanticize local culture as embodying noncapitalist ideals and values. In the organization's vision, subsistence production is far more palatable than competition in the market.

Over the longer term, neoliberal policies in Argentina—as, indeed, elsewhere—proved wildly unpopular. By the late 1990s, the Catholic Church as well as unions emerged as major opponents of neoliberal policies, and by extension, the Menem government. Unions, traditionally strong agents in Argentine politics, were able to effectively mobilize mass protests. The national Catholic Church, which had formerly been a very conservative actor in the political sphere, emerged as a site of resistance to neoliberalism, emphasizing issues of social justice. A series of mass demonstrations at the end of 2001 were largely protests against neoliberal policies, and ushered in a period of political instability, which finally resulted in the election of Néstor Kirchner in 2003, largely because of his commitment to reverse neoliberal policies.

The moral economic philosophy of the Catholic NGOs critiques Western capitalism, with its long history of exploitation and oppression, as well as specific neoliberal agendas. In a practical sense, this critique is played out in the form of an emphasis on economic self-sufficiency and autonomy. Both NGOs view participation in the larger capitalist economy—through commercial agriculture, herding, or wage labor—as culturally alienating for the indigenous groups. The indigenous societies are almost invariably understood as being *outside* of capitalism, not as integrated at the lowest level. The focus tends to be on *subsistence* practices—whether or not they are adequate at dealing with poverty in these contexts—rather than on "enterprise." The focus of projects is not on more integration with the capitalist economy, but on less. Both organizations respect and value traditional subsistence practices—small scale agriculture in the highlands and hunting and gathering in the lowlands. They schedule projects around the needs and schedules of traditional subsistence, while other projects are aimed directly at improving traditional subsistence activities. In both cases, there is an effort to reduce risk and ensure the reliability of subsistence in communities which are seen as having a precarious economy. In OCLADE's case this shows in an emphasis on nutrition, through child-feeding centers which are a major focus of its programming, and on meeting other basic needs, such as potable water and access to basic health care. For Fundapaz it has been channeled mainly through land claims, which are seen to provide a secure economic base. The emphasis on subsistence accords well with the theme that the indigenous societies are culturally vulnerable. The focus of projects is not on more integration with the capitalist economy, but on less.

Both NGOs see local economic change as a result of external forces impinging on local resources, especially land and labor. The "outside" world is rarely seen as offering anything beneficial in terms of change, but rather as a threat to local cultural integrity. Social change is seen to be driven primarily by the relationship of local villages with the external world, and is also viewed as a threat to the local culture. In keeping with liberation theology, economic development is promoted not as an end, but as a means to greater human dignity. Both NGOs were founded in this spirit, with a mission of supporting the communities where the founders worked. In their day-to-day administration, in their publications, and in their representation of the local communities, the organizations stress that local communities are oppressed, and need strong local organizations and structures. There is an emphasis on the need to work *together* to ameliorate conditions of poverty. Implicitly, creating local economic autonomy is one of the underlying goals of their development projects.

Inculturating Development

These religious NGOs have thus broadened the central ideas of liberation theology to include the ethics of cultural autonomy and self-sufficiency. The focus has shifted to protecting the inherent value of local culture *against* rationalizing global forces. Local cultures themselves are understood as emphasizing values that resonate with Christian beliefs rather than with market capitalism.

These NGOs have expanded on the central ideas of liberation theology to understand that cultural autonomy is key to human dignity. Dignity is understood as rooted in culture, building on local values and practices (Irarrázaval 2000). This may reflect a shift in Catholic discourse towards what is called the theology of inculturation (Orta 2004), although that term was never used by priests or lay leaders during my involvement in the communities. This recent Catholic theological movement has emphasized a celebration of indigenous cultures; it seeks to place all cultures, including or perhaps especially indigenous ones, on a theologically equal footing, arguing that God can only be understood by an individual within his or her own cultural context. This theological shift in Latin America has taken place within an extraordinarily complex context of indigenous political movements emphasizing indigenous rights, and has met with varying responses on the part of those local people whose cultures are suddenly being celebrated (see also Martínez Novo, this volume).

There can be little doubt that the ways in which the NGOs conceive of the cultures in which they work have a tremendous impact on their work. This conception shapes how the organization understands the causes of poverty as well as its visions of the future. It influences not only personal relationships between NGO staff and community members, but the kinds of programs that the NGO implements. In both cases in my study, the indigenous cultures that the organizations work with are seen as having a high intrinsic worth. Foremost in the literature and thinking of each is the uniqueness of the indigenous culture and the idea that these cultures are threatened or endangered. As each NGO theorizes economic development, the indigenous cultures' traditional lifestyles themselves represent an alternative model to global capitalism. At the same time, in Latin America, upward mobility for indigenous peoples often comes in the form of becoming urban mestizos. The religious NGOs are resisting this particular version of modernity and development.

Features of indigenous culture such as reciprocity, community labor, and even poverty are seen to model Christian ideals. OCLADE tends to romanticize an idealized "traditional" Kolla culture, an image which at times stands in the way of programs. Fundapaz, while very culturally sensitive, grapples with the question of what kind of economy is compatible with Wichí culture (even as the Wichí grapple with the same issue), while putting a great deal of emphasis on ecological sustainability. The NGOs share an implicit ideal that the local communities are closer to the communitarian ideals expressed in primitive Christianity.

This idealization of indigenous communities by a religious organization is a theme also found in Tara Hefferan's (2007) recent study of sister-parish programs between the U.S. and Haiti. Hefferan's study focuses not on development professionals, but on parishioners who become development workers through volunteer work in the church. As they see Haiti through their own eyes, they spontaneously create images of poverty, of deprivation, of the cultural Other that mirror those that have been critiqued in the wider development discourse. Yet Hefferan notes that the perspectives of Haiti created and recreated by parish partners are also shaped by a particular religious worldview that allows them to understand Haiti not just as a poor, underdeveloped Other but also as a site of spiritual and moral superiority. Noticing, or perhaps imagining, that which they find lacking or worthy of critique in their own culture, the Michigan parishioners balance the poverty of their Haitian counterparts with a cautionary tale of the excesses of capitalism, an ambivalence about the moral superiority of their own culture. This balance is rarely, or perhaps never, to be found in conventional notions of development. But OCLADE and Fundapaz similarly position the indigenous societies in counterpoint to contemporary Argentine culture and neoliberal economics, and in this comparison, the indigenous cultures, like the Haitians of Hefferan's study, occupy the more highly valued pole.

Both NGOs attribute the causes of poverty to the cultural divide between the indigenous cultures and the dominant society. The NGOs' emphasis on subsistence production accords with the theme that the indigenous societies are culturally vulnerable. Foremost in the literature and thinking of each organization is the idea that the indigenous culture is unique, and that it is threatened or endangered. The threat comes primarily in the form of poverty, as local economies seem to provide an increasingly inadequate level of subsistence. In Iruya, malnutrition and child mortality are taken as evidence that families live on the edge of hunger. In Los Blancos, the alternatives to subsistence agriculture—irregular wage labor and hunting and gathering—are both seen as inadequate to support families. In their programs, both NGOs stress local autonomy—subsistence production—as a way to ensure cultural survival. Projects thus focus on reducing risk and on ensuring a greater reliability of subsistence. Land ownership, together with local production which is not dependent on the market, is seen as ways for local people to maintain control of their own economic well-being.

Without economic change, in the forecast of each NGO, the indigenous culture cannot survive, beset by an array of difficulties: young people will leave their native communities in search of work; family ties and kinship networks will break down; norms of sharing and cooperativism will be lost as each household struggles to survive. Eventually, in the worst-case scenarios, under the flood of media images, the scant attention paid to indigenous cultures by the educational systems or the dominant society, and the increasing ease of transportation and communication, the cultures will disappear, subsumed into the underclass of Argentina. Survival of the indigenous culture is linked with the ability of its communities to be self-sufficient. Neither organization proposes that a wholehearted adoption of capitalism and the market will do—in part because of the economic and social marginality of both groups, and in part because of cultural issues. The market economy is seen at its base to be incompatible with the cultural values of the indigenous population, and to be intrinsically threatening to their way of life.

These NGOs come to the table with their own ideas about what constitutes "development" for the Wichí or the Kolla. An essential and fundamental element of their vision is that the future of these unique cultural groups not be complete assimilation, that development allow them to remain (or to become) self-sufficient, if not isolated. This idea of indigenousness is so ingrained that it may come to hinder negotiation, if it does not coincide with the visions that local people have of their own future. For both of these NGOs, the emphasis on preserving or maintaining the indigenous culture itself takes priority over strictly economic concerns. There is, of course, nothing wrong with this, as long as the NGO and the community share a similar vision. The key to success rests in the organization's ability to engage in a dialogue with community members about how they see their future, without becoming trapped in a static notion of saving a "traditional" culture.

Conclusions

Imagining a different kind of society based on the common good; a new concept of development that is sustainable and equitable and not limited to economic growth; participatory democracy and sound and credible institutions (Latin America Council of Churches [CLAI]).

In some ways, of course, a study of NGOs in Argentina represents a unique case. In particular, throughout the twentieth century the Argentine government offered a much greater level of social services than did many poorer countries of Latin America. Argentina has a large middle class and a diverse economic base. In other ways, the case here is similar to others, in the impact of neoliberalism and also in patterns of resistance to the changes that neoliberal policies imposed. While globalization through neoliberal reform meant to be a great equalizer, a creator of wealth, in some ways it has been quite the opposite—creating more wealth but also more poverty (and more contrast), creating hyperpowers and hyperinstitutions. It has proven to be singularly ineffective in creating social justice and equitability.

The religious discourse of development that is imagined and enacted by organizations like OCLADE and Fundapaz is distinct from mainstream development discourse. Rather than understanding the "poor" communities in which they work as backwards, or left behind, or having failed in some way to progress, they are seen as offering an alternative model to the dominant society and to global capitalism. The indigenous communities are more than a subset of "the poor"; they are distinct populations whose values and interests are seen as not just genuinely different but morally superior. Unfortunately, this romantic idea of subsistence economy is challenged and contradicted by real conditions, which the NGOs are highly aware of. Traditional subsistence economies are fragile and perhaps inadequate, given limited resources and ecological degradation. It is in fact these conditions of poverty and marginalization that prompted religiously motivated development organizations to improve the physical conditions of those communities as well as their access to centers of power.

Religious NGOs have an alternative discourse and praxis, one which is rooted in a particular vision of how the world is and how it ought to be. The religious NGOs that I have studied are not merely interested in economic development. They see economic development as an essential element of human dignity, one which makes it possible for individuals to lead more fulfilling lives. Therefore, the projects that they implement are in a sense the means to an end, rather than an end in themselves. While many secular agencies may also have an idea that economic development can be understood as part of a "whole life project" (Escobar 1995), this is a view that is fundamental to religious NGOs. "At heart, religion is transformational, not simply transitional. It looks upon the individual as a sacred being with the right to a life of dignity and worth. When religion informs social change, the effects of development transcend the material by reaching what is important to people" (Mayotte 1998, 69).

OCLADE and Fundapaz situate the problems of development not with "the poor" but with the dominant society that allows such poverty to exist. Working within a religious idiom of sacrifice, sin, and community, they challenge the dominant society to change its perspective on economic and social justice. The driving force is the idea that we have a moral obligation to care for our fellows. It is in this respect that they offer a truly critical assessment of neoliberalism. Most discourses of development ultimately blame the poor—for being uneducated, backwards, or otherwise resistant to the benefits of development. In sharp contrast, Fundapaz and OCLADE blame not the poor, but the rest of us.

Notes

1. About 4-5 percent of the Argentine population is indigenous, although official estimates may be somewhat low. See Occhipinti 2003 for further discussion.

2. The term Kolla is contested, however, and not everyone in the highlands claims an identity as Kolla. See Occhipinti 2003.

3. About 25 percent of total funding comes from some level of the government, the rest from NGO sources and direct support from the Catholic Church.

Works Cited

Benavides, Gustavo. 1987. Catholicism and politics in Latin America. In *Movements and issues in world religions*, ed. Charles Wei-hsun Fu and Gerhard E. Spiegler, 107-142. New York: Greenwood Press.

Berryman, Philip. 1987. *Liberation theology: Essential facts about the revolutionary movement in Latin America and beyond*. New York: Pantheon Books.

Bornstein, Erica. 2001. The verge of good and evil: Christian NGOs and economic development in Zimbabwe. *PoLAR* 24(1):59-77.

———. 2003. *The spirit of development: Protestant NGOs, morality, and economics in Zimbabwe*. New York: Routledge.

Escobar, Arturo. 1995. *Encountering development: The making and unmaking of the Third World*. Princeton, NJ: Princeton University Press.

Ferguson, James. 1994. *The anti-politics machine*. Minneapolis: University of Minnesota Press.

Fundapaz. 1989. Fundapaz annual report 1988/89. Buenos Aires: Fundapaz.

Grillo, R. D. 1997. Discourses of development: The view from anthropology. In *Discourses of development*, ed. R. D. Grillo and R.L. Stirrat, 1-33. New York: Berg.

Hefferan, Tara. 2007. *Twinning faith and development: Catholic parish partnering in the U.S. and Haiti*. Bloomfield, CT: Kumarian Press.

Irarrázaval, Diego. 2000. *Inculturation: New dawn of the Church in Latin America*. Maryknoll, NY: Orbis Books.

Kamsteeg, Frans H. 1998. *Prophetic Pentecostalism in Chile: A case study on religion and development policy*. Lanham, MD: Scarecrow Press.

Little, Peter. 1992. *The elusive granary*. London: Cambridge University Press.

MacDonald, Laura. 1995. A mixed blessing: The NGO boom in Latin America. *NACLA report on the Americas XXVIII* (5):30-35.

Mayotte, Judith A. 1998. Religion and global affairs: The role of religion in development. *SAIS Review* 18(2):65-69.

Occhipinti, Laurie. 2003. Being Kolla: Indigenous identity in northern Argentina. *Canadian Journal of Latin American and Caribbean Studies* 27(54):319-45.

———. 2005. *Acting on faith: Religious development organizations in northwestern Argentina*. New York: Lexington Books.

OCLADE. 1996. *Yareta*. Humahuaca, Argentina: Prelature of Humahuaca.

Orta, Andrew. 2004. *Catechizing culture: Missionaries, Aymara, and the "new evangelization."* New York: Columbia University Press.

Pigg, Stacy Leigh. 1992. Inventing social categories through place: Social representations and development in Nepal. *Comparative Studies in Society and History* 34:491-513.

Porter, Doug J. 1995. Scenes from childhood: The homesickness of development discourses. In *Power of development*, ed. Jonathan Crush, 63-86. New York: Routledge.

Samuel, Vinay, and Chris Sugden. 1982. Theology of development. In *Evangelicals and development: Toward a theology of social change*, ed. Ronald J. Sider, 19-42. Philadelphia: Westminster Press.

Shaw, Carolyn Martin. 1995. *Colonial inscriptions: Race, sex, and class in Kenya*. Minneapolis: University of Minnesota Press.

Sider, Ronald J., ed. 1982. *Evangelicals and development: Toward a theology of social change*. Philadelphia: Westminster Press.

Tsele, Molefe. 2001. The role of the Christian faith in development. In *Faith in development: Partnership between the World Bank and the churches of Africa*, ed. Deryke

Belshaw, Robert Calderisi, and Chris Sugden, 203-218. Oxford: Regnum Book International.

United Nations (UN). 2007. *UN millennium development goals*, www.un.org/milleniumgoals/ (accessed June 8, 2007).

Van Kessel, Joop, and Andre Droogers. 1988. Secular views and sacred vision: Sociology of development and the significance of religion in Latin America. In *Religion and development: An integrated approach*, ed. Philip Quarles van Ufford and Matthew Schoffeleers, 53-71. Amsterdam: Free University Press.

Yoder, Richard A., Calvin W. Redekop, and Vernon E. Jantzi. 2004. *Development to a different drummer: Anabaptist/Mennonite experiences and perspectives*. Intercourse, PA: Good Books.

Chapter 13
Building an Anti-Neoliberal Nation with the Indigenous Movement: The Salesian Missions of Ecuador
Carmen Martínez Novo

During his 2006 political campaign, the current president of Ecuador Rafael Correa, who received his Ph.D. in Economics from the University of Illinois, stated that he obtained his most important graduate degree while being a volunteer for a year in the Salesian mission of Zumbahua, located in the central highlands of Ecuador. President Correa used his knowledge of the Kichwa language profusely during the campaign, which was in part a strategy to distract attention from the fact that the indigenous party Pachakutik had decided against an alliance with him. He claimed to have learned Kichwa while speaking to peasants in Zumbahua, although he also took classes at San Francisco University, an elite college where he taught before becoming a politician. When he assumed power, he organized a symbolic event at the heart of the Salesian mission that was attended by presidents Hugo Chávez of Venezuela and Evo Morales of Bolivia. Correa dedicated the event to the indigenous and the poor of Ecuador, and used a stylized shirt with ethnic decorations. However, his relationship to indigenous people during the event was ambiguous. Zumbahuan peasants could not enter their own town's square because it was closed and reserved for important guests. They also had a secondary and mute role in the event. Correa highlighted the importance of his experience as a Catholic volunteer, and thanked the missionaries. In 2008 *Alianza Pais*, the political party created by Correa and his allies, finished a Constitution that enlarged the role of the state, kept government subsidies, restricted the subcontracting of workers and other neoliberal labor practices, required state control of foreign companies, and, thus, sought an end to neoliberalism as it had previously existed in Ecuador.

This has not been the only moment in which the Salesian missions have been at the center of Ecuadorian politics. Since the 1960s and 1970s, the missions have been key points of organization of the indigenous movement of Ecuador, one of the strongest social movements in Latin America in recent decades. Since its first nationwide uprising in 1990, the indigenous movement has been able to lead struggles against neoliberalism and even halt the implementation of structural adjustment reforms (Ospina and Guerrero 2003). Thus, I argue that the Salesian missions have been instrumental in creating a strong social movement with an antineoliberal agenda that has been able to transform the nation.

The formation of this antineoliberal political culture has been intimately linked to the development work carried out by this Catholic order. Their understanding of development has been multidimensional, focusing on protection of indigenous peoples' territories, land acquisition, access to credit and technical knowledge for agricultural and animal husbandry development, education, political organization, and, of course, evangelization. An important focal point of Salesian work with indigenous peoples has been the formation of identities, which the missionaries perceived as an important goal of development. In the first half of the twentieth century, the Salesians emphasized that indigenous peoples should learn Spanish, Western ways, and become Christian as a way to "civilize" them and integrate them into the nation. After Vatican Council II (1962-65), the Salesians changed their strategies and attempted to preserve indigenous languages and customs—although purified by Christian ethics—as mechanisms to promote ethno-development as well as integration into the nation.

Although they are a transnational Catholic order with European as well as Latin American and local staff, the Salesians have had a close relationship to the Ecuadorian state. Since independence, the Ecuadorian state has lacked the infrastructure and perhaps the motivation to control the totality of its national territory. Frontier areas populated by indigenous and Afro-Ecuadorian peoples were delegated to the Catholic Church (Martínez Novo 2007) or even to evangelical organizations. This was just one aspect of a delegative state that had also ceded the administration of native populations to the private domain of haciendas from the abolition of Indian tribute in the nineteenth century to the agrarian reform in 1964 (Guerrero 1993). In 1893, President Luis Cordero (a Catholic indigenist who wrote the first Kichwa-Spanish dictionary) granted the Salesian Order authority over the southeastern lowlands to "civilize and Christianize the Shuar people," a grant that has been renewed several times up to the present. After the Agrarian Reform of 1964 distributed public *haciendas* to peasants, an absent state also delegated control of the area of Zumbahua in the central highlands of Cotopaxi to the Salesians. In these marginal areas, the Salesians have been in charge of building roads, schools, and hospitals, enhancing the local economy, and even organizing people to claim their rights from the state. As noted above, neoliberal reforms have only partially been implemented in Ecuador due to a resistant civil society. However, the unfinished withdrawal of the state has only enlarged those spaces occupied by the Catholic Church as well as by other faith-based and non-faith-based nongovernmental organizations.

A number of authors have acknowledged the important role that the Catholic Church played in the origins of the indigenous movement in Ecuador (Cornejo 1991; León 1991; Zamosc 1993; Martínez Novo 2004; Rubenstein 2005). Others have emphasized the role of the left (Guerrero 1993; Becker 2008). An emphasis on one external organizer or the other is linked to regional differences in the formation of the indigenous movement. However, it is widely held that once CONAIE—*Confederación de Nacionalidades Indígenas del Ecuador* (Confederation of Indigenous Nationalities of Ecuador)—was founded in 1986, the first national indigenous uprising took place in 1990, and the political arm of CONAIE, Pachakutik, was created in 1995, indigenous peoples became relatively independent from external agents (León 1991; Guerrero 1993). A desire to emphasize the recently gained political voice of indigenous people, or the fear of reproducing colonial images of Indians as passive and manipulated, seems to have precluded efforts to study in greater depth the relationship between the Church and the indigenous movement. While there are interesting ethnographies of the interactions between missionaries and native people in Ecuador (Muratorio 1981; Kohn 2002; Andrade 2004; Lyons 2001; 2006; Rubenstein 2005), most have focused only marginally on the political effects of this relationship (some exceptions are de la Torre 2002; Martínez Novo 2004; Rubenstein 2005). In addition, missionaries have been discussed most of the time as agents of "acculturation" and not of "inculturation," the task of evangelization through the preservation of indigenous languages and cultures.

The Catholic Church started to acknowledge the religious legitimacy of non-Western cultures and the need to respect and preserve them after the Second Vatican Council (1962-1965). More concretely, the Decree *Ad Gentes* on the missionary activity of the Church, written by Pope Paul VI in 1965, has been seen as one of the foundational documents of the theology of "inculturation," which has developed as theology and practice ever since, and which has been discussed in several Councils and bishops' conferences. The main idea behind inculturation is that the Church no longer considers non-Western cultures profane. Instead, these cultures are believed to contain the "seeds of the word of God" (*Ad Gentes* 1965). Inculturation advocates that pastoral agents should identify "seeds," those elements within a culture which are positive from the point of view of Catholic ethics or that can be used for evangelization purposes, such as solidarity, love for mother earth, spirituality, and so on. Pastoral agents should learn the language and other cultural elements of the people among whom they work, and should use them for evangelization and Catholic rituals. This theology has led to the development of particular branches of the Church specializing in indigenous peoples, the African Diaspora, and other subaltern groups. Although this theology focuses on respect for diversity and cultural preservation, the Decree *Ad Gentes* argues that cultures should be purified from those elements that are negative from the point of view of Christian ethics. This document is an interesting example of the tension between the global identity of the Catholic Church, whose very name means "universal," and the desire to accommodate and incorporate difference.

I will focus in this paper on the work of the Salesian Order as it attempted to mold collective identities that the Salesians understood as important goals for development and as necessary tools for political organization. Moreover, I will argue that the missionaries perceived political involvement as a precondition for substantial improvement in the standards of life of indigenous people and, thus, as a requirement for economic, social, and spiritual development. I have done fieldwork since 2002 in two areas of influence of the Salesians: the Amazonian province of Morona-Santiago and the Salesian Mission of Zumbahua, in the central highlands of Cotopaxi.

Development, Identity, and Politics in the Salesian Missions of the Ecuadorian Amazon

In 1893 the Ecuadorian government granted the Salesian Order the authority to "civilize and Christianize the Shuar" in Ecuador's southeastern lowlands and, in the process, to ensure Ecuadorian presence along the highly contested border with Peru (Botasso 1986; Rubenstein 2005; Audiovisuales Don Bosco n.d.). The Shuar were called Jívaros by Spanish conquerors, adapting the word Siwar, meaning "people" in Shuar Chicham, to Spanish phonetics (Taylor 1994). According to Anne-Christine Taylor (1994), the Jívaro were perceived by the conquerors as an anarchic group that rejected any form of authority or social hierarchy beyond the family, inhabited dispersed habitats, and were in a permanent state of internal war. This lack of hierarchical social organization in a large group endowed with a more or less coherent culture puzzled the conquerors. On the other hand, European travelers were fascinated by the Shuar custom of reducing the heads of dead enemies to make *tsantsas*, the native word for shrunken heads. At the end of the nineteenth century, the rationalism, materialism, and perceived lack of spirituality and rituals of this group irritated missionaries. Missionaries called the Shuar "a barbarous and atheist race . . . resulting from all the savage forces combined like cascades, ravines, the claws of beasts, and the venom of snakes" (Taylor 1994, quoting Pierre and Alvarez, 84), and argued that Shuar culture was of satanic inspiration. For the missionaries in this period, cultural change was a way to eradicate the work of Satan. The Salesians were also preoccupied with what they saw as a lack of sexual morals of the Shuar, which they associated with the custom of polygyny.

However, by the 1960s the Salesians had begun to reflect on the importance of preserving an indigenous culture that was seriously threatened both by Salesian educational strategies of Westernization and by the massive colonization of Amazonian regions that started following the 1964 Agrarian Reform and Colonization Law. Thus, the missionaries resorted to strategies of agricultural and animal husbandry development in order to prove that the land was already occupied and, therefore, not susceptible of colonization by newcomers from the highlands. Their strategy of development for the Shuar also involved political organization to defend their territory and culture from colonizers. The Salesians led a process that resulted in the formation in 1964 of one of the first modern indigenous organizations in Latin America: the *Federación Interprovincial de Centros Shuar* or FICSH (Interprovincial Federation of Shuar Centers). This organization, however, did not seek a return to an indigenous tradition. According to Steve Rubenstein (2005) the hierarchical character of FICSH, its well-defined territorial limits that mimicked the Ecuadorian state, and the concentration of the population in towns or centers contrasted with traditional Shuar understandings of diffuse authority and vague territoriality.

In 1972, the Salesians and the Shuar Federation created the Radio System of Bicultural Shuar Education (*Sistema de Educación Radiofónico Bicultural Shuar*, SERBISH), one of the first experiences of this kind in Ecuador and Latin America. In order to educate a population dispersed in the rainforest and to intensively use scarce human resources, a "radio-teacher" transmitted the lesson through radio, and a radio-teacher assistant reinforced the lesson directly in the community. With the help and financial support of the Salesians, the organization printed teaching materials in both Shuar Chicham and Spanish. This system was the seed of intercultural bilingual education in the Amazonian province of Morona-Santiago. Today, for a number of reasons including the allocation of more human resources for intercultural education, modernization processes in the region, and the fact that the radio technology imported by the Salesians became obsolete, education is being carried out directly by teachers in regular schools. As happened with other pioneer experiences in indigenous education in Ecuador, when the National Direction of Intercultural Bilingual Education was created in 1988, there was some tension over who would control the educational system: the missionaries who implemented it in the first place or the indigenous organizations, which have been in charge of the national office since 1993. According to interviews that I conducted in several schools, Shuar parents prefer the supervision of the missionaries because they feel that mission education entails greater discipline and higher quality. The Shuar school system created by the Salesians has been a powerful tool for political consciousness raising, political organization, and socioeconomic development, as the teachers were required to become multidimensional leaders in their communities and in the indigenous organization. According to the official regulations of SERBISH (2000, 57) besides their educational duties, teachers were also required "[t]o be active in community development work."

Despite the later interest of the Salesians in the preservation of indigenous language and ways, the profound transformations effected in Shuar culture and social organization during the first half of the twentieth century could hardly be reversed. José Vicente Jintiach, a historic leader of the Shuar Federation and one of the first to access higher education at the Catholic University in Quito, published his reflections on the difficult adjustments facing the Shuar youth who entered Salesian boarding schools (Jintiach 1976). Jintiach's book portrays the Shuar as a people fully integrated into, and fond of, modernity, who enjoyed the music of The Beatles and the few movies to which they had access in the town of Sucúa. Evoking the egalitarian traditions of Shuar culture, Jintiach is highly critical of Salesian authority. According to Jintiach, Shuar adolescents find the lack of personal liberty and the sexual repression they encounter in the boarding schools particularly painful. However, Jintiach unambiguously recognizes the importance of the opportunity that the Salesian schools provide for Shuar to educate themselves in the dominant culture. This book portrays both a process of culture change and also cultural continuity because, according to ethnographic accounts, the Shuar had been traditionally attracted to influences from outside their own culture (Descola 2005).

Rosana Pichama and her father Carlos Pichama, an eighty-six-year-old Shuar man who grew up in the Salesian Mission of Sevilla Don Bosco, explain the transformations of Shuar culture and the role played by the Salesians in the following way. Rosana notes,

> When we went to school they did not want us to speak the Shuar language. We spoke Shuar with our classmates because we did not speak correct Castilian, but the nuns thought that we were insulting them. Today, they do not want us to speak Spanish. "Speak Shuar," they say. They used to call the parents and tell them that they [the Salesian nuns] commanded us to speak Castilian. And because we were little, we gradually lost our language. Today, our kids at the Shuar centers speak only Spanish. We still know a little, but our children don't. And now they [the Salesians] want us to return to our past. Of course, I identify as Shuar. Wherever I go I say: "I am Shuar, I am from the Amazon, I am Ecuadorian." And people look at me with surprise. However, it is also unfair that today's schools teach only Shuar. How can children learn if they don't teach them good Spanish? When we went to school we had well-prepared teachers from Quito and Guayaquil. At least thanks to those teachers we learned to speak good Spanish. We want to get education for our children. Because we do not have good education, we get delinquency. They [the Salesians] taught us well. They taught us how to do things, how to cook, how to greet people, how to eat properly, how to use the broom . . . But, today schools don't teach children good manners. That is why I say that there is a lot of corruption. There is corruption in our own race (Interview, February 19, 2006).

This quote illustrates some of the complexities of the process of cultural transformation and development endured by the Shuar. The Shuar are first forbidden to use their language and customs, and when the process of cultural change is almost complete, they are asked to retrieve them. As seen in the quote, both processes are perceived as an imposition. However, the process of political organization that started in 1964 with the help of the Salesians has been successful in this regard: Rosana is proud to identify both as Shuar and Ecuadorian. This informs us that both identities, ethnic and national, are not mutually exclusive for her, but reciprocally reinforcing, as the Salesians intended when they created the Federation (Rubenstein 2005, Martínez Novo 2007). Rosana indirectly criticizes indigenous organizations that took some control of intercultural bilingual education since the creation of DINEIB (*Dirección Nacional de Educación Intercultural Bilingüe*, National Directorate of Intercultural Bilingual Education) in 1988, and which as recently as 2005 attempted to eliminate the role of the Salesians as tutors of the school system. She perceives a decline in the quality of education that she associates with the turn from the teaching of "civilization" and "good Spanish" by foreign or urban Ecuadorian priests to the teaching of indigenous language and culture by indigenous teachers. However, this process of change should not be explained by greater distance from the missionaries. We should be aware that the Salesians were behind this transformation, which reflected the changes within the Catholic Church described above. Even the greater independence of the organizations from the missionaries is an effect deliberately sought by inculturation theology. With her critique of cultural recovery in schools, Rosana is communicating to us the role that many indigenous people think that formal education should have: to make children able to deal with the dominant culture and society. Like Jintiach (1976), she argues that the process of cultural transformation has been painful but ultimately useful for the Shuar, because it helped them integrate into, or survive within, the dominant culture. However, her comments seem to be also informed by internalized prejudice against her own traditions and people.

Her statements are paradoxical, however, if contrasted with the practice of intercultural bilingual education in the Upano Valley, the most urbanized region of Shuar territory in the province of Morona-Santiago. Indigenous language and culture are hardly taught or debated in intercultural schools, which also explains why children are not knowledgeable in the language and culture of their ancestors. The Shuar language is not used to teach different areas of knowledge, as stated in the official intercultural bilingual education model (MOSEIB) approved by the Ministry of Education in 1993. It is only taught as a special class approximately two hours a week. In addition, there are contradictions in how culture and language are taught in schools. For example, I was observing a Shuar language class in a school in the community of Asunción, close to the city of Sucúa, where a Shuar teacher was asking children to memorize the days of the week and the months of the year in Shuar. When I asked whether the ancestors of the Shuar counted time that way, he responded no. "So then," I asked, "how do you have Shuar words for units of time that are not of Shuar origin?" The teacher responded that the Salesians together with the Shuar Federation had invented those words.

At this point the teacher was uncomfortable, not because I was questioning his teaching of Shuar culture, but because he seemed to think that he was wasting his time with me. The stated purpose of his lesson was to have children memorize the words he had written on the board, not to discuss their relation to Shuar culture. Intercultural education has reproduced the authoritarian methods of traditional education, its focus being on repetition and memorization instead of critical thought. On the other hand, the teacher is also reproducing another Western tradition while trying to teach Shuar culture: the missionary strategy of using indigenous languages to introduce Western concepts to native peoples.

Rosana's father, Carlos Pichama, also makes reference to the misunderstandings enmeshed in the process of cultural recovery undertaken by the missionaries. He complains of the new Catholic mass implemented by the Salesians that makes use of Shuar language and music in the liturgy. Carlos notes,

Here, they celebrate the mass in Shuar. If God had been here and had made a miracle, if God-Arutam [a Shuar deity] had said, "come with me," I would believe. But I don't. That Father said that Arutam is God. He is writing a Bible [in Shuar]. I don't want the Shuar mass. My father and my grandfather used to sing that music [that they use in mass] when they killed. They are singing a song from the times of the hard *chonta* [kind of palm of the Ecuadorian Amazon]. My father would drink *chicha* and sing that song with our own rhythm. The priests should not use that [in mass]. That song is what they sing when they kill a person. I told the Father that the Bible that God wrote couldn't be amended. We cannot change what Christ has written. What Christ said, we must follow. But now they are writing another book, a book with Arutam, Iwia and what else. My father and grandfather use to say that Iwia [a mythological Shuar giant] ate people . . . And, there he was, Father José, I came in and he was there, standing and singing "Ahhhhh." Then, he raises the holy host and he invokes Arutam and Christ. If Christ were that powerful, why would he need Arutam to help him? Then, I said that's enough, I won't come back to mass. If they would sing in Shuar, speaking about God that would be nice. But they mix everything. The song that they sang when they killed humans and made *tsantsas* [shrunken heads], the song that they sang to attract women, songs for demons and snakes . . . [they use in mass]. I say no. I told them to be careful with Arutam. Arutam is a powerful Demon. They [the Salesians] taught us that. They told us that Arutam was a Demon almost equal to God. Arutam knows how to deceive. We did not know well before. All the Salesian priests and nuns who have sung to Arutam have died or become ill. That Arutam gave strength to commit crimes. That is why I say that this is not a mass. They already fed us that there is only one God. Why do they have to bring in Arutam now? (Interview, February 19, 2006).

Carlos Pichama highlights again the contradictions of the colonization process. First their culture is stigmatized and changed. Later, the Salesians want to retrieve it. However, they do so as if one culture were equivalent to another, as if one God were equal to another God. Probably the priest is using the Shuar word Arutam to say "God" in the native language. Carlos's sharp exercise in cultural analysis tells us, however, that cultures are not equivalent. They cannot be translated one into another literally, and they cannot be mixed without cultural consequences. Furthermore, the missionaries have convinced the Shuar that there were negative elements in their own culture, particularly those related to violence. Thus, it is problematic to return to these elements both for the Church and for the organizations. Moreover, Carlos refuses to accept the new stereotyped and stylized version of his own culture that the Salesians seem to be attempting to promote in their search for "cultural preservation." He says, "I know everything, nobody can lie to me because my grandfather told me: 'This is like this, and that is like that . . .' And, now they are creating a new law. That is why I don't like when they do Shuar things." He rejects the "purification" of culture proposed by the theology of inculturation as inauthentic. Consequently, this Shuar elder perceives the process of "preservation and recovering" as yet another colonial imposition, or, in his own words, as a new "law."

Development, Identity, and Politics in the Salesian Mission of Zumbahua

Much later than their missions in the Amazon, the Salesians created one in the town of Zumbahua, located in the central Andean highlands of Ecuador around 4000 meters above sea level, and populated by peasants who spoke the Kichwa language and some Spanish (this town has been studied by Weismantel 1988; 2001). Unlike the Amazonian missions, this one, started in 1971, was informed from its start by liberation theology and the philosophy of inculturation.

From the sixteenth until the beginning of the twentieth century, Zumbahua was a large hacienda property of the Augustinians, another Catholic order (Weismantel 1988). Due to the high altitude of most of its lands, the hacienda consisted largely of pastures used for sheep raising, an activity that provided wool for a textile factory that the order owned close to the provincial capital, Latacunga. In 1908, with a law that nationalized Church assets, Zumbahua became the property of Social Assistance, a public institution that rented lands to finance hospitals, orphanages, and other charities for the urban poor. Paradoxically, labor conditions were often harsher on public haciendas. The Zumbahua hacienda subjected its workers to the systems of *concertaje* and later *huasipungo*, contracts based on custom through which the worker exchanged his and his family's labor for the usufruct of a small plot of land (*huasipungo*), a nominal salary that most of the time was not paid, and some other benefits (Weismantel 1988; Guerrero 1991). In 1964, with the first agrarian reform law, Zumbahua, like other public haciendas, was distributed among the Kichwa peasants. Social differences that originated in the hacienda period were reproduced in the land distribution process, causing inequalities and tensions. The Salesians had to confront these tensions in their search for a more egalitarian peasant society.

The Salesians sought to combine peasant evangelization with human development. They understood human development as helping and advising peasants in their struggle for access to land and for the better exploitation of this resource.

In order to make the agrarian reform law effective, or to get government credit, or to have access to development funds and technical advice, peasants needed to organize. Therefore, the Salesians promoted social and political organization indirectly through intercultural bilingual education and directly through creating and strengthening peasant organizations.

From the point of view of rural development, the Salesians had goals that may seem contradictory: they sought both to promote a self-sufficient peasant community based on the Kichwa tradition *and* to modernize agriculture in the style of the green revolution. Among the first goals of the mission were the improvement of roads, the introduction of enhanced seeds and new agrarian techniques, the selection of animal species, and so on. These noble goals and intentions, however, confronted important limitations due to the low quality of land, the difficulty of cultivating steep slopes, and the small size of plots. Given these limitations, peasants in the Cotopaxi highlands have not been able to live solely on agriculture. They typically combine several economic activities that include trade, smuggling, temporary construction work in cities, crafts in the case of Tigua, and incipient tourism. Despite this reality, the Salesian priests perceived the inhabitants of this area as peasants and criticized migration as a source of social disorganization, violence, and destruction of traditional culture. This "peasantist" focus is reflected in the kind of education promoted by the mission, which focuses on rural needs. The Salesians educate rural teachers and experts in agrarian and animal husbandry techniques. This curriculum has been questioned by young highland residents who prefer a professional urban education based on the use of computers and knowledge of English and other languages. In their own words, highlanders want to be ready for what they perceive as the "modern" world. However, they seek this kind of education while also advocating the study of the Kichwa language and culture, as well as radical politics, useful for young people's insertion into the indigenous movement, an important source of social mobility in the last two decades. It is important to note, to the Salesians' credit, that mission education has adapted to the desires of the youth, offering classes in computers and languages. Again, the Salesians have not perceived a contradiction between the reinforcement of ethnic traditions and the modern education of youth.

Nevertheless, the Salesians still think in terms of a peasant-oriented project. To confront the agrarian crisis of the Zumbahua area they propose reforestation and the migration of highland peasants organized in cooperatives to subtropical land. The Salesians do not perceive craft production, tourism, or migration to cities as valid alternatives. This enduring representation of indigenous people as subsistence peasants is also reproduced by scholars and indigenous organizations and has important political consequences; more complex economic realities and identities are not taken into account in the movement's political strategies. Even educated leaders who live in the city and return to the countryside only on weekends and vacation periods pretend to be peasants in order to be perceived as "authentic" Indians.

Since the 1970s, the Salesians have sponsored intercultural bilingual education in an area where 70 percent of men and 95 percent of women had been illiterate (Manangón, Baltazar and Trávez 1992). The Salesians started with informal literacy programs in Kichwa in 1976 and continued with a network of elementary schools. *Jatari Unancha*, a high school to graduate rural teachers, was created in 1989. Finally, the Salesians opened the Cotopaxi Academic Program, a branch of the Polytechnic Salesian University, to educate rural teachers and agrarian engineers in Zumbahua.

As happened in the Shuar case, the Salesians of Cotopaxi felt that organization under an ethnic banner was an appropriate way for indigenous peasants to articulate themselves into the nation. In 1971, the Salesian Zumbahua project noted: "It is important to create a new rural school that preserves and develops the culture that exists in the indigenous world and that achieves in this way integration to the national culture" (Costales Samaniego et al. 1971). Furthermore, the name of the high school created by the Salesians, *Jatari Unancha*, means "raise the flag" in the Kichwa language. This is a way to put a nationalist thought in native words. The peasants of the area agreed with the Salesians on this point because they too perceived intercultural bilingual education and ethnic political organization as ways to be recognized by the Ecuadorian state. Indigenous teachers not only wished to be officially recognized, but to become employees of the state. This is understandable since official recognition carried economic benefits: the state pays bilingual educators the salaries and benefits that *mestizo* teachers already enjoy.

Although the Salesians' motivations for integrating highland peasants into the nation while reinforcing their indigenous culture may have been largely idealistic in the beginning, peasants kept projects and programs grounded. As Salesian Father Javier Herrán notes:

> We did well because before the start of the [national] literacy program we had already got economic help for the literacy teachers through the Provincial Directorate. There was a lot of interest on the part of the people. That is why they learned. But we could not give them their official elementary school certificates. Then, the Provincial Directorate in Cotopaxi gave us a hand because the Provincial Director was a good guy, because I did not find opposition or difficulty but support. He accepted that we gave a special examination . . . and the supervisors were thrilled. They felt that the kids knew a lot, even more than those graduating from regular schools. And then, they gave them their elementary education certificates. That provided a lot of strength to the people. Then the indigenous schools started to gain prestige for the community. Because the teachers were not *cholos*, mestizos, or white, they were *runa* [indigenous Kichwa]. And they said, "That *runa* does not know anything because he is *runa*." But when they started to find official certificates . . . Then, their attitude changed (Interview, August 2002).

What is interesting here is that bilingual education and ethnic political organization are seen not as ways of becoming separate from the state (i.e., some form of ethnic separatism), but as a form of inclusion in the national arena.

What, then, did the Salesians understand by promoting indigenous identity and what impact did these ideas have on the political culture of the indigenous movement? The Salesians thought that one important reason to promote cultural identity was to reinforce the self-esteem of peasants. The missionaries taught the Kichwa language and philosophy, but they did not extract this knowledge from the indigenous peasants. On the contrary, they believed that peasants' Kichwa was corrupted with influences from Spanish and sought to teach a purified, more classic version of the language, one used by university-based linguists and priests. They felt that Kichwa culture should be preserved while purifying it from those elements considered by the Salesians contrary to ethics or development, such as the oppression of women. A Salesian priest, for example, noted that the well-known trait of Andean reciprocity should be transformed into the Christian value of gratuity: in other words, when a person does something for another person, she should not necessarily expect something in return. In short, the Salesians sought to change those cultural aspects that collided with their modernized and ethical Christian utopia. As the *Ad Gentes* Decree (1965, 7) states:

> [Mission activity] liberates from evil traits all the truth and grace that existed among the peoples as the veiled presence of God and restitutes it to its author, Christ, that subdues the presence of the Devil and separates wickedness from sinners. Thus, all that is good in the heart and mind of men, in the rites and cultures of the peoples, does not perish, but is purified, elevated and perfected for the glory of God.

As in the Shuar case, this particular way to reinforce indigenous culture, which the Salesians connected with improving self-esteem, confronted resistance by indigenous peasants. Communities did not always trust indigenous teachers, and many peasants thought that teaching in Kichwa was a waste of time. Wasn't the whole point of going to school learning Spanish in order to become stronger, less vulnerable, in relation to the dominant culture? For instance, Rodrigo Martinez, a white-mestizo teacher who participated in the Salesian project for decades, states:

> Why did we emphasize the philosophy of bilingual education? Because indigenous people themselves were not convinced of the value of indigenous education. They always thought that it was a second-class situation. They were not convinced that an education that is relevant to the cultural reality could also be an education with possibilities to achieve quality. Then, we spent our time convincing them that the Indian is a person with value, that indigenous people are valuable as a people, that their culture includes valuable things. And so we spent our time, until they were able to consolidate their collective identity (Interview, July 2002).

The struggle for the land, rural development, and intercultural bilingual education had an impact on indigenous political organizations: to get land and credit peasants needed an organization that could become an interlocutor to the state and nongovernmental organizations. Intercultural education created a political consciousness based on ethnic pride and formed a new generation of leaders. The Salesians also promoted political organization in direct ways. The Zumbahua Project (Costales Samaniego et al. 1971, 20) gave priority to this:

> In order to solve the indigenous problem, indigenous peoples themselves have to become agents in liberating actions . . . through a consciousness raising process that leads them to transform every unfair socio-economic structure. Therefore, the main goal of all our action should be to guide the indigenous community to a true self-management. Our work as agents of change is just temporary, transient, and subsidiary.

Again, the Salesians did not aim to preserve indigenous social and political organization, but to transform it in ways that they saw as more just and efficient. For instance, the Salesians had to struggle against forms of exploitation and inequality among peasants that came from *hacienda* times, even though this made them a target of local *caciques*.

The style of the Church—promoting organization and social action and then retiring to the background to allow people to become independent—is one of the reasons why its role remains hidden from social scientists. In addition, indigenous and other leaders wish to emphasize their independence and agency. Father Javier Herrán (Interview, August 2002), however, highlights the outstanding role of the Salesians in the creation of the Indigenous and Peasant Movement of Cotopaxi (Movimiento Indígena y Campesino de Cotopaxi, MICC):

> We held a first meeting. It was in Chugchilán if I remember correctly. We [the Salesians] did everything. We called the people through the radio. We hired buses so people could come. After three and a half years, our role continued to be central. We conducted the meetings and were able to assemble the peasants. In that period, support for the struggle to acquire the land was central. In general, what we wanted was to create something that helped people to be able to make their own decisions. We did not see it appropriate to continue with the traditional organization systems of our area.

Through thirty years of sustained work, the Salesians have had a progressive influence in Cotopaxi. Although the process has not been without tensions and contradictions, the Salesians have successfully promoted indigenous organization and identity by tackling a series of quite concrete problems ranging from bilingual education, outdated agricultural techniques, and the development of infrastructure.

Conclusion

These examples of the work of the Salesians in different regions and with different native groups show that the work of the order reveals some common elements while not being homogeneous across time or space. An important element of development for this order has been the formation of identities, first Western identities, and later preserved and purified indigenous traditions. Since the 1960s, these indigenous traditions have been perceived as preconditions for political organization, and political organization as a requirement for the improvement of indigenous living standards.

The work of the order has differed according to the regions and the peoples with which it has worked. It has been less problematic to talk about cultural preservation from the point of view of a Kichwa peasant group whose customs are purportedly based on solidarity, reciprocity, and love for mother earth (an image that may be confronted with empirical evidence to the contrary), than for a society historically affected by internal warfare and generalized violence like the Shuar. However, in the Catholic Church's particular understanding of cultural preservation, both cultures have to be purified of their negative elements. This means that the cultural relativism of the Church has limits, imposed by the tension between its search for tolerance and intercultural dialogue and the historical universalism and ethnocentrism of the Church. After all, what the Church is spreading among other cultures is a particular cultural message. Moreover, because cultures have to be purified, the very indigenous peoples from whom these cultural traits originate may not recognize the images that result from this process. This may be one of the reasons why indigenous people, both in the Amazon and in the highlands, perceive cultural recovery as a somewhat alien project.

There are other reasons why native peoples resist the cultural agenda of the Church; for example, internalized prejudices resulting from the historical subordination of indigenous people, and the desire to integrate into the dominant society in order to acquire social mobility. Regarding modernization, the agendas of the Salesians and indigenous people coincide because it is clear for the Church that the cultural preservation project does not contradict the search for modernity. For instance, the Salesians specialize in technical training, and take advantage of the use of technologies like the internet, video, and radio for the purpose of evangelization. In the case of the Shuar, the radio was an important technology for both educational development and evangelization.

Both the Salesians and the indigenous people agree on another issue that may seem paradoxical and that relates to the tradition-modernity dichotomy: the idea that the reinforcement of ethnic pride should be combined with integration into and love for the nation. During my fieldwork in Mexico (Martínez Novo 2006) and Ecuador, I have learned that indigenous people are less worried about assimilation than about having been historically excluded from citizenship and from the nation. The idea that they reject the nation-state originates in an elite prejudice projected onto them, as Mercedes Prieto (2004) has shown. For instance, in all of the intercultural bilingual schools controlled by indigenous organizations in Ecuador, native children are proud to honor the national flag and to sing the national anthem in their native languages and Spanish. In contrast to what is often stated in the literature, indigenous people are far from being suspicious of or indifferent to the nation-state. The Salesians have efficiently filled the gaps left by the state, promoting both love for the nation and claims for a more inclusive citizenship.

Another aspect that emerges from the discussion is the important impact of the Catholic Church, and the Salesians in particular, in the creation of the indigenous movement. The Salesians, with the collaboration of the Shuar, formed the Shuar Federation in 1964 to protect this group from colonization. The Shuar Federation is one of the first modern indigenous organizations in Latin America, and a founding member of CONAIE, the first president of which was Miguel Tankamash, a Shuar. The Salesians were also instrumental in the creation of MICC, the Indigenous and Peasant Movement of Cotopaxi. Through the fight for agrarian reform and bilingual education, the Salesians gave shape to an active and assertive leadership and to one of the most active branches of CONAIE.

Through their work in agrarian reforms and development, intercultural bilingual education, and indigenous organizing, the Salesians have had an important role in promoting antineoliberal ideology and politics in Ecuador. The indigenous movement staged its first nationwide uprising in 1990. Through periodic uprisings that have taken place every other year, the movement has been able to hinder the complete implementation of the neoliberal model in Ecuador. As Ospina and Guerrero (2003) have noted, when different Ecuadorian governments have attempted to reduce subsidies or introduce neoliberal agrarian and other laws, social turmoil led by the indigenous movement has made it difficult to implement these reforms. Today, the indigenous movement has lost some of its ability to lead social processes, due in part to important mistakes made by CONAIE's leadership, and also because grassroots elements of the movement have been absorbed by the radical-populist project of Rafael Correa. Nevertheless, the radical-populist project of Correa is also intimately linked to liberation theology and particularly to Salesian theology, as noted at the beginning of this chapter.

Works Cited

Andrade, Susana. 2004. *Protestantismo indígena: Procesos de conversión religiosa en la provincia de Chimborazo, Ecuador.* Quito: FLACSO.

Becker, Marc. 2008. *Indians and leftists in the making of Ecuador's modern indigenous movements.* Durham, NC: Duke University Press.

Botasso, Juan. 1986. "Las nacionalidades indígenas, el estado y las misiones en el Ecuador." *Ecuador Debate* 12:151-59.

Cornejo, Diego, ed. 1991. *Indios: Una reflexión sobre el levantamiento indígena de 1990.* Quito: ILDIS, Duende, Abya Yala.

Costales Samaniego, Alfredo, P. Pedro Creamer, P. Javier Cattá, and P. Juan Botasso. 1971. Proyecto de Zumbagua. Salesian Archive of Quito.

De la Torre, Carlos. 2002. *Afroquiteños: Ciudadanía y racismo.* Quito: CAAP.

Descola, Philippe. 2005 [1993]. *Las lanzas del crepúsculo. Relatos jíbaros. Alta amazonía.* Buenos Aires: Fondo de Cultura Económica.

Guerrero, Andrés. 1991. *La semántica de la dominación: El concertaje de indios.* Quito: Libri Mundi.

———. 1993. La desintegración de la administración étnica en el Ecuador. In *Sismo étnico en el Ecuador,* ed. José Almeida, 91-112. Quito: CEDIME y Abya Yala.

Jintiach, José Vicente. 1976. *La integración del estudiante Shuar en su grupo social.* Quito: Mundo Shuar.

Kohn, Eduardo. 2002. Infidels, virgins and the black robed priest: A backwoods history of Ecuador's Montaña region. *Ethnohistory* 49(3):545-82.

León, Jorge. 1991. Las organizaciones indígenas: Igualdad y diferencia. In *Indios: Una reflexión sobre el levantamiento indigena de 1990,* ed. Diego Cornejo, 373-417. Quito: Abya Yala, ILDIS.

Lyons, Barry. 2001. Religion, authority, and identity: Intergenerational politics, ethnic resurgence, and respect in Chimborazo, Ecuador. *Latin American Research Review* 36(1):7-48.

———. 2006. *Remembering the hacienda: Religion, authority, and social change in highland Ecuador.* Austin: University of Texas Press.

Manangón, José, Ernesto Baltazar, and Pedro Trávez. 1992. Sistema de escuelas indígenas de Cotopaxi. In *La escuela india: ¿integración o afirmación étnica?* ed. V. H. Torres, 61-82. Quito: COMUNIDEC.

Martínez Novo, Carmen. 2004. Los misioneros salesianos y el movimiento indígena de Cotopaxi. *Ecuador Debate* 63:235-68.

———. 2006. *Who defines who is indigenous? Identities, development, intellectuals and the state in northern México.* New Brunswick, NJ: Rutgers University Press.

———. 2007.¿Es el multiculturalismo estatal un factor de profundización de la democracia en América Latina? Una reflexión desde la etnografía sobre los casos de México y Ecuador. In *Ciudadanía y exclusión: España y Ecuador frente al espejo,* ed. Víctor Bretón, 182-202. Madrid: Catarata.

Muratorio, Blanca. 1981. *Etnicidad, evangelización y protesta en el Ecuador: una perspectiva antropológica.* Quito: CIESE.

Ospina, Pablo, and Fernando Guerrero. 2003. *El poder de la comunidad: Ajuste estructural y movimiento indígena en los Andes ecuatorianos.* Quito: FLACSO.

Prieto, Mercedes. 2004. *Liberalismo y temor: imaginando los sujetos indígenas en el Ecuador post-colonial*. Quito: FLACSO.

Rubenstein, Steven. 2005. La conversión de los Shuar. *Iconos* 22:27-48.

SERBISH. 2000. *Reglamento interno del SERBISH y la unidad educativa experimental fiscomisional intercultural bilingüe shuar-achuar "Yamaram Tsawaa."* Sucúa: SERBISH.

Taylor, Anne-Christine. 1994. Una categoría irreductible en el conjunto de las naciones indígenas: Los jíbaro en las representaciones occidentales. In *Imágenes e imagineros: Representaciones de los indígenas ecuatorianos. S XIX y XX*, ed. Blanca Muratorio, 75-108. Quito: FLACSO

Vatican Council II. 1965. *Ad gentes* decree: On the missionary activity of the Church.

Weismantel, Mary. 1988. *Food, gender and poverty in the Ecuadorian Andes*. Prospect Heights, IL: Waveland Press.

———. 2001. *Cholas and pishtacos: Stories of race and sex in the Andes*. Chicago: University of Chicago Press.

Zamosc, León. 1993. Protesta agraria y movimiento indígena en la sierra ecuatoriana. In *Sismo étnico en el Ecuador*, ed. José Almeida, 273-304. Quito: CEDIME y Abya Yala.

Audiovisual materials

Audiovisuales Don Bosco. n.d. *Misiones en el Oriente*. Quito.

Index

About the Authors

Julie Adkins is a Ph.D. candidate in cultural anthropology at Southern Methodist University, where she serves as adjunct faculty in the Department of Anthropology and the Perkins School of Theology. She has been an ordained minister in the Presbyterian Church (USA) since 1986, holding the M.Div. from Princeton Theological Seminary and the D.Min. from McCormick Theological Seminary (Chicago). Her dissertation research is focused on homelessness in the city of Dallas, and, in particular, the city's response. In addition, she has recently become involved in a collaborative project with the Dallas Police Department, court system, and more than forty social-service providers in designing and implementing a project to offer alternatives to women in prostitution. Her research interests include the U.S. and Latin America, poverty and homelessness, faith-based organizations, and tourism.

Bretton Alvaré studied sociology and anthropology at the University of Richmond, VA and the Universiteit Leiden, NL and is currently a doctoral candidate in cultural anthropology at Temple University in Philadelphia, PA. He serves as an adjunct faculty member at LaSalle, Lehigh, and Temple Universities and is a graduate fellow at the Center for the Humanities at Temple. He specializes in the study of Rastafari religion and culture and has been conducting fieldwork with the National Rastafari Organization of Trinidad and Tobago since 2005. His other research interests include the political and economic history of the Anglophone Caribbean, NGOs and neoliberal governance, social movements, and political violence.

Jacqueline L. Angel received her Ph.D. in Sociology from Rutgers University and is a Professor at the LBJ School of Public Affairs and the Department of Sociology at the University of Texas, Austin. Her research deals with social structures, inequality, and health. She has published numerous articles and chapters on social policy issues as well as four books, *Health and Living Arrangements of the Elderly* (Garland Publishing, 1991); *Painful Inheritance: Health and the New Generation of Fatherless Families* (University of Wisconsin Press, 1993) and *Who Will Care for Us? Aging and Long-Term Care in Multicultural America* (New York University Press, 1997), jointly with Ronald Angel; and

The Health of Aging Hispanics: The Mexican-Origin Population, Co-Edited with Keith Whitfield (Springer, 2007). Angel is an active member of the NGO community.

Ronald J. Angel is Professor of Sociology at the University of Texas, Austin. For over twenty-five years his research and writing have focused on the social welfare and health care needs of minority populations, with a special focus on Hispanics. His work documents serious inequities in income, wealth, and health care access among Hispanic subgroups and relates those to structural factors, particularly those that result from labor market disadvantages. His recent research focuses on the role of non-governmental organizations in providing health and social services to poor individuals and families in the U.S. and Latin America. With Laura Lein and Jane Henrici he is author of *Poor Families in America's Health Care Crisi"* (Cambridge University Press, 2006), and with Jacqueline Angel, of *Painful Inheritance: Health and the New Generation of Fatherless Families* (University of Wisconsin Press, 1993) and *Who Will Care for Us? Aging and Long-term Care in Multicultural America.*

Suzana Ramos Coutinho Bornholdt received her B.Sc. in Social Science at the Universidade Federal de Santa Catarina (2000) and master's degree in Social Anthropology at the Universidade Federal de Santa Catarina (2004). Currently, she is a Ph.D. candidate atthe Religious Studies Department (Lancaster University - UK). She is a research fellow at the Religious Studies Centre (NUR/PPGAS) at the Universidade Federal de Santa Catarina. Her main research interest is focused on missionary activities, with previous experience on Christian mission on the Internet and also millenarianist/missionary perspectives of the Jehovah's Witnesses. Her current Ph.D research focus on the missionalising strategy of the lay Buddhism of Soka Gakkai in Southern Brazil.

Jill DeTemple served as an agricultural extensionist with the U.S. Peace Corps in rural Ecuador, and then earned an M.T.S in Christianity and Culture at Harvard Divinity School and a Ph.D. in Religious Studies at the University of North Carolina – Chapel Hill. Currently, she is Assistant Professor of Religious Studies at Southern Methodist University. Her research interests include Pentecostalism, faith-based organizations, ethnography, transnational religious communities, and Latin American religions. At present, she is at work on a book that explores negotiations of modernity in the context of faith-based development in rural Ecuador.

Erin Eidenshink is a student in the Honors Program at Southern Methodist University. Her research in Bolivia, along with Katrina Josephson, was funded by the Richter International Fellowship.

Tim Fogarty researches small transnational NGOs as contexts for constructing cross-cultural solidarity. Tim worked in Nicaragua in the late 1980s with Habitat for Humanity. He has a masters degree in religion from Fordham University and doctorate in cultural anthropology from the University of Florida, where he teaches about NGOs and grassroots development. As director of the UF in Nicaragua Program he brings students there to experience and analyze NGO practices. Tim is an adjunct professor in the Center for Women's Studies and Gender Research and in the Honors Program of the University of Florida. He serves on the board of directors of ProNica, a Quaker NGO working in Nicaragua. His research interests include the cultural production of masculinities, NGO mediated grassroots development, the interface between NGOs and popular social movements, and cross-cultural solidarity formation.

Tara Hefferan currently teaches in the Sociology, Anthropology, and Social Work Department of Central Michigan University. A cultural anthropologist, Hefferan earned the Ph.D. from Michigan State University. Her research interests include international development, globalization, and faith-based organizations in the US and Caribbean. Hefferan is the author of *Twinning Faith and Development: Catholic Parish Partnering in the US and Haiti*, published by Kumarian Press.

Emily J. Hogue is a doctoral candidate in Anthropology at Florida International University (FIU) in Miami, Florida, where she is a Presidential Fellow. A social anthropologist specializing in international development, her research focuses on faith-based development and processes of economic, religious, and social change, globalization, rural economies, ethnodevelopment, and Andean anthropology. She has worked as a consultant for development NGOs throughout Latin America and the Caribbean. Hogue also holds an M.A. in Comparative Sociology from FIU and a Graduate Certificate in Peruvian Studies from the Pontificia Universidad Católica del Perú. Upon completing her Ph.D. in December 2008, she will pursue work as a practitioner of applied Anthropology in the international development sector.

Katrina Josephson is a student in the Honors Program and a President's Scholar at Southern Methodist University. Her research in Bolivia, along with Erin Eidenshink, was funded by the Richter International Fellowship.

Carmen Martínez Novo is currently a Visiting Scholar in the Department of Anthropology at the Johns Hopkins University and Professor at the Latin American Faculty for the Social Sciences (FLACSO) in Ecuador. She obtained her Ph.D. in the Department of Anthropology at the New School for Social Research, New York. She had pre-doctoral grants from the MacArthur and the Wenner-Gren Foundations, and post-doctoral grants from Wenner-Gren. She is the author of *Who Defines Indigenous? Identities, Development, Intellectuals and the State in Northern Mexico*, published by Rutgers University Press. She has also published in Identities, Journal of Latin American Anthropology, and Bulletin of Latin American Research as well as other articles and book chapters in Spanish journals and books. She has done research on the interactions between non-Indians and indigenous peoples in Mexico and Ecuador in contexts of globalization and modernity.

Laurie Occhipinti is currently an associate professor of anthropology at Clarion University of Pennsylvania. Her research interests include economic development, faith based organizations, indigenous peoples, and religion in Latin America. She is the author of *Acting on Faith*, which focuses on the role of Catholic NGOs in economic development in indigenous communities in northwestern Argentina. Occhipinti obtained her Ph.D. and M.A. in Anthropology at McGill University in Montreal, Canada.

Javier Pereira is a Uruguayan sociologist, currently working at the Universidad Católica in Montevideo where he chairs the Social Science department. He is a PhD student at the University of Texas at Austin. His research focuses on the role of civil society organizations in the provision of social services to teenage mothers in Chile, Argentina and Uruguay. His interests relate to the challenges faced by traditional welfare systems in the Southern Cone countries in Latin America and the new emerging balances between states, markets and civil societies. Prior his graduate studies in the United States, Javier received his B.A. in Sociology at the Universidad de la República in Uruguay and took specialization courses in the field of Policy Evaluation in ECLAC (Economic Commission for Latin America and Caribbean) and the International Development Bank. His academic work has been supported by the Fulbright Program, the National Science Foundation and the Mellon Foundation.

Paul A. Peters is a Ph.D. candidate and Mellon Fellow in Latin American Sociology in the Population Research Center, Department of Sociology at the University of Texas at Austin. He has a Masters degree in Planning from the University of Waterloo in Ontario, Canada. His research interests include nongovernmental organizations, education planning, urban planning, and urban spatial segregation. He has several published articles in major journals on education planning, urban spatial segregation, housing policy, and the use of information technology for urban sociological analysis.

Ethan P. Sharp received his Ph.D. from Indiana University in 2004, and is Assistant Professor of Latin American Studies at the University of Texas – Pan American in Edinburg, Texas. He is the author of "Testimonies and the Expansion of Women's Roles in a Transnational Mexican Parish" in *Language and Religious Identity: Women in Discourse*, edited by Allyson Jule (Palgrave Macmillan, 2007) and *No Longer Strangers: Mexican Immigrants, Catholic Ministries and the Promise of Citizenship* (Indiana University Press, forthcoming 2008). His current research addresses the roles of faith and spirituality in Mexico's "war on drugs."

CPSIA information can be obtained at www.ICGtesting.com
Printed in the USA
BVOW030608280911

272276BV00005B/2/P